The Insights of Sociology

The Insights of Sociology:

An Introduction

HOWARD BOUGHEY

University of Toronto

Allyn and Bacon, Inc.

Boston   *London*   *Sydney*   *Toronto*

Third printing . . . August, 1979
Copyright © 1978 by Allyn and Bacon, Inc., 470 Atlantic Avenue, Boston,
Massachusetts 02210. All rights reserved. Printed in the United States of America. No part
of the material protected by this copyright notice may be reproduced or utilized in any
form or by any means, electronic or mechanical, including photocopying, recording, or by
any information storage and retrieval system, without written permission from the
copyright owner.

Library of Congress Cataloging in Publication Data
Boughey, Howard.
  The insights of sociology.

  Bibliography: p.
  Includes index.
  1. Sociology. I. Title.
HM51.B768   301   77-26977
ISBN 0-205-06011-0

Contents

Acknowledgments

I take pleasure in first giving thanks to my teacher and friend, Charles Page, who has provided me, not only with invaluable commentary and criticism on major portions of successive drafts of this manuscript, not only with a great teacher's insights and guidance into the labyrinth of sociological thought, but also with a model of intellectual rigor and strength of character that serves over the years as my personal touchstone and emulative goal. Page is one of those rare men whose life work finds its fulfilment mainly in the productive and satisfying lives of others he has deeply touched. I am but one among a host of sociologists who owe Charles Page this debt.

Four years back the broad outlines of this book were conceived over lunch with Gary Folven, the senior sociology editor at Allyn and Bacon, Inc. Folven's insight and encouragement have seen me through to completion, and much of whatever merit this work might have is due to his kind persistence. The sharp editorial brilliance of Allen Workman also has honed and polished every page. I find myself blessed with two good, strong friends in Folven and Workman as an unexpected reward at the end of the project.

The critical inspiration of my wife, Dr. Nirmala Cherukupalle, also infuses the pages of this book, as it does everything I try to do well. If a textbook can be dedicated, this one ought to be to her.

The critical reviewers of prepublication drafts have done yeoman service over the last three years, and have given abundantly of their experience as teachers and scholars in sociology. It is only a minimal acknowledgment of their contributions to list their names: Professor David Altheide, Arizona State University; Professor Peter Chroman, College of San Mateo; Professor Kenneth R. Cunningham, University of Alberta; Professor Jack Douglas, University of California at San Diego; Professor Eric Goode, State University of New York at Stony Brook; Professor John Horton, University of California; Professor H. Roy Kaplan, State University of New York at Buffalo; Professor Robert Lauer, Southern Illinois University at Edwardsville; Professor Barry D. Lebowitz, Portland State University; Professor Richard A. Minisce, Suffolk County Community College; Professor David Schneider, L. A. Pierce College; Professor Robert Winslow, California State University.

In addition, I have received unstinting advice and critical commentary from my colleagues at the University of Toronto, foremost among them, Helen Breslauer, Douglas Campbell, Barrie Green, John Hagen, Robert Mackay, Joe Pilotta, Edward Silva, and John Simpson.

Last, but by no means least, I thank my students, who have been willing to make their "inner voices" audible to me in reaction to my attempts to challenge them with sociology.

Of course, I alone must and do take full responsibility for the many failings and limitations of this text.

Introduction

We were at the 8,000-foot level in the Nilgiris (blue mountains) of South India when my eighty-four-year-old hiking companion, stopping to allow me to catch my breath, told me about *Ashtaavadhaana.* We had been hiking together regularly these mornings, and our conversation was of bits and snatches of modern sociological thought from me and healthy chunks of Sanskrit language, philosophy, and cultural history from him. *Ashtaavadhaana,* he said, was a word representing the normal, perhaps minimally required, level of awareness, alertness, or intelligent attention for the beginning scholar in the Sanskrit tradition. It means, literally, "the capability of being aware of eight things simultaneously." In olden times, he told me, a test based upon this word would be devised for the candidate to schooling in Sanskrit philosophy. A group of scholars and teachers would prearrange eight actions to be performed all at once the moment the candidate entered the room. Perhaps a bird or animal would be released, a gong of a certain pitch struck, a tone briefly sung, a piece of cloth of a certain color held up, a certain scent wafted, gestures made, and words spoken. Then the candidate, after a moment of reflection, had to list the eight events in precise detail. I thought this was wonderful enough, but my mind began to reel when my instructor continued, "There is another Sanskrit word, *Sataavadhaana.* It means "the capability of being aware of one hundred things simultaneously." "For this, too, there is a test. . . ."

As we looked out over miles of barren hills, fertile valleys, and parched red plains, the sounds of at least three different birdsongs mingled in our ears; the sweet smells of jasmine flowers and ripe jackfruit came, it seemed, from every direction; and my feet hurt. I was aware of thinking quietly about two or three different problems at the same time, as well. It became clear that perhaps *Ashtaavadhanna* is not such an unusual feat of consciousness, but might be close to the multilevelled awareness of any normal, wide-awake human being.

The idea of multiple levels of awareness, illustrated to me so neatly by my elderly Indian friend, came back to me later as I wrestled with the ambiguities, internal contradictions, and inconsistencies within my own intellectual discipline, sociology. Perhaps these inconsistencies were more apparent than real. Perhaps there are many different sociologies, not one; and for each sociology, there is a level of awareness about the social world in which we live that is made available only by that sociological perspective. The diversity of sociological viewpoints would then be the strength of sociology and not its weakness.

This three-faced introductory text is the result of following through with this line of thought. For an increasing number of sociologists teaching introductory classes, the standard texts are either useless or worse, a hindrance in trying to communicate to students the reality of sociology as they know it. The standard texts uniformly claim that their version of sociology is *the* sociology.

The failure of the standard texts to present a true picture of this multifaceted discipline is matched by their failure to meet the reality of student capabilities in the seventies. I believe, based on fifteen years of undergraduate teaching, that today's introductory student is fully capable of *Ashtaavadhaana* and more. This text's presentation is thus an attempt both to report authentically the complexity of the discipline and to respect the ability of today's student to see and grasp a multilevelled reality.

This introduction to the varieties of sociological thought rests on the philosophical assumption that our knowledge of the truth is never absolute, particularly the truth about social life. The truth is colored by the situation of its discovery, its recording, and its telling. The truth about people in society lies in the social actions of men and women; discovering this truth, recording it, and telling it are also social actions; therefore, at least a part of sociological truth is in the telling.

We are led then to examine the various ways in which different sociologists go about finding out the truth. No criteria are offered by which the student must decide definitely that *this* and not *that* version of the truth is the correct one. Each sociology outlined here has its difficulties, its built-in error factors, as well as its own validity and its unique strengths. The strength of sociology as a whole lies in the richness of this diversity, and in the robustness of the debate between different factions.

The aim of this text is to give students the feel of involvement in hotly disputed sociological issues, and to let them experience for themselves several of the current possibilities for viewing and analyzing their social world. I use two major devices to achieve this goal. Throughout the book, I present sociological problems from the perspective of three major schools of sociological thought. Quotes from classic and contemporary scholars bolster these points of view. Second, throughout the text I provide activities and projects for the students to carry out. Through these projects, students will become directly involved in *doing* sociology, from all three viewpoints.

The three sociologies presented in this text, it must be understood, are convenient fictions, just as fictional as the single sociology presented by standard texts. For the convenience of teaching and learning at the introductory level, I have artificially boiled down many sociologies into three composite sociologies. I feel that this "lumping and splitting" of the discipline's diverse viewpoints best draws the outlines or battle lines between contending factions. This assertion, however, like any other sociologist's contention, is debatable, and I invite and encourage such debate from my readers.

In capsule form, the three sociologies are distinguished as follows: *Sociology I* is the functional model, until recently so influential in the field that leading sociologists could claim that all sociology is functionalist sociology. Its characteristic orientation is summed up by the question, What forces (including conflict) generate and sustain the stability of the social system? *Sociology II* is the increasingly important activist sociology that advocates changing the social order through studying it. *Sociology III* is what this book will call naturalistic sociology, or the study of how subjective social realities are created, experienced, and described by social participants. Within each of these categories there are several distinct strains of inquiry, competing methodologies, and varying theoretical viewpoints, but each family of sociological theories has more in common within its categorical bounds than any member has with the other families. Taken together, they comprise the kaleidoscope that is today's sociology—turn the lens, and a different reality comes into view.

Perhaps even more important for students than learning about sociology by reading and talking about it is the *experience* of asking and answering sociological questions for themselves. That is why this text invites students not only to *read* but to *do*. At the end of each chapter is a section titled "Doing Sociology." This contains detailed instructions for carrying out in-class or independent exercises in sociology. In addition, a full chapter (Chapter 4) is devoted to the description of a series of semester-long research projects and activities to be undertaken by student work groups. This is in lieu of a chapter on methods such as might be found in a standard introductory text. Rather than merely describe the methods used by professional sociologists in their research, this chapter lays out the full range of sociological methods as instruments to be taken up by students, by means of which they can experience their world sociologically.

May we all strive for *Sataavadhaana*. It may be the minimum necessary for survival in today's world.

ELEMENTS OF SOCIOLOGICAL INVOLVEMENT

The four chapters in Part I present the basic elements of what it means to become involved in doing sociology.

Chapter 1, "One, Two, Three . . . How Many Sociologies?" states the premise of this text, that sociology is multifaceted and can be used to observe multiple social realities. It then goes on to outline in detail the three major sociological perspectives from which the student will learn to look at the world.

Throughout the text, a number of different "voices" are used in the exposition of the material. First there is the voice you are reading now, the views of the author of the textbook. A second voice will appear in the form of quotations from or paraphrases of relevant writings of the great original masters of sociological thought, the Founding Fathers. This voice will be marked off by a border of diamonds. A third voice will consist once again of quotations or paraphrases relevant to the textual issues at hand, but this time the ideas and findings come from contemporary sociologists, men and women of our day who have already distinguished themselves as Leading Lights. This voice will have a border of stars. A fourth voice, set off by yin-yang symbols, will echo the silent "Inner Voice" of the thoughtful reader as he or she contemplates the applicability of sociological ideas and techniques to the realities of everyday social life.

Chapter 2 is meant to be provocative as well as instructive. Making distinctions between "Social Problems, Sociological Problems, and Sociologists' Problems" often makes students and other sociologists angry. All three can be described as modes of involvement in social life, and therefore becoming aware of them is a form of self-awareness, which is always to some extent painful.

1

Self-awareness, self-involvement in society, and self-creation are the themes of Chapter 3, "Identity and Identification as Sociological Problems." An understanding of the relationship between the individual and society-at-large is a theoretical prerequisite to any study of social life, and a decision about the relationship between the sociologist's self and the truth about society he is searching for is a practical and moral prerequisite to doing sociology.

"Doing Sociology," Chapter 4, discusses methodology and suggests several specific group projects to be assigned and organized by the instructor. These projects will provide the student with the experience of revealing and participating in a variety of social realities, from a variety of sociological perspectives.

One, Two, Three . . .
How Many Sociologies?

1

More than anything else, sociology is a state of mind. One may do sociology, one may read and study it, one may join and profess it, or in rare and fortunate instances, one may be possessed by a sociological imagination.

The sociological imagination is what *every* self-respecting sociologist believes himself to possess; but for each one, the sociological imagination is a slightly or drastically different thing. It is this multiplicity of imaginations that we wish to explore.

According to one sociologist, the sociological imagination is

> A quality of mind that will help (people) to use information and to develop reason in order to achieve lucid summations of what is going on in the world and of what may be happening within themselves. . . . By such means the personal uneasiness of individuals is focused upon explicit troubles and the indifference of publics is transformed into involvement with public issues. (Mills, 1959, p. 5)

If you think that kind of imagination is likely to get you into trouble often and deep, you are right. Doing sociology in the style of C. Wright Mills does tend to get the doer into trouble, but that is just where he or she wants most to be, in order to see clearly what's going on, as we shall explain in full detail later on.

It may be added that for better or worse one might have sociology done to him. Victims of sociology include "subjects" of research projects whose answers to questions are misused, or subjected to interpretation for "hidden" meanings not consciously intended by the respondent; subjects whose emotions and human sentiments are manipulated or brutalized in sociological "laboratory" research (see "The Shocking Experiments of Doctor Milgram" in Chapter 3); all of us whose political or economic decisions have been swayed by the supposed objectivity of opinion polls; and, more seriously, the often fatal victims of counterinsurgency programs whose governments utilized intelligence data from sociological studies to identify and locate insurgents and potential insurgents (see the full description of "Project Camelot" in Chapter 2, and Horowitz, 1965).

But what is this "sociology" that may be done, read, joined or suffered? Here is our minimum definition of the subject: sociology is the application of scientific methods of inquiry to the puzzles of social life.

This appears to be the simplest and most straightforward definition possible, and most practitioners calling themselves sociologists could, I think, accept it as a minimal description of what they do. Yet a careful examination of each word in this definition reveals that it is neither simple nor straightforward. In fact, the practitioners agreeing on this description of what they do begin to part company as soon as any one of these terms—*application*, *scientific methods*, *the puzzles*, *social life*—is qualified with more precision. As the following scenario illustrates, there are many ways to skin a sociological cat.

Here lies before us the body of a man, certified by the local coroner to have died by his own hand. With us today we have three qualified professional sociologists, each of whom has agreed to explain for us the sociological significance of this man's death. Well, gentlemen?

Sociologist I: I see before me another case of suicide, one more to be added to the yearly total for this fine city of ours, which, divided into the population total, gives us a suicide *rate* of, ah, might I say, rather alarming proportions, comparatively speaking. As a sociologist I cannot, of course, even speculate as to the motivation of this particular individual, any more than a physicist can explain the path of a single molecule of water in an ocean wave. I am concerned with the social causes of social facts. That is why I *can* comment upon the likely causes and consequences of periodic changes or fluctuations in the suicide *rate*. In this context this corpse before us can be taken to represent the breakdown of orderliness in our society as a whole. The ever increasing rate of suicide we have been experiencing parallels the increasing rapidity and intensity of change in our social life, changes in social rules, social expectations, and social situations that more and more of us experience as serious disruptions. Over the whole of the social system, these changes have become too rapid and too severe for the normal reciprocating, balancing mechanisms in society to iron things out. As a result, more and more individuals find themselves socially dislocated, disoriented, rootless, and confused. More and more of these individuals become mentally ill, get divorced, commit crimes, or, at the extreme, commit suicide, their numbers indicating a sort of social despair. No doubt about it, as social order breaks down, the suicide rate goes up.

Sociologist II: On the contrary, my friend. It is the *lack* of change that is the problem, and the root cause of such despairing acts as this suicide. As you can see from his clothing and his calloused hands, this poor soul was a working man, a common laborer. No matter what unique, personal troubles might appear to his close associates to have driven him to take his life, the real causes for his suicide, as for other forms of anti-social behavior, such as crime, are to be found in the history of domination, oppression, and social injustice that is our true social context in this day and age.

This man's personal troubles stemmed from his inevitable involvement in great public issues—he has been ground down between gigantic contending forces in the world-historical framework. Specifically, he is a victim of the war between workers and owners that continues in advanced capitalist societies today. This man has been *alienated* to the fullest degree, to the death, in every possible sense: his control over his own work; his awareness of his brotherhood with all other workers; his natural impulses to do meaningful work, to develop and to grow fully as a human being in all possible directions—all of these have been taken away from him by an oppressive society that refuses to move forward toward a truly human, truly just future for humanity. The sickness of this society results in alienated death, not only for this particular victim, but for many others, including those who may think they are the winners in this deadly social game of dog-eat-dog. Suicide is one way out of a sick social order, where there is no hope for meaningful participation, for real change. This man is not a victim of social change, as my learned colleague would have it, he is a victim of the *lack* of revolutionary change, an alienated reject of a stagnating system of monstrous injustice. His blood cries out for the overthrow of this corrupt social order! We must write his name upon our banners, and mobilize for justice in his honor. This man died for *us*, my sisters and brothers. Justice *now*!

Sociologist III: To those of you who remain in the audience, I would like to apologize for my complete lack of interest in the motive, cause, or responsibility for this man's death, or rather, this apparently male corpse. I *am* curious in general about the social practices, procedures, and mutually constructed meanings that make up the social reality of this society we live in and make together, and in this case the question of suicide is for me, as well as for my colleagues, a puzzle of social life that needs to be unraveled. But for me, the question is how did this particular death become classified and accepted as a suicide, and what is the social order revealed and the social activity exhibited in the work of those who do such classification? I am interested in what suicide in general and this suicide in particular *means* to variously situated people in this society, and how these meanings change or are stabilized.

How did the coroner know, for instance, that this man's death qualified for certification as a suicide? What are the set of criteria he uses to decide such things? What particulars did he observe or what was he told by witnesses and others about this particular death? How did he match these up with his criteria to make the final disposition? What are the consequences of the coroner's decision to the victim's family, to the neighborhood and district, to the insurance company, to the police department, to the coroner's employers? Does the coroner's definition of this death correspond to that of the victim's relatives and friends? Perhaps everyone has his own reasons for assuming that a suicide is a suicide and that's that, but frankly, I'm skeptical about the whole business of counting the number of "suicides" in order to come up with a rate. I think the variety of meanings attached to any one suicide in various social contexts is what needs studying.

Three sociologists, all practicing under the basic definition, "the application of scientific methods of inquiry to the puzzles of social life," and yet we get three very different interpretations of the same puzzle. How can this be?

AN INNER VOICE

Three sociological imaginations? It's the same dead body lying there, isn't it? All three sociologists seem to be saying that this suicide, and suicide in general, is the product of society, or social forces, or social definitions. Yet the three explanations of how society produces suicides are so totally different from one another. Which sociological imagination am I supposed to learn and use? Are there more possibilities than these three, and would that still be sociology? Which explanation is correct, and which are wrong? They can't all be right, can they? Are they all equally scientific, and are they all dealing with what society really is? It looks like we've got many more questions than answers so far.

The sociologists practicing under this broad definition can construe "science" in a number of different ways to build their version of "scientific methods of inquiry." They can choose among several competing images of what social life essentially is. Within that chosen image, they can select which questions, issues, or problems they wish to define as the fundamental "puzzles," and which are peripheral or irrelevant. Even then they are free to choose or invent a rationale for their research activity—in whose interest, if anyone's, is their research to be done, and toward what ends, and to what uses should their findings be put? The combination of these choices—which model of science, which image of social life, which focal puzzles, and toward whose and what goals—determines which sociology the sociologist will practice.

There are many sociologies being practiced today, some more popular than others, some that are growing in strength and influence, and others that are on the wane. The beginning student of sociology ought to be fully aware that the field is not a uniform, integrated discipline, but a many-headed Hydra. Let us return to our first example, suicide, and examine the ideas of two real, not imaginary, sociologists on the topic.

FOUNDING FATHERS

Emile Durkheim's Sociology of Suicide

Emile Durkheim (1858—1917) provided the first model for the use of social statistics to explain individual actions in his book, Suicide. Durkheim demonstrated statistically that any theory that attempts to explain the causes of suicide as individual in nature contradicts the facts. The general theory that best fits the statistical information available on suicide is that lack of social integration, or the breakdown of normal social order, correlates positively with a high rate of suicide in any population. For instance, there are more suicides among unmarried than among married persons, and within the married group, more suicides among those without children than among those having children. In this instance, it would appear that the more integrated and responsibly related one is in a familial grouping, the less vulnerable one is to suicide. Further, Durkheim found that during periods of economic or political change and upheaval, suicide rates increase, even if the changes are for the better.

Durkheim's three major points are best made in his own words:

a. *"Society is not only something attracting the sentiments and activities of individuals with unequal force. It is also a power controlling them. There*

is a relation between the way this regulative action is performed and the social suicide-rate."

b. *"It is a well-known fact that economic crises have an aggravating effect on the suicidal tendency . . . .if therefore industrial or financial crises increase suicides, this is not because they cause poverty, since crises of prosperity have the same result; it is because they are crises, that is, disturbances of the collective order."*

c. *"Every disturbance of equilibrium, even though it achieves greater comfort and a heightening of general vitality, is an impulse to voluntary death." (Durkheim, 1897)*

Subsequent studies have challenged some of the details of Durkheim's findings, and confirmed others, but they have by and large shared a basic acceptance of Durkheim's fundamental sociological claim: it is a social fact that suicide rates correlate with other statistical fluctuations relating to the same population aggregates. In addition, this finding leads to an understanding of suicide as a symptom or a consequence of social forces operating throughout the entire integrated social system.

★★

LEADING LIGHTS

Jack Douglas' Sociology of Suicide

Seventy years after the publication of Durkheim's Suicide, Jack Douglas came out with the first total rejection of Durkheim's theory. His book, The Social Meanings of Suicide, offers an alternative explanation of that phenomenon—in short, an alternative sociology of suicide.

Douglas attacks Durkheim and his intellectual heirs (comprising most of Douglas' contemporary colleagues) for assuming that "social facts," like suicide statistics, are facts of the same sort as the "facts of nature" compiled and studied by natural scientists. In fact, Douglas argues, suicide rates, or any other rates, are not among the "observables" that would make up the basic data of a true natural science of social life. The only social activity that can be observed and studied in relation to such rates is the creating of statistics through the bureaucratic compiling, coding, and investigation of deaths. The statistics themselves are socially produced meanings, and they are not the only meanings people in societies attribute to phenomena like suicide.

Douglas proposes that it is the variety of social meanings attached to any social phenomenon that needs scientific study by sociologists. What are the competing meanings, how are they produced, how does one set of meanings attain dominance or acceptability as "the truth" over others? These are the questions sociologists need to ask, and the questions left unanswered by Durkheim's mode of analysis.

Exploring the social meanings of suicide, Douglas makes the following five major points:

a. People everywhere are ambiguous about the meanings, including effects and causes, of suicide. It is an emotionally charged issue, and never simply a case of the facts speaking for themselves.

b. "The meanings of suicide" are not equivalent to the meanings of specific suicidal acts. Ambiguous as poeple are about the meanings of suicide in general, there is even more confusion surrounding each actual suicide that occurs.

c. Meanings of any suicidal act vary, from what it means to the suicidal actor to what it means to professional and lay observers, some of whom will have been implicated in the act (for instance, by being blamed for the suicidal act, or held responsible for preventing it).

d. People are basically ambiguous about causes of suicides—are they to be found in the actor or in his situation? Or both? The traditional psychological argument that the causes of suicide are essentially within the person taking his own life denies too much of what "everyone knows," that there are causes outside the person that "drive" him to suicide. The Durkheimian "sociologistic" argument denies the other half of common knowledge—that suicides commit suicide for their own personal reasons.

e. "The structure one finds in the meanings of specific suicidal phenomena is not given by the transmitted culture, though some of the specific meanings and criteria that make this structure possible are so given, but . . . the individuals involved construct this structure of meanings . . . . The only way we can go about scientifically studying the means of suicidal phenomena (or any other social phenomena) is by studying the specific meanings of real-world phenomena of this socially defined type as the individuals in-volved construct them: we must work from the clearly observable, concrete phenomena upward to abstractions about meanings in any culture . . ." (Douglas, 1967, p. 254).

Douglas presents detailed case-study

materials, which he claims are the only truly "scientific" data we can get on suicide, and analyzes the variety of specific and culturally generalized meanings he finds in them. Just as he rejects the Durkheimian social facts as unscientific, other sociologists reject his find-ings as impressionistic and subjective.

★★★

Two sociologies of suicide, well and good, but there are *many* sociologies, alive and well, in this creatively divided and factious field. The number of possi-ble sociologies, given the choices of scientific model, image of social life, major puzzles, and goals for research faced by sociologists at any point in their careers, is astronomical. Many more sociologies are still to be created in the near future, quite possibly by readers of this book. Today there are a dozen or so sociologies practiced in North America, and a few more in Europe and the other countries of the world. This number is still too large for full and adequate presentation in an introductory textbook, however, so we shall resort to a very common but intel-lectually dangerous device—generalization, or lumping many different ideas into a few handy categories. The danger of this practice is that we may be guilty of what is called *reification*—treating what is only an idea as if it were a concrete thing. We shall have much more to say about this concept further on in the text.

When we describe three sociologies, we are constructing three handy categories with which to compare and contrast some of the major diversities in sociological thinking and inquiry. If we avoid the reification found in most texts—treating "sociology" as a single existing thing—we still risk the possibility of creating *three* sociologies in the minds of students. To avoid this outcome, we rely on two methods of prevention: this *caveat*, or consumer's warning, that the sociologies constructed here are indeed fabrications; and secondly an urgent in-vitation to the course instructor to identify his or her own sociological orientation to the class, and to argue, against this text, *his or her* own way of categorizing sociologists and sociologies.

In this text, we arrange the sociologies into three broad categories, calling them Sociology I, Sociology II, and Sociology III. Each of these categories in-cludes a number of contending sociologies that diverge from one another on very serious grounds. Their proponents would be acutely discomforted to find themselves in the same category with each other. But like members of an inter-nally combative family, they have much more at stake in their conflicts with the outside world, and therefore in what they share in common.

It is important for students to see and understand sociologies as perceptual and analytic *tools*, by means of which they may come to see and understand social life. Sociology can be likened to a complex camera with many lenses, many filters, many focal planes. Turn the lens, and a new focus is available for the mind's eye. With each sociological lens, a distinct social reality, a different level of truth about society, is brought into view. The multiplicity of our discipline mirrors and clarifies the plurality of social worlds in which we live. Our view is thus a constantly shifting *kaleidoscope*, bringing totally new images into view with each shift of the lens.

This is not the first book in the literature to acknowledge and assert that there are several sociologies, not one, though it is perhaps the first introductory text to do so. "There are, then," wrote sociologist Alan Dawe, "two sociologies: a sociology of social system and a sociology of social action. They are grounded in the diametrically opposed concerns with two central problems, those of order and control. And, at every level, they are in conflict" (Dawe, 1970). Without stating it explicitly, Dawe asserts a third sociology, his own: "In summary, one views action as the derivative of system, whilst the other views system as the derivative action. *And the contention here is that sociology has developed on the basis of the conflict between them.*" How would you describe Dawe's *third* sociology, implicit in this statement?

Sociologist George Ritzer outlines three sociologies in a recent book (Ritzer, 1975), but they are not the same three sociologies to be presented in this text. Ritzer calls his sociologies "paradigms" (distinct, fundamental patterns of a science's subject matter that define what should be studied and how), and delineates "the Social Facts paradigm," "the Social Definition paradigm," and "the Social Behavior paradigm." The Social Facts paradigm, following sociological founding father Emile Durkheim (see Durkheim, 1895), explores the impact of institutions and organizations upon individual actions. The Social Definition paradigm, following sociological founding father Max Weber (see Weber, 1904) examines and interprets the ways in which the rules and values of society, having become "internalized" by social actors, shape their actions and define their situations. The Social Behavior paradigm, following the contemporary behaviorist B. F. Skinner (see Skinner, 1971), calculates the determination of individual behavior by the immediate social rewards and punishments, the "contingencies of reinforcement" of the social actor's situation. In the case of each of these three sociologies, it is the system—in the form of institutions and organizations, as culturally transmitted rules and values, or as situational contingencies—that determines individual actions.

Sociologist Nicholas Mullins sees American sociologists as divided up into eight distinct "theory groups," clusters of practitioners who take each other's work seriously and disparage everyone else's (Mullins, 1973). His book's thesis is that sociological theories, or complete sociologies, emerge from the interactive work of such theory groups. Mullins' eight sociologies are called "Standard American Sociology," "Symbolic Interactionism," "Small Group Theory," "The Social Forecasters," "Ethnomethodology," "New Causal Theory," "The Structuralists," and "Radical-Critical Theory."

Two, three, or eight sociologies? The point of all this is not to decide how many sociologies there really are, nor to assign the names of various sociologies for memorization, but simply to document that the existence of several sociologies is widely recognized in the field. This multiplicity is not due to the fact that some sociologists see social reality correctly whereas the others are wrong, or less correct in their view. The development of many sociologies reflects the growing awareness that there are many different levels of truth about society that can be approached sociologically. There are many different worlds of social life that overlap and interpenetrate like a series of Chinese boxes. The puzzles of social life are complex, and multiform, and the variety of sociologies mirrors this complexity.

Social reality consists of worlds within worlds. Learn to see through the special lenses of the various sociologies, and a variety of these worlds will come more sharply, more distinctly, more consciously into view. But let the merely curious beware. Once you take up and use this powerful set of instruments, seriously, you will be changed, perhaps never to observe your own social life in the same way again. The sociological lenses will become a living part of your own eyes, your own awareness, your own perceiving self.

Sociology I, Sociology II, and Sociology III are three distinct ways of performing "the application of scientific methods of inquiry to the puzzles of social life." Each involves choices of and deep commitments to different versions of science, contrasting images of social life, separate agendas of puzzles to be solved, and discordant goals. The three major sociologies to be described here could be said to be practiced by three major *types* of sociologist. We shall call them the Functionalists, the Activists, and the Naturalists.

Most sociologists are exclusive and ardent proponents of one or the other of these sociological modes. But many creative contemporary sociologists, and a surprisingly high proportion of the classic "Founding Fathers" of sociology, would have to be classified as belonging to two, or even all three, of these categories. This is because some practitioners have changed their minds drastically over the course of their careers about the subject matter of their discipline and ways to go about studying it. Thus a sociologist might in his "youthful" days practice as an Activist, but settle down to be a Functionalist in his maturity, or some other combination. Others have consistently made contributions to more than one sociology. C. Wright Mills, for example, was both a Naturalist and an Activist throughout his career (Mills, 1940, 1951, 1959). Wilbert Moore has consistently contributed to both Functionalist and Naturalist sociologies (Moore, 1962, 1963). And Alvin Gouldner has made lifelong contributions as a Functionalist and as an Activist (Gouldner, 1970, 1973). We will examine the work of some of these contemporary "Leading Lights" in detail below. Finally, in the work of the "Founding Fathers" of sociology all of sociology can be found in a complex, ambiguous mix, as we shall see later on.

But before the glass becomes too cloudy with the richness and ambiguity of the work of the distinguished sociologists, let us clarify the differences between our three sociologies. Let us take up the lenses one by one, and ask, what are the social realities revealed by the different sociologies?

SOCIOLOGY I
Social Life as the System

Sociology I includes among its practitioners, whom we are calling the Functionalists, probably the largest single group of sociologists. It can also be referred to as establishment sociology, orthodox sociology, or conventional sociology. In 1959, Functionalist Kingsley Davis wrote that the "structural-functional analysis" done by Functionalists is, "in effect, synonymous with sociological analysis" (Davis, 1959). Since that time Sociology I has come under attack by ever increasing numbers of sociologists, and it is perhaps on its way out as the "dominant" sociology, but it still commands the loyalty and interests of many of sociology's best minds.

In brief, here are the choices making up the boundary lines of Sociology I: Functionalists choose the analytic, empirical model of science, based on the physical science standards of Newtonian mechanics, mathematical and experimental physics, and biochemistry. They choose to see social life as a great system of interlocking, interdependent parts, a system that can be theorized about as a whole, or experimented upon in its tiniest particles. The central problem, as the Functionalists see it, is how the social system manages to hold together, even as it tends to fall apart into its atomistic components, human individuals. This can be succinctly stated as "the problem of order." The chosen rationale for their endeavors is to be able better to predict the social consequences of our actions, with the second-order goal of increasing rational *control* over these consequences. In the words of Founding Father Auguste Comte, the goal is, "savoir pour prevoir; prevoir pour prevenir," "to know in order to predict; to predict in order to control."

Each of these distinguishing features of Sociology I must now be carefully examined in its turn, keeping in mind the key question, "What kind of social world are we likely to see if we look at it in this particular way?"

The Application of a Physical Science to
Social Life

It may appear contentious to say that there can be more than one correct answer to the question, "What is science" and perhaps it is. We are here following the contemporary German thinker Jurgen Habermas' distinction between three kinds of science, one empirical-analytic, with the aim of prediction-control; the second hermeneutic or interpretive, directed toward the enrichment of consciousness; and the third critical, directed toward liberative social change (see Habermas, 1972).

The most successful form of scientific activity to date is physics. The structure and dynamics of matter have been revealed by a majestic procession of theorist-experimenters from Newton to Einstein to Bohr; the laws of organization they formulated have been proven to hold uniformly throughout the universe as we know it, from the microcosm of the atom, to the macrocosm of the galaxies. In practical terms, the successive discoveries of the physicists have generated spin-offs that make possible all of our modern technology—including the means for total self-annihilation. Physics has brought humanity the power to radically transform the material world to suit itself.

This success perhaps explains why so many sociologists have chosen to borrow those features of scientific thought and method characteristic of physics. What are these methods, and what features of social life become magnified and clarified through a lens so structured?

Sociology I models itself on physics by applying four basic intellectual tools: generalization, objectification, quantification, and experimentation.

a. Generalization. Physics is the most general of the sciences. Its subject matter is *all* matter, everywhere, for all time, however it may be circumstantially organized in any instance. It is in this light that the "Social Physicist," or Functionalist, searches for the basic laws of all social life. The Functionalist strives to produce theoretical generalizations with the power and quality of physics' universal laws of matter. These laws would have to be statements about people in society, therefore, that would hold true independently of the particular circumstances of any person or any society. They would have to be statements independent of time and space, and in the social sphere, this means independent of history and geography.

Three of the leading Functionalists, Parsons, Bales, and Shils, at one time even proposed the direct application of Newton's Three Laws of Motion to the general examination of social action: the Principle of Inertia, the Principle of Action and Reaction, and the Principle of Effort (Parsons, 1953, pp. 102, 103). Another, William Catton, cites three similar "sociological axioms," one of which reads, "Every social pattern continues to manifest itself in constantly recurring social action at an unaltered rate unless some social force modifies the rate of pattern of such action" (Catton, 1966, p. 235). Compare this with Newton's original: "Every body continues in its state of rest, or of uniform motion in a right line, unless it is compelled to change that state by forces impressed upon it."

Sociology I, in its search for general laws to explain all of social life, also emulates physics by striving for logical coherence and consistency. It is an attempt to understand social life once and for all.

b. Objectification. The level of abstraction attained by the physical sciences allows for the greatest emotional distance from the subject matter—a maximum of objectivity. As an element of Sociology I, the standard of abstract objectivity demands the objectification of social activities, and of people themselves. In addition, person-as-object can only be studied scientifically by an objective scientist—one who systematically subdues any tendency to react with human biases to the situation of one's fellow human beings. Therein is the double objectification required by Sociology I for a "scientific" sociology. Treating social life as a collection of objects, and viewing them without personal bias, together form what is called the "value-free" or "value-neutral" stance taken by sociology toward its human subject matter. We shall confront some of the contradictions involved in this requirement in Chapter 2.

c. Quantification. Further objectification is involved in Sociology I's attempt to become an "exact" science like mathematical physics. The use of mathematical logic and formulae requires precision of measurement and the quantification of units. "Only what can be counted, counts" in such a social calculus. Those features of social life that can be readily measured, counted, and recorded, come to be seen as society's only characteristics. As in the case of Durkheim's treatment of suicide cited above, the decision to accept as "social facts" only quantitative data—rates, statistical totals, averages, or the proportion who answered yes or no to a question on a questionnaire—began with Durkheim and has continued to be one of Sociology I's defining characteristics. This might be compared to philosopher George Santayana's famous four-word definition of a dog's universe: "What don't smell, ain't."

d. Experimentation. The measurement of social life in terms of quantities and rates is the empirical task of Sociology I, as the formulation of logically coherent universal laws of social life is its theoretical endeavor. What links these together is the fourth major element borrowed from the methodology of physics and chemistry, experimental logic and practice. Experimentation is the way in which empirical data is gathered to test theoretical propositions. Functionalists frame questions about the social world in the form of predictions which, if accurate, should confirm or deny their hypotheses about social life.

Taken together, these four principles enable the sociologist to view social life as a whole entity—an integrated, empirically observable, numerically measurable, and experimentally predictable *system* of interacting parts.

Social Life as the System

Sociology I begins and ends with the image of social life as a great system composed of a variety of parts or subsystems. Because of the way the parts are organized, movement, change, or activity in any part leads to reactions in other contiguous parts, reverberating ultimately throughout the whole. The general tendency to be observed in all such actions, reactions, and reverberations is that the system acts to restore itself to a state of equilibrium or balance.

Practitioners of Sociology I have used various analogies to the physical sciences to describe social life as a system. Some, starting perhaps with Herbert Spencer (1820—1903) in England, have described this system as a living organism, in which each organ plays its part in maintaining the metabolism of the organic whole (Spencer, 1898). Others have compared it to a chemical-physical system, like a liquid in a vacuum flask—push in the cork, and the density, temperature, volume, and liquidity or solidity of the substance within will all change until, through mutual adjustment, an internal balance or equilibrium is restored (Cannon, 1932; Parsons, 1951; Demerath, 1967). Again, beginning with Marx, the revolutionary systematist, society has been seen as a great engine exploding internally class against class or conflict group against conflict group, in a vast reciprocating ("dialectical") motion through history. But all systematists perceive the significance of the *parts* of the social system primarily in terms of their contribution toward the persistence, the destiny, or, simply, the wholeness, of the whole.

There are Functionalists who concentrate on the workings of social systems as wholes—the social *macrocosm*. Others focus close in on the elemental particles or atomistic units of social interaction making up the larger whole—the social *microcosm*. Still others specialize in widespread if not completely generalized relationships between major system components—the *middle range*. Thus sociologists who compare the suicide rate in one society to that in another, sociologists who produce instances of individual perceptions being distorted by group pressures in laboratory experiments, and sociologists who inquire into the relationships between the kind of educational system found in one society and the kind of political system, all are working within the system image, and all are practitioners of what I have called Sociology I.

From perspectives large, small, and middle range, Sociology I reveals a social universe in which we are all constrained to live out our lives as social beings. It is a universe of systematically intertwined relationships in which our personal actions toward one another always bear the imprint of the system. Functionalists scientifically measure, analyze, and lay out for our inspection the social mechanisms we most commonly refer to as the mysterious "them" who make it impossible for us to do otherwise than we do. We are the products of the system, and at the same time we are fundamental components.

The Problem of Order

Which of the "puzzles of social life" shall the sociologist single out as the major focus of attention? For the sociologist doing Sociology I, on large or small scale, the question that demands a measured, scientific solution, over and over again, is "How is the orderliness of the social system maintained?" What motivates men and women to follow the rules their societies lay down—even willingly to subscribe to the rules, often even to over-conform? How does the social system manage to control its members' behavior so that it is then predictable by scientific observers?

The Functionalists look around themselves, and everywhere observe and are wonder-struck by the relative peacefulness, routine, and cooperation displayed by most social participants most of the time. But why is this orderliness and mutual coordination such a difficult thing for the Functionalist to understand or simply accept as the natural order of things human and social? Implicit in the

Functionalist's concern with "the problem of order" is a belief about basic human nature, namely that Homo sapiens in its natural state, without the restraints of social structure and social control, is a bloody, savage beast. Homo sapiens is by nature a disorderly, anarchic creature, and left to the creature's own devices, its behavior would be unpredictable, chaotic, and out of control. It is the view of human nature held by Thomas Hobbes, who set the terms of the "problem of order" as it is still viewed by Sociology I today.

FOUNDING FATHERS

Thomas Hobbes on the Natural Condition of Mankind

"Nature hath made men so equall, in the faculties of body, and mind; . . . when all is reckoned together, the difference between man, and man, is not so considerable, as that one man can thereupon claim himselfe any benefit, to which another may not pretend, as well as he. . . . From this equality of ability, ariseth equality of hope in the attaining of our Ends. And therefore if any two men desire the same thing, which nevertheless they cannot both enjoy, they become enemies; and in the way to their End, (which is principally their own conservation, and sometimes their delectation only) endeavor to destroy, or subdue one another. . . . Herebye it is manifest, that during the time men live without a common Power to keep them all in awe, they are in that condition which is called Warre; and such a warre, as is of every man, against every man. . . . Whatsoever therefore is consequent to a time of Warre, where every man is Enemy to every man; the same is consequent to the time, wherein men live without other security, than what their own strength, and their own invention shall furnish them withall. In such condition, there is no place for Industry; because the fruit thereof is uncertain: and consequently no Culture of the Earth; no Navigation, nor use of the commodities that may be imported by Sea; no commodious Building; no Instruments of moving, and removing such things as require much force; no Knowledge of the face of the Earth; no account of Time; no Arts; no Letters; no Society; and which is worst of all, continuall feare, and danger of violent death; And the life of man, solitary, poore, nasty, brutish, and short." (Hobbes, 1881)

The continuing problem for the survival of any social system, then, is to protect its members against their own natural brutishness toward one another. By controlling its members, the system maintains its own stability, organization, and wholeness. The basic function of a social system is to restrain everyone's antisocial tendencies for its own, and their own, good. How people become "socialized," how they sustain and are sustained by social order, are the major questions addressed by Sociology I.

The Goals of Prediction and Control

Sociology I shares the goals of technologically applicable physical sciences as well as many of their methods. In the long run, modern science, applied in technology, has reversed the relationship between human beings and the forces of nature. Humanity was once at the mercy of natural forces; now it has nature, as it were, on her knees, begging for relief from exploitation and destruction. Analogously, many see humanity today as still the victim of uncontrolled social forces—war, overpopulation, tyranny, social upheaval, economic depressions, crime—and hope that social science, in the long run, will give us the power over human nature that physical science has given us over physical nature.

Functionalists generally have no specific, applied humanitarian goals in mind when they do sociology. They wish simply to increase and improve our objectively verifiable knowledge about the social systems in which we all live. Those who fund and subsidize such research, however, do believe that improved knowledge of the social system and its parts will result in an improved technology of control over the vagaries of human nature. Just as Copernicus' astronomical measurements and inferences replaced the commonly held but erroneous notion of an earth-centered universe, Sociology I seeks to correct and improve our conceptions about the social world through the research of "pure science." But just as Copernicus' improvements in astronomical calculation had immediate practical "spin-offs" for navigators and later made possible the conquest of space, there are practical consequences expected from Functionalists' work, at least in the long run.

The main goal of Sociology I is to improve our ability to predict the actions of persons and groups on the basis of measurable factors, or "variables," that determine those actions. This increased predictability will enhance the ability of the social system to control those actions in the interest of its survival as a system, and to protect people against the consequences of their uncontrolled, or unforeseen, actions. Which specific values the social system should embody, or which of our actions need to be controlled and which encouraged, the Functionalists claim are not their decisions to make. The society itself, through its own particular form of organizing the making of decisions and choices, chooses and proclaims its ultimate values and goals; Sociology I can only provide the scientific means toward those goals, whatever they may be.

ᘯᘯᘯ

AN INNER VOICE

It would be great to increase the predictability of social events, and bring things a bit more under control than they are now. A so-ciety where you never know what's going to happen next, whether in the world at large or among my own group of friends, is a bit too *chaotic and disorderly. But would the success of this sociology mean that some Functionalist is going to predict when I'm ready to commit suicide, or help to control my behavior through the system so that I don't? And for whose benefit will this control be exercised? This sociology seems to give me all the freedom of choice of a puppet on a string. I wonder how controlled by the system my behavior is. Am I as free as I feel? Or have I maybe internalized the system's own hooks and levers? And if so, am I then at all responsible for whatever I do? I've got to look more closely at what I do from day to day in social situations, and why I do it. How much of a robot have they made out of me?*

SOCIOLOGY II
Social Life as the Arena

The Activists make up a growing minority of today's sociological fraternity in North America and Europe. They range from Neo-Marxists to Critical Theorists to Naderite reformers to counter-cultural anarchists, but all are proponents of Sociology II in that they have made the following choices in the "application of scientific methods of inquiry to the puzzles of social life":

The Activist sociologists' implicitly or explicitly held model of scientific inquiry is more like medicine or psychoanalysis than like physics or chemistry; their working model of the subject matter, social life, is of a great arena, in which, symbolically or literally, the great battles that comprise the events of human history are fought. Their chosen problem area within this model is the single, but multifaceted, issue of social justice versus social injustice, and their goal is the furtherance of the "good society," or at least a better society. The single trait that proponents of Sociology II most characteristically share is a commitment to change the society they study by means of scientific inquiry. This is exemplified in Karl Marx's proclamation: "The philosophers have only *interpreted* the world, in various ways; the point, however, is to *change* it" (Marx, 1845, p. 245). From this commitment their own distinctive sociological orientations flow quite logically.

This commitment to change the social order is the fundamental difference between proponents of Sociology II and their more detached colleagues, the Functionalists and the Naturalists. There are Functionalists who emphasize the study of change, and other Functionalists who see change and conflict as the core reality of the social system, the so-called "conflict school," but they remain within the same basic intellectual framework of Sociology I. The Activists consciously violate the principles of objectivity on which the Functionalists rest their claims to validity. Sociology II denies and rejects any separation between applied and pure social science, or between a person as a sociologist and as a morally involved actor in social struggles. To know social reality scientifically, they claim, one must become involved in changing it. In an important sense, Comte's sociological credo is totally reversed, or stood on its head, by Activist sociologists. It is not, "*savoir pour prevoir, prevoir pour prevenir*," but, "you must intervene in social processes in order to make accurate social predictions, because that only will come to pass which you and others in concert make to happen, and only then, when you have succeeded in bringing your own predictions into being, will you have achieved realistic knowledge of the social system."

◆◇◆

FOUNDING FATHERS

Lester Frank Ward's Social Ameliorism

Early pioneers of American sociology were forthrightly activists in terms of commitment to change society. Lester Ward, for instance, set out with Christian social conscience and reformist moral zeal to cure modern society of its ills, which were seen as inherent in the capitalist industrial system, through scientific diagnosis and rational reform.

Ward's chief aspiration was to create a social science that could form the proper basis of intelligent social action. Ward himself was essentially a reformist placing his faith in the "scientific" control of society. He did not view science as an end in itself. Truth for the sake of truth, or knowledge for its own sake were, he held, unwarranted principles. Science has "always an ulterior purpose, and that purpose is ethical. . . ." "Human happiness" is the ideal end of all social effort, but the system of classes in our society stands as a great barrier in the way of its attainment. It becomes the task of a dynamic sociology to develop appropriate means to gain this ideal (Ward, 1906, pp. 287, 318. Cf. Page, 1964, Ch. 2).

◆◇◆

The Application of the Medical Model to Social Life

The medical scientist utilizes relevant techniques and findings from all the other sciences, including physics, biology, chemistry, and zoology, but medicine has its own principles, methods, and procedures, its own appropriate line of scientific inquiry. This line begins with *diagnosis*, leading rationally and logically to proper *treatment* (or prescription) for the diagnosed illness, and thence to *evaluation* of the effects of treatment. Proof of the ameliorative effect of the treatment is the scientific "truth" sought.

Like medical science, Sociology II also proceeds from diagnosis to prescriptive treatment to evaluation of the results, but, as the title of an Activist's book of a generation ago puts it, with *Society as the Patient* (Frank, 1948). Likewise, Activism is receptive to and compatible with any scientifically formulated information germane to the problem, whether borrowed from other sociologies or other social sciences, such as economics, psychology, political science, etc.

The initial task of social diagnosis draws the practitioner of Sociology II into confrontation with social issues, problems that are seen as symptomatic of the underlying illnesses in the society. The Activists' moral awareness equips them to make fundamental judgments about social health and social illness. Their training and their ability to utilize scientific methods and findings enable them to choose and prescribe proper treatment for the ills they identify. In the words of C. Wright Mills, the leading sociological Activist of the 1950s, the diagnostic task of the sociologist is to transform "the personal troubles of milieu" into "public issues of social structure" (Mills, 1959).

In order to carry the diagnosis of social ills forward into treatment, Activists find they must involve themselves as advocates of those social characteristics and forces that they have identified as social health, and further that they must enlist as partisans on the side of a particular group of people who are struggling on what they have defined as the right side of the issue. As long as they only prescribe cures from a distance, proposing ameliorative actions that others should carry out, the sociologists are not behaving like true Activists, and according to Activist theory, they have no chance to approach the truth about society. It is only when they themselves are involved in the struggle that they may experience directly the consequences of the treatment they have prescribed. It is only when the doctors are willing to take their own medicine that the validity of their science can be accepted by others.

As "medical" scientists, the Activists are more oriented to particular, flesh-and-blood cases of social illness than to the abstract laws of social structure that dominate the work of Functionalists. While Sociology II does relate particular social ills to their historical context, assigning them places in the worldwide struggle of humankind, it is nevertheless seldom able to reach the heights of abstraction sought by the Functionalists.

The Activists' scientific "objectivity" is also modified somewhat by this "medical" orientation: like physicians, and unlike physicists, Activist sociologists *care* deeply about the "objects" they study, and cannot achieve emotional distance from them for purely intellectual or analytic purposes. In diagnosing and treating social "patients," they are inevitably involved with them subjectively. The Activists maintain, however, that it is only through a clear-eyed self-awareness of such subjective involvements, and a hard-headed analysis of one's own subjectivity, that true scientific objectivity about society can be achieved at all.

Thus Activists cannot study the social causes and consequences of the war in Vietnam without producing information that is damaging to the U.S. government and helpful to the antiwar movement, and they must fight that battle through to the end as antiwar partisans, in order to complete their inquiries; they cannot study the exploitation of the natural environment without attacking the exploiting corporations and fighting on the side of the conservationists; they cannot investigate relations between the sexes in modern society without becoming feminist partisans; and they cannot study poverty without supporting the poor in their struggle against the rich.

Such diagnoses and proposals for treatment tend to land Activists in trouble much of the time, as we shall detail more fully in the next chapter. But that is precisely how the Activists see the social world: not a smoothly running system with a few wrinkles to iron out, but a strife-torn arena full of conflict.

Social Life as the Arena

As scientists, the practitioners of Sociology II professionally *intervene* in the historical processes of social change and development they study. They focus their scientific lens on the contending parties and contradictory forces of social life.

People come to the attention of medical scientists only as patients, only when a conflict between health and illness in the body seriously threatens their well-being or their lives. The doctor's view of the world therefore tends to divide things up between health and its enemies. Similarly, sociological Activists are sensitized primarily to the conflicts rending the social fabric, the physical, moral, and intellectual battles being fought between the forces of social health and the forces of social illness.

They move to the center of the action and try to diagnose the social illness and to prescribe or apply treatments for it. From this position, the image of social life that is most clearly revealed, and out of which Activists operate cognitively, is that of a vast arena, a public battlefield or theater of operations in which the important issues are decided. The quality of social life hangs in the balance. For Sociology II, the only way to study this arena is to plunge into it and fight.

By identifying forthrightly and actively which side of the struggle they are on, Activists are able to see clearly which side the others in the arena are on, as well. *From the perspective of Sociology II, this defines a person's primary social identity.* The combatants in any particular issue may be identified by Activists as the strong against the weak, the rich against the poor, men against women, imperialist nations against presently or formerly colonized peoples, one race against another, the elite versus the masses, the owners versus the workers, the state versus the individual, corporations against communities or persons, or even, the system against people.

Identification of the major combatants or contending forces in the social arena is the first step in the Activists' diagnostic work, but it follows from their earlier perception of the "puzzle" to which they find they must dedicate their energies. Activists are caught up in the agonizing question asked by men and women in every age, "Why do the iniquitous triumph over the just, and how can this be rectified?"

The Issue of Social Injustice

The Activist equivalent of physical illness in medicine is social injustice. The puzzles studied by Sociology II are formulated as issues—racism, poverty, imperialism, sexism, militarism, environmentalism, censorship, prison reform, police violence, corporate irresponsibility, public miseducation, and so on. All of these are localized or historically specific versions of the one great issue—how may social justice be achieved, restored, or protected; how may social injustice be exposed, understood, rooted out. The symptoms of social disease are exhibited by its primary victims—the oppressed, the poor, the alienated, the suicidal, the despised, the ghettoized, and the incarcerated—in short, the underdogs. And so the underdogs become the Activists' direct clients. They enter the lists as champions of the victims' cause by first exposing the fact that they *are* the victims, and second by identifying the villains of the piece.

But we are all in the Activists' social arena and they do not fail to remind us that injustice threatens everyone's social life. In a sick society, no one is socially healthy. Therefore any attempt to restore social justice in any particular instance should benefit, in the long run, the oppressors as well as the oppressed. One example is the feminist insistence that the liberation of women from male domination and exploitation, though it requires some painful self-awareness on the part of the men at the outset, will in the long run liberate and enrich their lives as well.

Here again, the Activist version of sociology not only diverges from Functionalist sociology, it runs up against it headlong and forms a bitter opposition to the sociological "establishment." Practitioners of Sociology I cannot possibly see the social reality of the arena, Activists claim, because they are the hired propagandists for the corporate elite in the West and the bureaucratic elite in the socialist countries. The system image dominates Functionalists' minds because it is the antagonist in the arena who benefits from the status quo, who needs the system to continue to dominate the masses he controls. It is this antagonist who hires Functionalist sociologists to do "objective" research. By simply identifying the antagonists and their associates, therefore, Activists strike a damaging blow against their colleagues, the Functionalists.

✚✚

LEADING LIGHTS

Martin Nicolaus' Remarks to the American Sociological Convention, 1968

Following the Secretary of Health, Education and Welfare to the speaker's platform at the Sheraton Hotel in Boston, Mr. Nicolaus spoke for the radical sociology caucus:

"It is no secret and no original discovery that the major and dominant sectors of sociology

today are sold—computers, codes and questionnaires—to the people who have enough money to afford this ornament, and who see a useful purpose being served by keeping hundreds of intelligent men and women occupied in the pursuit of harmless trivia and off the streets. I am not asserting that every individual researcher sells his brain for a bribe—although many of us know of research projects where that has happened literally—but merely that the dominant structure of the profession, in which all of its members are to some extent socialized, is a structure in which service to the ruling class of this society is the highest form of honor and achievement. . . . The honored sociologist, the bi-status sociologist, the book-a-year sociologist, the sociologist who always wears the livery—the suit and tie—of his masters: this is the type of sociologist who sets the tone and the ethic of the profession, and it is this type of sociologist who is nothing more or less than a house servant in the corporate establishment, a white intellectual Uncle Tom not only for this government and ruling class, but for any government and ruling class—which explains to my mind why Soviet sociologists and American sociologists are finding after so many years of isolation that, after all, they have something in common." (Quoted in Horowitz, 1971, p. 15.)

✶✶✶

The Goal of the Good Society

Like medical men, Activists are adept at recognizing and treating instances of social illness, but also like medicine, Sociology II is both vague and reticent about stating specifically what a state of good health is. Behind their commitment to eradicate social injustice, logically assumed in every recognition and diagnosis of a social issue, Activists have a vision of utopia: social life with perfect justice, the good society. It is this ideal, or this hope for the future of humankind that drives them into the arena to work toward realization of the good society.

Admitting that they are working toward the good society is the hallmark of the Activists' professionalism. The Activists are positive in their view of human nature, and optimistic about the future of humanity, and also in a principled way forthright about their positive bias, their "nonscientific" reasons for doing social science. However, the least developed area of Activist sociology is an explicit statement of what the good society would be like were it to be achieved.

Activists criticize Functionalists for claiming to be perfectly objective and value free, while in fact projecting a veiled image of "the good society" from the viewpoint of those now in power. According to this critique, the job of the Functionalists is to convince the oppressed that they are living in the best of all possible worlds.

Karl Marx is a major founding father of Activist sociology because he saw the possibility of utopia only through the overthrow of the power relationships between capitalists and workers, after which the workers would take power, and the reorganization of society, into their own hands. Marx comments here on the commune as the ideal form of organization for the good society, and on communism as its organizing principle.

❖❖

FOUNDING FATHERS

Karl Marx on Unalienated Society

"Yes, gentlemen, the Commune intended to abolish that class-property which makes the labour of the many the wealth of the few. It aimed at the expropriation of the expropriators. It wanted to make individual property a truth by transforming the means of production, land and capital, now chiefly the means of enslaving and exploiting labour, into mere instruments of free and associated labour. But this is Communism, "impossible" Communism! Why, those members of the ruling class who are intelligent enough to perceive the impossibility of continuing the present system—and they are many—have become the obtrusive and full-mouthed apostles of cooperative production. If cooperative production is not to remain a sham and a snare; if it is to supersede the Capitalist system; if united cooperative societies are to regulate national production upon a common plan, thus taking it under their own control, and putting an end to the constant anarchy and periodical convulsions which are the fatality of Capitalist production—what else, gentlemen, would it be but Communism, "possible" Communism?"

The working class did not expect miracles from the Commune. They have no ready-made utopias to introduce par decret du peuple. They know that in order to work out

their own emancipation, and along with it that higher form to which present society is irresistibly tending by its own economical agencies, they will have to pass through long struggles, through a series of historic processess, transforming circumstances and men. They have no ideals to realize, but to set free the elements of the new society with which old collapsing bourgeois society itself is pregnant." (Marx, 1871, p. 518)

"In a higher phase of communist society, after the enslaving subordination of the individual to the division of labour, and therewith also the antithesis between mental and physical labour, has vanished; after labour has become not only a means of life but life's prime want; after the productive forces have also increased with the all-round development of the individual, and all the springs of co-operative wealth flow more abundantly —only then can the narrow horizon of bourgeois right be crossed in its entirety and society inscribe on its banners: From each according to his ability, to each according to his needs!" (Marx, 1875, p. 24)

(Throughout the text, page references for quoted material will refer to the modern, more available, edition of the work cited in the References.)

❖❖

The dream of a good society shared by Activists has many common elements much like those expressed here by Marx—emancipation of and rule by the underclasses, a sort of participatory democracy, equality between physical and mental labor, concern with distribution of society's goods to those who need it, the opportunity to develop one's personality fully, and to make the maximum contribution of one's talents and skills to one's society.

But more recent Activists have been even less explicit about the exact character of the utopia to follow the eradication of injustice. Activists are therefore often accused of negativism, of being able to state much more clearly what they are against than what they are for.

The goal of the good society, as well as the diagnosis of what is wrong with present society, are value judgments that Activist sociologists make, and must make, for themselves. Unlike the Functionalists, who offer scientific means toward goals chosen by the society they serve, Activists, in the very act of diagnosis and prescription, in the ideal of social health they hold up against the social reality they view, choose goals and decide on ultimate values. They claim that anything less is dereliction of every thinking person's ethical duty, and anything less forthright is a built-in distortion of scientifically observable social reality.

AN INNER VOICE

The Activist social world as an arena certainly squares with all the conflicting forces I can see around me and in the news every day. And getting involved must be a more effective way of coming to grips with these conflicts. But, it sounds like the Activists are saying I must become active on behalf of justice if I want to study society, or even to live in it happily. It's like Eldridge Cleaver's saying, "If you're not part of the solution, you're part of the problem." There's freedom possible here, in this image of how society works, but its freedom I've got to go out and fight for. I don't know if I'm any more comfortable with this image than with the last one. Does everything in society have to be a struggle, a war, a battle in the arena leading toward revolution? At least it's not watertight and confining like the system of the Functionalists, but maybe it's an exaggeration in the other direction—too open, too chaotic, too much emphasis on change and upheaval. How do I live a quiet, normal life and still remain free?

So, am I naturally a Functionalist or an Activist? Do I think basic human nature needs to be controlled, or that it has to be liberated? I don't even know if there is such a thing as "human nature." I wonder if the third sociology has any answers? Probably not. If the first two are any indication, Sociology III will probably just make it harder to even ask the same questions.

SOCIOLOGY III
Social Life as the Gallery

A growing number of sociologists are doing sociological work that is neither Functionalist nor Activist in basic orientation. There is a wide diversity among them, and no agreement at all on what the new sociology they are doing should be called. Some of them call what they practice Action Theory, Chicago School Sociology, Cognitive Sociology, Dramaturgical Analysis, Ethnomethodology, Interactionism, Interpretive Sociology, Labelling Theory, Phenomenological

Sociology, Social Definitionism, Social Ethnography, Sociolinguistics, Sociology of the Absurd, Sociology of Everyday Life, Symbolic Interactionism, Wild Sociology, and other titles. The diversity and controversy among and between these sociologies should always be remembered and stressed, but I find several important elements that all of them have in common, that distinguishes them as a group from Sociologies I and II and earns them my label of Sociology III, the Naturalists.

The new breed of what I call sociological Naturalists descends from a long and respectable intellectual ancestry in the field, but it is regarded as a band of the most radical upstarts, *enfants terribles,* by professional peers. To its practitioners, Sociology III is the wave of the future in sociological inquiry, to its opponents, a short-lived, useless fad, but it is based on the most ancient of impulses toward a social science—the urge to observe the actions of one's fellow men and women intensively, to describe them carefully in full complexity and detail, and to be impressed with their elegance and skill—in short, to *wonder* about humanity. If the be-all and end-all of social science for the Functionalist is to predict and control social behavior; if the basic commitment of the Activist is to change society through scientific study; then the characteristic and defining impetus of sociological Naturalists is to enhance their own and others' *appreciation* of social life.

The second major element that Naturalists hold in common with each other is a belief about human nature in relation to social life that is truly different from either the Functionalist's beast who needs social control or the Activist's gentleman who needs liberation from a beastly social system. For the Naturalist sociologist, people are basically, observably, the *creators* of day-to-day social reality, including the day's prevailing theory about human nature. It is people making themselves and their society in social interaction that the Naturalist observes, analyzes, and comes to appreciate.

Drawing on scientific traditions of an interpretive nature, practitioners of Sociology III attempt to work scientifically toward a science of social life in the mode in which linguistics is a science of language, or in the way in which natural history is a science of plant and animal life in its ecological environment. Working in this way, Naturalists describe and present instances of social life in the form of specimen exhibits, rather than as samplings of data or as confrontations with issues. The whole of social life then takes on the image, through the Naturalist's lens, of a vast gallery of independently interesting exhibits, which can be organized and reorganized in the viewer's mind. The central puzzle of social life examined case by case through this imagery is called "the mystery of intersubjectivity." In brief, it is considered mysterious that from day to day all of us who participate in social interaction can simply take it for granted that events occur in their normal ways, that you meant by what you said what I heard you to mean, that I am who I claim to be, that society, my family, our relationship, the gross national product exist as social facts. It is a mystery how all of these things appear to be realities we experience in common because we know that each and every one of us experiences things, interprets things, and distorts things, in his or her own unique way.

My experience of the world is private, and cannot be known or experienced by any other being. Yet the appearance of normality, of business as usual, that underlies and certifies all of our social life as genuine and practical rests on the unshakable assumption that my experience of most things most of the time is just like yours, and that *because* our experiences are the same, the common object or event we are experiencing is, immutably, what it is. Naturalists ask of social life, "How is this ongoing appearance of normality, of commonality, and of mutuality of experience created and sustained by social participants?" And, as was said above, the goal, the rationale for this kind of social scientific endeavor is neither the certainty of prediction nor the justice of change, it is something almost shameful to have as an ambition in this pragmatic age: the desire to know and appreciate, as an end in itself.

The Naturalist is seeking merely to fulfill the passion of idle curiosity. Because this is the only promise that Sociology III holds out—the satisfaction of knowing how something works, the gratification of a deeper appreciation of the social life constructed day by day by ordinary men and women—perhaps it would best be pursued as a hobby, a leisure-time activity, rather than as a paid, professional activity with official standing. Naturalist sociology probably never did anyone any good, and never will; on the other hand, it has never harmed anyone either, which cannot be said of the other sociologies.

◆◇◆

FOUNDING FATHERS

Georg Simmel on Society and Sociability

In the opening speech at the first meeting of the German Sociological Society in Frankfurt in 1910, Georg Simmel said:

"There is an old conflict over the nature of society. One side mystically exaggerates its significance, contending that only through society is human life endowed with reality. The other regards it as a mere abstract concept by means of which the observer draws the realities, which are individual human beings, into a whole, as one calls trees and brooks, houses and meadows, a "landscape." However one decides this conflict, he must allow society to be a reality in a double sense. On the one hand are the individuals in their directly perceptible existence, the bear-ers of the processes of association, who are united by these processes into the higher unity which one calls "society"; on the other hand, the interests which, living in the individuals, motivate such union: economic and ideal interests, warlike and erotic, religious and charitable. To satisfy such urges and to attain such purposes, arise the innumerable forms of social life, all the with-one-another, for-one-another, in-one-another, against-one-another, and through-one-another, in state and commune, in church and economic associations, in family and clubs."

What identifies Simmel as a Founding Father of the Naturalist approach is what he then did with this "conflict." In setting up the dichotomies between individual and society, between interests and associations, asking whether society is made up of individual persons of economic and ideal interests, or of groups and associations, posing the possibility that the reality of the individual is prior to the reality of society not vice versa, Simmel named most of the philosophical controversies in which other sociologists are regularly embroiled. But Simmel has no interest whatsoever in the resolution of these controversies. He is not out to argue that either side of any of these dichotomies is more probable or more logically correct than the other. Rather, Simmel goes on in his talk to outline the processes of everyday social interaction within which people enact, argue, try out, and realize (in the dual sense of make real and become aware of) all the sides of these conflicts. Simmel calls this the process of "sociability." Simmel transforms what have been traditionally seen as the problems of social scientists and social philosophers into the practical problems ordinary members of society face daily in their interactive lives.

Sociability, Simmel observes, is that portion of our social lives in which we interact with others just for the pleasure of each other's company, not as a means to some end. Conviviality, chit-chat, flirtation, and aimless talk characterize the activities of sociability. It is during these periods of interaction that we are free to play with the social and personal forms and definitions whose existence is the serious business of the rest of our social lives. When they are being sociable, Simmel claims, our fellow men reveal to the observer (who must of course at the time also be a participant in the sociability) the reality, the paradox, and the transformability of the "social facts" that form the basis for social life. Individuals consciously demonstrate their independence from and priority to social constraints; at the same time, the formal, mask-like quality of social identity is brought into play most openly, and participants can feel relieved of personal responsibility for their actions because they are only "playing the game." In his analysis of sociability, Simmel tries to show how people in their everyday lives raise and resolve the sociological conflicts and paradoxes stated above. This is the fundamental approach of the Naturalist (Simmel, 1910).

The Application of Interpretive Science to Social Life

Sociology III is a sociology that at one and the same time takes seriously Max Weber's definition of social action as consisting solely of the subjective meanings actions display to social participants (Weber, 1904), *and* insists on a natural science or natural history approach to these social meanings. A naturalistic study of social meanings? What kind of a science is this?

Sociologist Matthew Speier proposed

that the student of social life adopt a very simple working method for his investigations. It is a method we might call naturalistic, in the same sense that biologists use that term for the study of natural history. The objects of study in a natural history approach to the sociology of everyday life consist of social phenomena that are amenable to naturalistic observations, i.e., the ongoing stream of naturally occurring social activities. . . . *The formulation of sociological problems has to be responsive to the data of observation.* In fact, the noted paleontologist, George Gaylord Simpson, argues that, if there is any one basic feature to the so-called scientific method, it is observation. (Speier, 1973)

The Naturalist begins with the claim that science, any science, must be fundamentally based upon observation. The theories developed by that science must then be built step by step upon the foundation of observation, and must always remain true to the phenomena that has been and is being continuously observed. Naturalist social science thus represents a return to the social things themselves for closer scrutiny, and a rejection of the sociological ideas that have been developed without a basis of careful observations.

The first thing Naturalist social scientists do, then, is carefully observe social life as they see it, day by day, and record their observations. The second step they must take to make sense of their recorded observations is a *reflexive* analysis of what they have seen, and more importantly, *how they have seen it.* This is demanded of them by the nature of social phenomena, insofar as they are observable phenomena. Sociological Naturalists can only record what their observations have *meant* to them, as social participants like other social participants. Their "data" then must always consist of meanings, and subjective meanings at that. To be scientifically objective about social life means to the Naturalist, paradoxically enough, to realize that all of social life consists in the subjective interpretation of meanings.

Like botanists or zoologists, sociological Naturalists first describe in minute detail the specimens of social life they have observed and collected. They then organize and categorize these specimens, and attempt to penetrate through their outward appearances to the system of meanings or the process of constructing meanings that may lie underneath. In searching for a grammar of such meanings, they borrow from the science of linguistics.

But the focus of investigation is on *how* people display the meaningfulness of the world, or how they construct meanings for their own and others' actions. From this perspective, Functionalist and Activist sociologists appear to be deluded, practicing in a prescientific or folkish manner, because they take the meanings of "social facts" for granted. That is, they accept the meanings everyone else attaches to behavior, and try to go on from there with quantification and logical theorizing to make better sense out of social life. The Naturalist, on the other hand, suspends belief in the taken-for-granted meanings of social actions and social facts, and asks, how do these actions come to have these meanings for these participants, and how do these social facts come to be formulated as facts? The Naturalist sociologist, in other words, inquires into the processes by which the "naturally occurring" facts of social interaction come to be produced.

★★★

LEADING LIGHTS

Alfred Schutz on the Problem of Multiple Realities

Alfred Schutz is the major exponent of the idea that there are many social realities, and that each can be seen and understood with the appropriate viewing lens. By stating the problem of multiple realities, and providing some solutions for it, Schutz has had an important influence on American sociology and has provided much of the theoretical foundation for contemporary sociological Naturalism, or Sociology III.

Schutz started with the insight that reality, as we perceive it and deal with it in our social lives, is a social construct, something people interactively construct together. Different individuals, different social groups, and different collections of groups construct and experience different realities, or versions of reality, and each of these is totally valid and real for those experiencing it.

Society appears to all of us to be relatively orderly, however, an organization of meanings that seems to be pretty much the same thing for you as it is for me. If there are multiple realities, how is this orderliness and this commonality of social reality possible?

Schutz theorized that for the purposes of order and sanity in our lives, we take for granted certain ideas about reality and about other people. A central one of these is the "reciprocity of perspectives" whereby we assume that the other person's view of reality is determined by their social position, and that if we were to exchange positions, we would then see things essentially as they do. Through speech and other forms of interaction we work to make our separate and different realities congruent with one another, and through that work we mutually create a social world-in-common out of our multiple realities (Schutz, 1962).

★★★

Social Life as the Gallery

The image of social life emerging from the varied researches of the Naturalist sociologists is that of a vast, ever more fully explored, yet ever richer and more unknown, gallery or museum-hall, lined with exhibits of social life's varieties. Sociology III describes and holds up for our wonderment a series of specimens from the exotic and bizarre to the most commonplace and everyday. The life-as-the-gallery image unites these diverse spectacles by announcing a frame of mind within which our common social life may be viewed anew, as a world of totally familiar, yet curious objects needing explanation.

There are great similarities between this image and the practice of anthropologists for the past two centuries. The great difference between anthropology and Sociology III, however, is crucial: for two hundred years anthropologists have been bringing back to "civilized" countries detailed descriptive reports of the habits, customs, and practices of peoples of other cultures, other social worlds, implicitly characterized as reports on the activities of strangers. What the Naturalists attempt is to describe to us *our own* exotic customs, like breakfast, lunch, and bureacracy, to make us strangers to ourselves. In this way we can view our social realities as products of our efforts rather than as givens somehow existing in the environment.

Descriptions already available in Sociology III's gallery include specimens such as the art of walking as a social activity; how the patients organize a mental hospital into their own place; how nurses transform the handling of dead bodies into mundane, routine parts of their daily worklife; how caseworkers transform welfare clients' untidy life situations into neat case histories; how a woman manages the day-to-day feat of convincing others she is in fact a woman; how urban blacks create a new language and use it to make an oral literature; how telephone calls are properly or improperly begun; and many, many others (see Turner, 1970; Sudnow, 1972; Douglas, 1969).

The Puzzle of Intersubjectivity

The sociological Naturalists, in describing social life's exhibits, find themselves perpetually returning to their central "puzzle," the question of intersubjectivity, or, how do separate individuals manage to experience in common the same realities, specifically, social reality? The creation of social experience out of private experience is the primary mystery they explore. Why is this a mystery?

Naturalists believe that all of sociology must be concerned, in one way or another, with the study of meaningful social action. As Max Weber defined it, meaningful social action is "human behavior when and insofar as the acting individual attaches a subjective meaning to it" (Weber, 1904). This puts the sociologist in the difficult position of interpreting what the social participants he observes might *mean* by their actions, and what those actions mean to the other participants toward whom they are directed. The Naturalist realizes, however, that this is not only the sociologist's problem; it is *everyone's* problem in trying to make his or her way through everyday life. We all work to make ourselves understood to one another; we all seek to understand what the other person means by his or her actions. This work is the task of constructing social meanings we can share as our conjoint definitions of our situations.

Let us look at the analogous problems involved in the relationships between the artist, his work, the public viewing the work, and the art critic, to try to shed some light on our general situation as social participants. The artist works to shape his or her work of art into the significant form that, to the artist's satisfaction, embodies the meanings he or she wishes it to convey. When it is finished and on public display, the public may observe it, enjoy it, respond to it, and interpret, each observer in his own way, what it "means." Might they misinterpret it? Certainly there will be members of the public who attribute meanings to the work that were never intended by the artist, often meanings the artist would vehemently deny. But there may well *be* meanings in the work that the artist did not intend, meanings even the artist perceives only after it has been completed. Over time, successive reinterpretations of the work might show that it continues to acquire new meanings for a succession of publics, so that, even long after the artist's death, the work appears to take on a meaningful life of its own. Who is to decide what meanings the work of art really has? The good art critic does not take it upon himself to make such final judgments about meaning. The critic serves as a guide for the public's appreciation of a work by analyzing in detail the ways in which it can be interpreted. By elucidating the work's internal structure, by elaborating on the technical, cultural, and historical contexts within which the work as a whole and in its parts may be viewed, and by laying out step-by-step the various procedures for interpretation that may be used to unravel a work's meanings, the critic enhances and enriches public art appreciation.

Now imagine each and every one of our daily actions in society as a tiny, mostly conventional but often innovative or highly individualized, work of social art. Social life is then a vast gallery of such small works, and each of us is alternately artist and public, at once shaping and presenting, viewing and interpreting, what we are doing, and what we mean by it.

In this analogy, the sociological Naturalist serves in the role of the art critic. He encourages fellow shapers and interpreters of meaningful actions to look at them anew, in a variety of interpretive contexts, to examine their structure and their history, but most of all, to become consciously, appreciatively aware of the artfulness we all share in the making of social meanings. Somehow we get through our social lives with the sense that we "understand" one another's actions, even though we are as distant from and as mysterious to one another as is the long-dead artist from generations of publics. This is the remarkable human social achievement that the practitioner of Sociology III would have us more deeply appreciate.

The Goal—Satisfaction of Idle Curiosity

Naturalists claim neither to improve the reliability of social knowledge, as Functionalists do; nor to help establish social justice, as Activists do. Naturalists offer neither superior wisdom nor diagnosis and cure. Is there liberation inherent in heightened awareness? Is there hope for a better future in the enhanced appreciation of social artfulness? The sociological Naturalist cannot say for sure. One does the work anyway, for the satisfaction of one's idle curiosity, and perhaps for the pricking of yours. Perhaps they cannot state a clear goal for their endeavors because they are driven by a sense of wonder about social life, and are willing to let it lead them wherever it may. The payoff will have to be found in the journey itself. Sociology III strives only to increase appreciation of social life, as a joyous end in itself.

AN INNER VOICE

Well, at least this sounds safer than Activism, and it grants me the freedom to create my   *own social reality, along with others, a freedom denied me by Sociology I's system* dominance over my life. But is idle curiosity really a worthwhile goal? Wouldn't I just be a dilettante if I devoted my life to going around appreciating everything, but leaving it alone? Perhaps none of the three sociol-

ogies is the answer in itself. Maybe the most hopeful course would be to pick up and lay down each of these "lenses" in turn to look at different aspects of social life. Then I could try to put it all together, myself.

FOUNDING FATHERS

The Three Sociologies of Comte, Marx, and Weber

Briefly, we shall illustrate the point that all three sociologies can point to the same founding fathers of sociology to warrant the historical continuity of their different views by outlining the diverse contributions of three great sociological masters: Auguste Comte, Karl Marx, and Max Weber.

Auguste Comte of France (1798—1857) is acknowledged by most scholars to be virtually a Founding Grandfather of sociology. Comte invented the word sociology by combining the Greek logos with the Latin socius to produce a linguistic bastard meaning "the science of companionship." The most often cited foundation for modern sociology to be found in Comte's works (Comte, 1855) is the functionalism that predates Sociology I. Comte pictured society as an organic whole, with social institutions and social classes as the organs or interdependent parts. But there is also in Comte a commitment to reform, reorganize, even revolutionize society, if necessary, in order to establish social justice and harmony. This is cited by the activists of Sociology II as support for their position. The bulk of Comte's voluminous writings, however, is what he saw as only the beginning of the encyclopedic task of sociology to carefully describe and categorize social action in all of its varieties and forms. This, of course, is the project of Sociology III's naturalism.

Karl Marx (1818—1883), the German who wrote in England and published in the United States as well, attempted himself and

exhorted others to change society through scientific study, and thereby obviously grounded the work of sociological Activists (Sociology II). But Marx was not only a revolutionary sociologist, he was also one of sociology's great systematists in his construction of the theoretical relationships between the major components of whole societies. Marx saw society as inevitably divided along class lines, but he also proposed a picture of society as a structured whole. The parts making up the whole were the substructure—means and modes of production such as businesses, factories, and workers' organizations—and the superstructure—religion, education, and the arts and sciences. He can therefore be considered a Founding Father of Sociology I as well. Finally, the "humanistic" Marx is cited by Naturalists (Sociology III) as the true Marxian perspective, giving historical grounding to their version of sociology. Along this line, Marx emphasized the importance of social actors being conscious of the meanings of their actions and relationships in shaping the course of social struggles (see Marx, 1845, 1871).

The German sociologist Max Weber (1864—1920) also comes easily to mind as a Founding Father. Weber's great comparative studies of the relationship between religion, economics, and politics in various historical societies made it possible to conceive of truly objective, scientific research into the workings of whole societies as systems (Sociology I). On the other hand, his delineation of the rise of bureaucracy as both the bane and backbone of modern social life can be seen as the key diagnosis of what ails our social structure, and what we must surgically destroy in order to cure it, and ourselves (Sociology II). At the same time, Weber is consid-

ered the first writer to insist that sociology, if it is to study social action, must always and everywhere be concerned with interpreting the subjective meanings actors attribute to their actions. Sociologists must strive for a sympathetic understanding of the social actor's own point of view, or as Weber termed it in German, Verstehen (Sociology III).

◆◆◆

A Further Note on Reification

We've said that *reification* is the kind of fallacy whereby one treats an idea or an abstract category as if it were a concrete, sometimes even a living and breathing, thing. Any claim that an idea, theory, or style *came* from somewhere and went elsewhere, that it "has its origins" in such and such a place or time, or that it "emerged" or "developed" in such and such a way is a reification.

My favorite example of this pitfall, the one that reminds me how easy it is to make this intellectual slip, and yet how ridiculous it is, is a cartoon I recall from the *New Yorker* magazine in the late 1950s. A young, hip urban father, wearing sunglasses and the most currently fashionable hairstyle, is sitting on the edge of his little son's bed. The son is peeking out of the covers and saying, "Tell me the one again, daddy, about how Jazz came up the river from New Orleans."

Now, it's a bed-time story to tell how Jazz came up the river from New Orleans, but it's equally reification and a bed-time story to tell how structural-functionalism came from France to Germany to England to America, or how Marx's thought swept over Europe, or how modern sociology emerged from the work of Georg Simmel and a few others. Forebears can be found for every sociology if one looks hard enough. In this textbook, we wish to keep reality clearly in mind, and not be deluded by reifications of any kind. Therefore, let us reject and abandon all origins myths, and accept the fact that ideas and theories are creations of their current proponents. That includes, of course, the three sociologies constructed here for our mutual purposes. We have constructed these three sociologies to reflect the major cleavages and solidarities among sociological ideas and activities now in vogue. They are not real things. Not one of our sociologies ever did, or ever could, come up the river from New Orleans. Dig?

The three sociological lenses presented here do not thus restrict any sociologist, established or potential, to one single categorical mold. Each may be picked up for a distinctive viewing of the social world, and each sociologist may combine the elements of these perspectives in his or her unique manner. As for me, it should become clear to the reader from all that has been said thus far that the author of this text is himself a practicing sociological Naturalist with strong

Activist leanings. Let it remain to be debated between students and instructors whether the opposed orientations have been given equal and fair play in the text throughout.

DOING SOCIOLOGY

1. Using library sources (and carefully citing your sources) compile a list of ten major "social facts" that may be stated numerically, and that outline the structure of the society in which you live. Remember that the facts do not speak for themselves. You must state why they are "major."

2. Making your own diagnosis, compile a list of the ten major issues of social injustice confronting your society today. Speculate on a reasonable solution for each of the ten issues.

3. a) Reflect back on the facts you have compiled for Question 1. How were these "facts" created, by what agencies, for what purposes, why are these records kept and not others. What kind of a society keeps this kind of records about itself?

b) Reflect back on the problems you have defined and the solutions you have proposed as answers to Question 2. Try to see the person behind this list. What does your selection of problems and solutions tell you about yourself? Does it tell you whose side you are on?

2

Social Problems, Sociological Problems, and the Sociologist's Problems

Two related topics are to be explored in this chapter. The first is the relationship, and the important differences, between social problems as they are commonly understood and sociological problems as they are specially defined. The second is the particular and peculiar kinds of relationship that develop between sociologists and their subject matter. These two topics are related because it is in the very attempt by sociologists to translate commonplace social problems into specialized sociological problems that the sociologists establish, consciously or implicitly, their modes of involvement with the social realities they study.

As I will illustrate in some detail, there are at least three very different ways in which social, as opposed to sociological, problems can be distinguished from one another, corresponding to our three sociologies. We shall therefore be able to examine three quite distinct modes of involvement between sociologist and subject matter. But, for all of the intramural differences between sociologists, there are still recognizably *sociological* ways of viewing and interpreting the social world, commonly accepted by all in the discipline. There is a way of looking at the world that is distinctively sociological, as differentiated from practical, moral, aesthetic, or traditional perspectives on social issues. It is the *perspective* that differentiates social problems from sociological problems, and it is the peculiarly sociological perspective that relates the sociologist in a special way with social life.

Anyone can take up the sociological perspective on social problems, and translate them into sociological problems. Many people do so quite unselfconsciously, without even knowing they are acting like sociologists. What is this perspective, and within this perspective, what are the various alternative viewing lenses? Further, what is the consequence for the viewer of taking up this perspective, of peering through these particular lenses? If there are social problems that can be re-viewed as sociological problems, what problems does this viewing cause for the viewer?

SOCIAL PROBLEMS

Everyone sees and has problems in social life, many of which can be called social problems, such as the commonly understood problems of racial strife, unemployment, crime and immorality in high places and low, poverty, divorce, overcrowding, unfair treatment because of age, sex, ethnicity, sexual preference or any other social characteristic, and the like. The daily newspapers are full of reports of specific instances of these problems, and of the rise or (seldom) the decline in the rates of such chronic problems as suicide, homicide, theft, assaults, divorce, mental illness, poverty, deaths due to alcoholism, etc. Depressing news like this is what we pay for each day, and what we eagerly read in our free moments.

Such problems are generally seen as your problem if they directly and negatively affect you, and other people's problems if they don't. They are generally perceived as primarily *moral* problems emanating from the evil intent and immoral character of at least some of the actors in the daily drama: either the victims of the problems are themselves "at fault" because they "bring it upon themselves," or somebody else is personally and damnably "doing it to them." Social problems are generally seen as localized and self-contained issues, matters that can be solved by experts or by agencies directed toward their specific solution. Crime control is thus a matter of better law enforcement by law enforcement agencies; divorce is the province of lawyers, marriage counsellors, and sex therapists, and an increasing number of suicides is met by the creation and staffing of suicide prevention centers (see Merton, 1961, pp. 697—737).

THE SOCIOLOGICAL PERSPECTIVE ON SOCIAL PROBLEMS

All of the sociologies distinguish themselves from such everyday, commonsense views of social problems by taking a major mental step back, a retreat, for the time being, from the mind's "normal" involvement in social problems and social issues, to a position from which these problems can be viewed anew. This is an importantly different position for each of our three sociologies, but there are also important elements of it held in common. Here is a short description of this position and some of its varieties.

Seeing the Larger Picture

In general, the three sociologies outlined here relate social problems as perceived by you and me and the man in the street to the larger pattern of social organization. It is this larger, or historically deeper, pattern, and how the social problem fits into it, that is the sociological problem. But each sociology talks about different kinds of parts, different kinds of wholes, different ways of relating them, and different overall patterns. In a nutshell:

a. Sociology I depicts social problems as *indices* or markers of the strain points and potential breakdown areas of the social system as a whole, and therefore as helpful information toward solution of its sociological problem: how is the orderliness of the social system sustained over time? The Functionalist often finds that some form of behavior or some social arrangement that appears as a social problem to most people in fact operates to keep the system balanced. A frequently cited example is that of the political "ward heeler," or "influence peddlar," whose corruption of the legal and political process has been considered in various times and places to be a serious social problem. The Functionalist points out that such illegal and perhaps even immoral activities often serve the "latent function" of making both the legal and political systems work for underprivileged or otherwise less powerful segments of the population, and thus allow the "legitimate" social system to operate more effectively (see Merton, 1949, Ch. 1).

b. Sociology II views the same problems as symptoms of a deeper, underlying illness of the society. The major sociological problem as the Activist sees it is: how is this illness, enmeshed in the larger fabric of human history, to be correctly diagnosed and treated? Social problems are seen by the Activist sociologist as *issues,* symptomatic parts of the larger ongoing struggle for social justice. The Activist invites all of us to transform our personalized, localized consciousness of troubles and problems in the social milieu each of us inhabits to an awareness of these problems in the larger scheme of history. The history of society's struggle toward health, in the form of social justice, is the larger picture for Sociology II.

c. For Sociology III, social problems are primarily a matter of *social definitions.* Recognizing and examining these problems helps the Naturalist understand the society's grammar of negative and positive social meanings. Members of the society mutually define certain events and certain situations as problematic, as social problems needing to be solved, as opposed to everything else that occurs in society that is seen and defined as "normal," or as "business as usual," or just "the way things are." The Naturalist notices that what is "normal" and what is "a problem" varies from society to society and from time to time through history. Sociology III tries to trace the process by which the problematic things got to be defined as problems. The Naturalist wants to know how problems are distinguished from the normal and the natural, and how it is that what is a problem and what is not comes to change over time, like fashions and fads. The larger sociological problem for Sociology III is, how is normality established and maintained as the prevailing "definition of the situation" (see Thomas, 1951) in the society? Social problems, and how they are created and solved by social participants, thus produce insights into the Naturalist's sociological problem by illustrating definitional contrasts to the normal. If social problems are indices of strain points in the larger system for Sociology I, and symptoms of the underlying social disease for Sociology II, for Sociology III they are grammatically crucial terms in the language of social meanings.

Involvement in the Search for Truth

The first general feature of the sociological perspective on social problems, then, is that distinct, localized problems are placed in context in the larger picture, the more comprehensive sociological problem. A second feature of the commonly held sociological perspective is the primacy of the search for the truth about social problems through transforming and translating them into sociological problems.

Truth is what sociologists first and foremost seek; hence their dedication to the use of scientific methods. Whichever version of science one adheres to, science has proven itself to be the most reliable truth-finding device available.

a. The Functionalist is engaged in the mind-boggling task of simultaneously measuring the immeasurable parts and pieces of social life, and of logically sorting them into their proper places in the unthinkably complex whole of the society, or the social system. It is the truth value of that measurement, and the higher truth of that sorting, that he is really after, and not the solution of any social problem in and for itself. Sociology I calls the measuring, *research,* and the sorting, *theory.* As we have discussed, if the Functionalist is measuring suicide, it is as a feature of the coherence of the social system, and not as "the social problem of suicide," itself. Social problems are solved by the production of moral solutions; sociological problems are solved by the production of scientifically validated truths. It is the hunger for such scientific truths that drives on the true sociologist.

b. Though it may not be obviously so, the Activist too is primarily hungry for the truth about social life, even as he struggles for social justice. The basic theoretical principal of Sociology II is that the truth about social life is only available to those who are engaged in the critical social struggles of their times, and that it is only their full and conscious engagement that produces scientific truth about society. Further, the Activists believe that it is only through working out the scientific truths about social relations in struggle that social justice can ultimately be achieved.

c. The Naturalist is the sociologist most clearly driven to his work solely by a sense of wonder, by a lust for truth about social life, since there is no other visible motive or rationale for his work. The Naturalist doesn't promise to do anyone any good, even in the long run. Whereas the Functionalist seeks the truth of prediction, which can lead to more efficient control over social processes, and the Activist seeks the truth of social justice, which must at least benefit those now deprived, the Naturalist seeks only increased appreciation, awareness, understanding of social life. This is a form of truth whose only foreseeable "payoff" is the joy one feels in reaching it. As in art or in sex, you can talk all you like about how it is "good for you" to enjoy it; the simple truth remains that the enjoyment itself is all there really is to it. So it is with the Naturalist, a hedonistic, rather than a practical or moralistic, luster after truth.

I think it is common to every sociologist to be driven by an inner "demon," a "demon who holds the fibers of his very life," in Max Weber's phrase, (Weber,

1946, p. 155). This demon drives the sociologist on toward truth of various kinds. It is beyond the power of any true sociologist to help himself against the demands of the demon; and the demon grabs hold of anyone who seriously puts on the lenses of the sociological perspective. Consider Peter Berger's description of the kind of person the sociologist becomes, and the kinds of places and situations he gets himself into when in the grip of the demon.

★★

LEADING LIGHTS

Peter Berger on the Natural Habitat of the Sociologist

Berger invites to what he calls the game of sociology "a person intensely, endlessly, shamelessly interested in the doings of men. His natural habitat is all the human gathering places of the world, wherever men come together." This might include the grimy public toilets where homosexuals meet to practice their peculiar forms of social interaction (see Humphreys, 1970). It might include participating as a patient in the world of the mental hospital (see Goffman, 1961). It might be the street corner where a gang of unemployed urban blacks spend their time (see Liebow, 1967). But wherever he finds himself, the sociologist's "consuming interest remains the world of men, their institutions, their history, their passions." The sociologist will be fascinated by people's do-ings, large and small, he will feel reverence and respect toward them, "but this reverence will not deter him from wanting to see and to understand. He may sometimes feel revulsion or contempt. But this also will not deter him from wanting to have his questions answered. The sociologist, in his quest for understanding, moves through the world of men without respect for the usual lines of demarcation. . . . Thus his questions may lead him to all possible levels of society, the best and the least known places, the most respected and the most despised. And, if he is a good sociologist, he will find himself in all these places because his own questions have so taken possession of him that he has little choice but to seek for answers." (Berger, 1963, p. 18)

★★

𝓮𝓮

AN INNER VOICE

So, if I put on these sociological lenses, I will be able to see how my problems, and the problems of the people around me, fit into the larger picture. I'll also find myself in the grip of a demon that urges me to search relentlessly for "the truth" above all else as the "solution" to these problems. It sounds to me as if there are serious disadvantages as well as advantages to this. There's some-thing unhuman, isn't there, about dealing with the immediate, flesh-and-blood problems of my friends and associates in the abstract—whether it's as part of the system or part of history or part of the grammar of meanings. On the other hand, there's something all too human about being driven to find the truth by some demonic force. It almost begins to sound like a religious quest, or maybe just a neurosis. I'm sure that social life is much more comfortable without the larger picture in view, that I'd be more at ease if I just dealt with things one day at a time, one problem at a time as it comes along.

❦❦❦

THE SOCIOLOGIST'S PROBLEMS. THREE MODES OF SOCIOLOGICAL INVOLVEMENT

Each type of sociology carves out its area of concern, its particular collection of sociological problems, in its own way. The manner in which a sociology makes this distinction between social and sociological problems defines as well the mode of ethical, practical, and political involvement that sociology will have with its subject matter. To put it more personally, this determines how sociologists will come to relate, as persons and through their work, with their "subjects," the other people in the society they study, and with "colleagues," the other sociologists engaged in the search for the truth about social life.

The two relationships mentioned above are usually treated as totally separate topics in sociological writing and discussions—in fact, there are *three* traditional issues involved that are hardly ever discussed in combination: a) the stance toward social life taken from different sociological perspectives; b) the ethics of the sociologist's involvement with "subjects"; and c) the controversies between sociological "colleagues" about such issues. Here we will deal with these three questions all together, in their proper interrelationship. Of each of our three sociologies we now ask, a) what is the sociologist's involvement with the subject matter in doing this sociology? b) what are the ethical problems arising out of this mode of involvement? and c) what do the *other* sociologies have to say about this?

The Functionalist Involvement: Moral Disengagement as Objectivity

Functionalist sociologists, the still dominant faction of the squabbling sociological family, have consistently championed the necessity for "scientific objectivity" in the study of social life, with science taken to mean the predictive, quantified operations borrowed from physics or chemistry. The proper relationship between the social scientist and his "data" from this perspective is one of emotional, political, and judgmental *detachment*. It requires the use of the same cold, calculating, distinterested eye that physical scientists cast on the chemical beakers, microscopic or telescopic observations, or computer read-outs of their measuring instruments.

In order to achieve what they take to be a truly scientific standpoint for their sociological analysis, Functionalists attempt to rid themselves of their personal prejudices, political biases, and unconsciously acquired cultural values with regard to their subjects. Scientific objectivity is the primary goal here, and there can be no objectivity so long as subjective values are allowed to seep into the scientific perspective. Functionalists can remain disinterested in the moral or political implications of their findings only by standing outside the arena of passionate dispute among men. Through the disengagement of their critical, moral, and emotional faculties, they reach a state of "value-neutral" detachment, an analytic frame of mind in which the researcher has no personal preference for any of the human alternatives being studied and compared.

The manner in which Functionalists transform the particular issues and problems of the society—crime, revolutionary movements, divorce, suicide— into general, abstract questions in the study of any society, or society in general, is essential to this neutrality. Crime, revolution, divorce, suicide, are not to be seen as problems in themselves—issues of moral concern for the social participant—but as problematic features of the orderly development and balancing of an integrated social system. Sociology I transforms moral problems into technical problems.

Two of the greatest sociological masters, Max Weber and Emile Durkheim, are commonly cited in works of Sociology I as authorities for this perspective. Max Weber, despite his own intense involvement in the political and philosophical issues of the Germany of his time, insisted upon a "value-free," or at least a "value-neutral," social science. This entails an objective, impersonal handling of social data, data that Weber himself defined as consisting of the subjective meanings social actors attach to their own and others' actions. Science has an ethic of its own, Weber claimed, and science demands that the scientist not claim any validity for his own value judgments about his subject matter. This neutrality must be maintained even when that subject matter consists primarily of other people's value judgments, and even when the scientist's subjects demand that the scientist too take a stand on the issues that concern them.

FOUNDING FATHERS

Max Weber on the Separation of Scientific and Practical Duty

"The capacity to distinguish between empirical knowledge and value-judgements, and the fulfillment of the scientific duty to see the factual truth as well as the practical duty to stand up for our own ideals constitute the program to which we wish to adhere with ever increasing firmness."

"There is and always will be—and this is the reason that it concerns us—an unbridge- *able distinction among (1) those arguments which appeal to our capacity to become enthusiastic about and our feeling for concrete practical aims or cultural forms and values, (2) those arguments in which, once it is a question of the validity of ethical norms, the appeal is directed to our conscience, and finally, (3) those arguments which appeal to our capacity and need for analytically order-*

ing empirical reality in a manner which lays claim to validity as empirical truth."

"It has been and remains true that a systematically correct scientific proof in the so- *cial sciences, if it is to achieve its purpose, must be acknowledged as correct even by a Chinese . . ." (Weber, 1904, p. 58)*

◆◆

Of course the critical reader of Weber will notice the value judgments, the Western ethnocentrism, expressed even in this statement on the need for strict objectivity. As stated, it is an inherently ambiguous position. Weber himself was repeatedly ambiguous about this question of subjective versus objective involvement. He states both sides of the paradox in two almost contiguous sentences in the essay excerpted above:

> There is no absolutely "objective" scientific analysis of culture—of "social phenomena" independent of special and "one-sided" viewpoints according to which—expressly or tacitly, consciously or unconsciously—they are selected, analyzed and organized for expository purposes." And then, the contradictory sentence, "The type of social science in which we are interested is an *empirical science of concrete reality.*" (Weber, 1904, pp. 58, 72)

There is the dilemma. Objective methods, subjective data. Naturalist sociologists resolve this dilemma by trying to develop a different kind of science, a science adequate to the handling of subjective social phenomena. Most Functionalist sociologists, on the other hand, try to resolve this dilemma by following the lead of Emile Durkheim, and developing a different kind of data. If subjective social life can be first transformed into objective "social facts," then it can be adequately handled by the methods of objective natural science without self-contradiction.

◆◆

FOUNDING FATHERS

Emile Durkheim on the Observability of "Social Facts"

Durkheim defined "social facts" as distinct from biological, psychological, or historical facts, as follows:

"A social fact is every way of acting, fixed or not, capable of exercising on the individual an external constraint; *or again,* every way of acting which is general throughout a given society, while at the same time existing in its own right independent of its individual manifestations."

But how are these facts, these "ways of acting" that exercise constraint upon us, which are general societal facts and exist as independent entities outside of any individual, to be observed by social scientists?

"The first and most fundamental rule is: Consider social facts as things." *Social facts are not just ideas, not just chimera. They are real, natural things in the world, and therefore natural science method is applicable to*

them. Social facts "qualify . . . naturally and immediately as things. Law is embodied in codes; the currents of daily life are recorded in statistical figures and historical monuments; fashions are preserved in costumes; and taste in works of art."

In order to treat social facts objectively, only the most external of their characteristics should be observed and considered factual, such as officially recorded statistics and codified rules and regulations. In some instances, it will be only the effects of the social fact that can be objectively observed. For example, "we note the existence of certain acts, all presenting the external characteristic that they evoke from society the particular reaction called punishment. We constitute them as a separate group, to which we give a common label; we call every punished act a crime, and crime thus defined becomes the object of a special science, criminology." In this way social problems become transformed into sociological problems for Sociology I (Durkheim, 1895, pp. 13, 14, 16, 35).

◆◆

The dilemma of involvement inherent in this sociological perspective still requires this kind of Durkheimian solution. Functionalists are engaged in the search for truth about subjective meanings, yet they have limited themselves to the use of scientific methods designed only for the study of physical objects, which in themselves are without subjective meaning.

Durkheim insisted that the meanings *individuals* might attach to their actions, even to the ultimately personal action of suicide, are too varied, too evanescent, and in any case too psychological to be studied scientifically as social meanings. In order to sustain scientific objectivity and at the same time deal with human actions as social facts, not merely personal ones, Durkheim set Sociology I on a course of collecting and analyzing publicly documented rates of the occurrence of social phenomena. The number of suicides per 1,000 persons per year in France, compared to the number of suicides per 1,000 persons per year in England, is thereby a comparison of suicide as a social fact in French society with suicide as a social fact in English society. Why does a person commit a crime at time x in city y? This the Functionalist does not claim to be able to answer, since it is not a social fact but a personal one, and therefore cannot become part of a sociological problem for him. But ask the question, "Why does the crime *rate* fluctuate from month to month and year to year in the same city, and why does the crime rate vary from city to city, or from subgroup to subgroup within the same society?" Then you are asking about social facts, or at least about crime as a social fact.

Since publicly documented facts such as these are already quantified, their analysis allows the researcher to remain completely detached from the individual emotional or evaluative implications they might otherwise appear to have. Concretely, the social scientist in this mode is handling only numbers as data, and theorizing about their mathematical relationships. Social theory of the most abstract, purely logical type can deal with the mathematical relations between rates, and thereby link theory with "empirical findings."

By defining publicly recorded rates as the "social facts" *par excellence,* Durkheim provided sociological Functionalists with the perfect rationale for performing empirical research into "dangerous" social issues while keeping their hands clean.

The Functionalist thus maintains the ideal of detachment by collecting and analyzing only nonevaluative information about society. Sociology I does not intentionally provide support for any social policy or any solution to a social problem. It merely provides information on the basis of which informed judgments may be made by those with the responsibility to make them.

The Activist Involvement: Commitment to Justice as the Path to Truth

The Activist vociferously opposes such detachment, or rather, opposes the *claim* to detachment as the warranty for scientific objectivity. Functionalists delude themselves and mislead everyone else when they claim that self-interests, value judgments, and distorting bias have been exorcised from their sociological findings, according to the critique of Sociology II. When it comes to social issues, there is no such thing as neutral information. Every statement of a "social fact" is a combative move in the war game of the social struggle. To claim objective neutrality for your statements is simply to try to add weight to the blow you are swinging at your opponents, and to try to hide the fact that you, too, are right in the thick of the fighting.

Commitment to a position is the necessary form of involvement for Sociology II. Social problems and sociological problems converge, for the Activist, in the large-scale movement of human history, in which, over the long run, both the scientific truth about society, and human potential for a just, humane social order, will unfold.

To struggle for social justice here and now in full awareness that this localized struggle is related to the worldwide development of humanity through history, is Sociology II's manner of translating social problems into sociological problems.

The Activist is of course also committed to the use of science in the search for truth, as well as to the alleviation of suffering. This dual commitment presents Sociology II with a logical dilemma in the face of Sociology I's insistence that science requires detached objectivity. In a variety of ways, Activists strive to resolve this dilemma by showing that the search for truth and the struggle for justice are necessarily one and the same activity.

The Activist faction refers most often to the sociological and philosophical groundwork of Karl Marx. For Marx, as indicated in Chapter I, it was not enough merely to study and understand society, it was morally and intellectually incumbent upon the researcher to change it.

The study of society, for the Activist, requires a mental movement not toward detachment, but through self-aware commitment to a position of value-reflexivity. In this position the sociologist realizes that any activity engaged in by a scholar will inevitably have some effect on the society being studied, so one might as well make that effect count on the side of justice.

American sociologist Alvin Gouldner, who has made contributions to both Sociologies I and II, calls this position of value reflexivity the moral and political responsibility of every sociologist. The truth of Eldridge Cleaver's dictum, "If you're not part of the solution, you're part of the problem," leads Gouldner to reject Weber's goal of "value-neutral" social science as a "myth" (Cleaver, 1969).

★★

LEADING LIGHTS

Alvin Gouldner on Value Reflexivity and the Myth of Value-Free Social Science

In a much reprinted article quoted here and later at length (Gouldner, 1970), Gouldner attacks the "myth" of a value-free sociology as part of the ideology of sociologists. (As used by many sociologists, ideology means a set of general statements that proclaim themselves as factual, but which are actually cover ups and justifications for the hidden interests of the speaker or the speaker's sponsors.) In doing this, Gouldner identifies himself as an Activist. He criticizes Functionalists and Naturalists for what he says is their belief that the sociologist, as a scientist, does not and should not make value judgments about human affairs. Weber's painstaking distinction between value judgments and statements of fact, which he said clearly were both necessary to social science, has been distorted by most contemporary sociologists, according to Gouldner.

"What to Weber was an agonizing expression of a highly personal faith, intensely felt and painstakingly argued, has today become a hollow catechism, a password, and a good excuse for no longer thinking seriously. It has become increasingly the trivial token of professional respectability, the caste mark of the decorous; it has become the gentleman's promise that boats will not be rocked."

The "value-free" rule of science has become the excuse for sociologists not to be-

come actively, forthrightly involved in the issues of their societies. Hiding behind claims of "objectivity," sociologists veil the fact that their work does serve the interests of the status quo, or of the social elite that funds and directs the research they do. Gouldner calls this doctrine an ideology because it is not only a falsehood and a distortion, but it also serves the material interests of those sociologists who profess it.

"It is useful to those . . . who live off sociology rather than for it, and who think of sociology as a way of getting ahead in the world by providing them with neutral techniques that may be sold on the open market to any buyer. . . . From such a standpoint, there is no reason why one cannot sell his knowledge to spread a disease just as freely as he can to fight it. Indeed, some sociologists have had no hesitation about doing market research designed to sell more cigarettes, although well aware of the implication of recent cancer research."

By contrast, Gouldner offers a different ethic for sociology, the Activist's version of proper sociological involvement: That the sociologist state and acknowledge the value preferences inherent in all research, and in his or her own work in particular, and admit to students and readers that only a person with subjective biases, moral leanings, and complete social involvement, can do soci- ology.

"If we would teach students how science is made, really made rather than as publicly reported, we cannot fail to expose them to

the whole scientist by whom it is made, with all his gifts and blindnesses, with all his methods and his values as well." (Gouldner, 1962)

★★★

Activist value reflexivity demands that all social scientists look at their own involvement in the political struggles in which they are inevitably engaged, and then state their positions, with all of their moral and bias implications, as part of their research presentations. If one believes in the necessity and importance of the continuity and the perpetuation of present political and economic relationships in the society, one should say so, and warn the reader that the "findings" within may well be biased in favor of this belief. On the other hand, if the sociologist wants change toward greater justice in society, in the form of greater political freedom or greater economic equality, this should be stated, and the reader warned that this work, in theory and in research methods, might well be biased toward those ends.

No sociologist is exempt from this moral and political demand, insists the Activist, on scientific or any other grounds. Activist analysis of social life brings the sociologist face to face, again and again, with the human conflict that is at the heart of moral and intellectual life in any society. The critique against Sociology I is therefore a logical and scientific as well as moral and ideological one: anyone claiming to do a value-neutral study of social life is not only bound to provide support for the status quo under the cover of neutrality, he or she is also bound to remain blind to society's contradictions, being unable to face up to the contradiction in his or her own life and work.

The Activist takes other people's claims that they have problems quite seriously. The task, in transforming these social problems into sociological ones, is to diagnose the deeper-lying contradictions from which these problems emanate, to see the disease beneath the symptoms. The Activist is in this sense literally a radical social analyst—one who takes surface problems to their root causes. By seeing the possibilities for movement toward health on the long-term scale of human social history, the Activist proposes solutions with equally radical implications: not band-aid patch-up cures, but proposals for the total and fundamental transformation of the present system into a just and healthy society. The Activist's involvement is, ultimately, taken to its logical conclusion, to become a conscious, intentional revolutionary, because desired change can only come about through revolution.

> [Only] where change occurs in the sense of a new beginning, where violence is used to constitute an altogether different form of government, to bring about the formation of a new body politic, where the liberation from oppression aims at least at the constitution of freedom can we speak of revolution. (Arendt, 1965, p. 28)

The Activist is involved in society as a revolutionary critic. Because of the kind of commitment Sociology II demands, and because of the sociologist's personal values, the Activist must oppose the society's most deep-seated injustices. Inevitably, these will be the very sources of power tapped by the elite, the props holding up the status quo. To find the truth about society, the Activist must expose the hidden power sources, the veiled con games, the secret deals, that enable those in power to exploit the rest of us. This very exposure is a revolutionary act.

The Naturalist Involvement
Bemused Hyper-awareness as an End in Itself

The Naturalist finds his or her own personal involvement in the social world to be a continuing source of wonder. Since one is inevitably *embedded* in the social reality being studied, one must perpetually try to understand how it is that one is able to perceive and interpret social reality. If the Functionalist is detached from and the Activist engaged in the social world they study, we may say that the Naturalist is primarily *bemused* by it.

★★★

LEADING LIGHTS

Lee Rainwater on the Sociologist as Naturalist

In response to Irving Louis Horowitz' request to write an essay outlining "the most uniquely defining characteristics of your way of doing sociology," Lee Rainwater, a sociologist who has made contributions to each of Sociology I, II, and III, wrote an article entitled, "The Sociologist as Naturalist." It begins as follows:

"The principle attitude which directs my work is one of puzzled curiosity. I have always felt that I don't understand the people around me very well, and with that feeling has come a strong curiosity to try to figure out exactly what they are doing and why they are doing it. This attitude is perhaps not particularly distinctive to me, but the form by which I have sought to resolve that puzzled curiosity during my professional life is perhaps more distinctive. I have always been drawn to styles of sociological and

psychological work that partake of the naturalist's approach—that is, an approach in which there is an effort to observe the forms and behaviors in which one is interested until one feels one understands how they hang together, and then to depict as accurately as possible what one thinks he has observed so that others may apprehend that reality, and perhaps by replicating the observations validate it."

Among the reasons Rainwater presents for why this kind of naturalistic sociological description and observation is "socially worthwhile, as well as personally gratifying," "the first, and I suspect the most enduring for me, is a belief in the intrinsic, almost esthetic value, of an accurate and penetrating depiction of reality" (Rainwater, 1969, pp. 91, 100).

★★★

Note the personal level at which Rainwater discusses his involvement in the search for sociological truth, as he sees it, as well as the respect he expresses for the knowledge about themselves and their society that ordinary people possess. Also, note the emphasis on description and accurate depiction of phenomena that pique the observer's curiosity. These are the distinctive features of the Naturalist sociologist's involvement with social life.

The Functionalist's claims to value-free detachment and the Activist's admission of judgmental involvement are taken by the Naturalist to be sociological problems in themselves, needing to be examined and explained as two of the many ways people can take a stance with regard to social reality, and two of the many ways in which "truth" about society can be constructed. How do participants in social life come to define only certain things as "social problems" when everything about social life, especially its most "normal" features, are problematic? This is the primary sociological problem for Sociology III.

We have said that the Activist demands that sociological work be "value reflexive," that it openly reveal the interests and biases of the researcher. The Naturalist introduces a second, deeper reflexivity into social science. For the Naturalist, sociological reflexivity asks us not only to look at ourselves, but since self-observation is itself a social phenomenon, to carefully look at ourselves looking at ourselves.

The Truth in the Mirror.   First, the Naturalist version of reflexivity directs the social scientist to look at himself as a participant in the very social reality he is studying. There is no exemption and no scientific detachment available here, nor is there any ground on which a committed activist could take a moral stand "outside" of the connivances, the compromises, and the comforts of social life.

But further, this deep reflexivity consists in seeing that the ways in which social scientists perceive, organize, and communicate the truth about the social reality they study are essentially the same ways *all* social participants perceive, organize, and communicate the truth about their social reality. Further—and here's the kicker—ultimately social reality can be seen to consist of nothing but *the ways in which all participants perceive, organize, and communicate reality*. The subjective perception of social reality; the mutual organization of those perceptions into patterned wholes that make sense to people as members of collectivities; and the modes and means of communicating, recording, and establishing as mutual reality these organized perceptions are the basic elements of social reality from the Naturalist perspective.

The involvement of the sociologist with his "data" from this perspective is therefore total and inextricable. The sociologist *is* the data, in large degree, because one must study oneself in the act of studying the social world. The Naturalist must admittedly *make* the data, in that he must use the same reality-perceiving, organizational, and communicative processes that everyone else uses, and these are the very processes being studied.

★★

LEADING LIGHTS

Ken Stoddart on the Naturalist's Sociological Reflexivity

Naturalist Ken Stoddart set out to study the specialized slang, or argot, used by a subcultural group of narcotics users and dealers in California. He began to compile the terms used by his informants in their conversations with one another, such as "pinched" for being arrested or picked up by the police for questioning. As he collected and began to use these terms himself, he realized that the group began to recognize him as "one of us" as opposed to "one of them," the outsiders in the straight world and the police. He also began to realize that he was increasingly identifying himself as one of the "insiders."

Stoddart's research report describes in de-tail, not the argot and its use from an objective ethnographer's viewpoint, but the process by which his increasing familiarity with and use of the group's special language made him, to the others and to himself, an increasingly involved member of the group. His most important point is that it is only by becoming recognized as a trustworthy and in the know member that the full and accurate meanings of the slang terms are made available to his understanding. Thus his study illustrates the basic naturalist claim that the sociologist must become the data in order to know and report it (Stoddart, 1970).

★★

The basic Naturalist critique of other sociologists is that they, too, must by necessity manufacture their data through the procedures of inquiry they use, but they continue to behave as if their data were produced by a social reality "out there." The Functionalist of course acts as if the "system" and its "functional requirements" were a reality beyond our perceptions and our agreements with other participants on "normality." The Activist comes closer to the Naturalist's acknowledgment of the inquirer's participation, because the Activist acknowledges that only through self-aware participation in the struggle will knowledge of the truth of social life emerge. The Activist, however, continues to affirm the independent reality of "history" as a mass of social forces and conditions limiting everyone's actions, whereas the Naturalist insists that history too is the product of people's definitions of the situation.

The ultimate logical development of sociological Naturalism in this direction is a version of sociology that is called "ethnomethodology." Its practitioners reduce the field to the study of *nothing but* how people communicate social reality (see Speier, 1973).

The Durkheimian notion of achieving objectivity through the use of statistics is rejected explicitly by this notion of reflexivity. As we have seen in Chapter 1, Jack Douglas produced a Naturalist sociology of suicide by showing how the public officials who create statistically recorded "facts" do so for official purposes of their own. Suicides are thus only "social facts" when and where there are bureaucratic reasons for recording certain types of deaths as suicides. The means and reasons for recording vary from time to time and place to place. The same is true of other statistically verified social facts, such as crime rates. The interesting thing for Naturalists is how the social reality of a "crime wave" is constructed through the cooperative interaction of police officials, media reporters, and sometimes even Functionalist sociologists.

For the Naturalist, to study the ways and means by which the "factual base" of such a social problem as suicide rate, murder rate, etc., gets established, changed, reinterpreted, and used, is to study the establishment and maintenance of "social order." Social order from this perspective is to be found in the creation of the facts. The Functionalist who "improves" the gathering, recording, and analysis of such "facts" by the use of scientific method is therefore, from the Naturalist's perspective, not *studying* social order, but *making* social order, with all of the moral and political connotations that the phrase "law and order" has come to carry in modern society.

The Naturalist agrees here with the Activist, that the development of social information is in itself a form of moral involvement in social issues, the sociologist must come down on one side or another of every question, and that the social researcher must state his own preferences and biases in order to give the reader a chance to "read between the lines."

The difference is that Naturalists enter social life with a special kind of humility. They see both the Functionalists and the Activists as blinded by their own arrogance. The Functionalists are convinced that, informationally, factually, and methodologically, they "know better" than the people being studied what their real problems are, what future consequences of their present actions will be, and how they ought to alter their behavior if they wish to reach their desired ends. The Activists are convinced that, morally and historically, they "know better" than the masses of "patients" they wish to cure of their fundamental social disease. Naturalist sociologists, on the other hand, are convinced that the subjects they study know better than any expert can ever hope to know how their social lives are organized and made meaningful, because it is they who organize social life, and make it meaningful.

The first decision as to "whose side are we on?" (Becker, 1976) is therefore, for the Naturalist, in doing our research, do we side cognitively with the experts, or do we side with the lay persons, those who make no claim to expert knowledge or scientific method, but who operate on the basis of "common sense"? The respect of the Naturalist always goes to the nonexpert. It is the magnificent complexity, creativity, and power of everyday "common sense" that Sociology III approaches as its subject matter, with awe and wonder. The scientific knowledge one can hope to accumulate can only, at its very best, be a pale reflection, a mere hushed appreciation, of the rich living reality that is "amateur" social life.

The value choice reflected in this focus cuts across the choices made implicitly and explicitly by Sociologies I and II. The Naturalist has equal respect for the skillful scheming of elites and for the cunning wiles of underdogs managing to get along. It is the style of the action that the Naturalist admires and studies, rather than its content.

AN INNER VOICE

Sociology III could turn out to be a really extreme sort of involvement. I mean it sounds like there is no sure line of distinction between me and what I'm studying here. You could get absorbed, literally, by the subject matter. I've heard about the fallacy of thinking that a mind "in here" contemplates a world "out there," but this Naturalist sociology appears to be putting it into practice, and the prospect I must admit is a bit frightening.

Intellectual Crossfire

The Naturalist's worst enemies turn out to be their Functionalist and Activist "colleagues." Sociologies I and II both come down hard on the uselessness, and even the alleged moral perniciousness, of Sociology III.

Functionalists deny the validity of any Naturalist study that is based on the subjective impressions of the social scientist, and which does not display proper scientific "controls." From the point of view of Sociology I, Naturalist sociologists are engaged in merely journalistic reporting, because they do not take the system as a whole as their frame of reference, but merely concentrate on microscopic instances of social life that can be thoroughly observed and described in detail. Description is not seen by Functionalists as a worthwhile scientific activity in itself. The fact that Naturalists admire and respect the knowledge possessed by the everyday person in his or her everyday activities *over* the projections, predictions, and generalizations of the social science "expert" appears to the Functionalist to be absurd wrong-headedness.

Activists castigate those who take the Naturalist stance as moral "cop-outs." To see social problems not as moral issues, but as language games and definitional puzzles, is to trivialize the great struggles in which we are all, willy-nilly, engaged, says the Activist. And to study the common sense of the unenlightened masses is merely to strengthen "false consciousness," and thereby to help keep the masses in thrall to the power elites. Respect for the ignorance of the masses is not respect for humanity, but contempt for social justice.

But real, flesh and blood sociologists do not make these choices in an intellectual vacuum. They do these things in "real life," with real life consequences for themselves, for each other, and for the social world in which they live and work. Enough of theoretical or hypothetical description. Let us look at three real cases of the interrelationship of social problems, sociological problems, and sociologists' problems.

THREE CASES OF EXTREME INVOLVEMENT

Project Camelot: the Death of a Functionalist

Let us put the objectivity versus involvement dilemma of Sociology I in a specific framework: *Is it possible to study revolution as a social event in general, and the rise of revolutionary movements in contemporary societies in particular, without either fostering or hindering actual revolutions, without acting as a revolutionary or counter-revolutionary oneself?*

The answer to this question is crucial to the continuation and the validity of Functionalist theory and research for two reasons. First, to study the problem of order in society, the Functionalist requires empirical knowledge of the outer limits of order, the point where order completely breaks down. To understand social order, one must develop an understanding of the processes leading to its breakdown, and the subsequent establishment of a new order. This is precisely what is meant by the term *revolution*. Clearly, the study of revolution is a necessary prelude to understanding social order in the Functionalist mode of sociology.

Second, scientific knowledge of revolutions and revolutionary processes, in the sense meant by practitioners of Sociology I, requires a study of revolutions from the outside. The phenomenon must be studied by sociologists who are not themselves involved in the processes, who are not committed either for or against the revolutionaries. If the phenomenon to be studied is necessarily dramatically changed by those who study it, then objective study of revolution, and hence of social order, is impossible.

What conditions set the stage for revolutionary activity, what conditions precipitate it, and what inhibit it? The ideal way to research this question empirically would be to study many societies simultaneously, over a period of time. The societies to be compared would have to be roughly equivalent in size, wealth, and level of development. They would have to vary clearly in the degree of revolutionary pressure faced by their established regimes. If one could study almost all of the societies of South America, plus a few equivalent systems in Europe, Africa, and Asia, the comparative picture just might yield that truth. This was the ambitious goal of Project Camelot.*

Project Camelot was a vivid example of the interaction between social prob-

---

*This account is based on three sources:
1. My own experiences as a graduate student of Rex Hopper, the director of the project, during the two years prior to its inception,
2. *The Research Adventure* by Myron Glazer (1974), and
3. "The Life and Death of Project Camelot" by Irving Louis Horowitz (1965).
As Horowitz himself says in a footnote, "(this article) has been reprinted in ten anthologies and translated into three foreign languages; which indicates the continued interest in the implications of the project both domestically and abroad, particularly Latin America."

lems, sociological problems, and sociologist's problems in Sociology I. It was a major test case of the question of value neutrality and it provided a decisive answer in the negative.

The study was launched in the early 1960s under the scholarly leadership of Rex Hopper, a life-long student of revolution and revolutionary movements. Most importantly, this project had the vital ingredient prior attempts to study such a vast problem had lacked—money. Six million dollars of U.S. federal funds backed the research.

Project Camelot was primed and loaded. A group of prestigious scholars were assembled. Theoretical questions about order versus disorder had been carefully framed, and the comparative, empirical research required to answer them had been carefully blocked out. Questionnaires and interview schedules were ready. Segments of the population in each society needing to be sampled had been identified. Methods were honed to a knife edge.

But not one sampling was drawn. Not one question was asked. Not one interview was recorded. Not one iota of information about revolutionary potential was acquired. Before it even began, Project Camelot was cancelled, the U.S. government was made to apologize to foreign governments, and many sociologists were disgraced and humiliated before their colleagues for their role in the affair. Why was this research project such a disaster?

Camelot misfired upon making the first tentative contacts with social researchers in the first of the countries scheduled to be researched, Chile. The Chilean scholars were at first suspicious of the intentions of the researchers from the U.S.; then, as they looked a bit further into the documentation for Project Camelot, they were outraged.

The Camelot researchers wanted to gain the cooperation of local sociologists and other scholars to further the research. They even wanted to hire large numbers of them at generous wages to carry out the technical functions of data gathering. But the ungrateful Chileans protested to their government that these *yanquis* wanted to do research in Chile that was funded by, controlled by, and served the interests of—the United States Army! The purportedly objective research project was seen by the Chileans as a counterinsurgency project inspired by the U.S. Army, whose self-appointed mission seemed to be to protect the world from revolutionary change. The Chilean government protested to the U.S. ambassador, who had himself never been briefed on the funding and aims of Project Camelot. In the ensuing fracas between the U.S. State Department and the U.S. Defense Department, Camelot was cancelled.

But the flack did not stop there. Back home, there was a flurry of letters, journal articles, and newspaper accounts. Most of them were bitterly critical of the involvement of Camelot's social scientists in what had been exposed as an army plot to suppress foreign revolutions. It was revealed that Camelot had indeed been inspired, right into the methodology and research aims, by army aims rather than by abstract scientific curiosity. Participants in the project and other defenders of its scientific integrity insisted on the "value-neutral" quality of the intended research.

Rex Hopper in particular came under heavy and vociferous personal attack. Many of his former friends in sociology, who had counted him at least a "left-leaning liberal" if not a radical activist, now accused him of betraying them and all of his formerly expressed ideals, of selling out to the U.S. Army for the mouth-watering six million dollars in research funds. In both private and public forums, Hopper fought back, insisting that free social inquiry had much more to gain from Camelot than the army could ever hope for, that the sociologists involved were totally independent of army control, and that the findings to be acquired would have been freely available information, useful to either or any side equally. Hopper died soon after the death of Project Camelot. There are those who say that the stress of this controversy over the possibility of value-neutrality in a totally politicized world (the dilemma that so tortured Max Weber) hastened Hopper's death.

It was my experience as his student that Rex Hopper believed profoundly in the separability of social problems from sociological problems, in the possibility of an objective, value-neutral study of the most explosive social issues. His critics claimed that no one could really believe this, and therefore Hopper acted as a willing conspirator in a military plot, or at least as a collaborator and front man for U.S. foreign policy objectives.

Hopper's belief is fundamental to Functionalist sociology. It is also the fundamental issue on which Activist sociology opposes all such research. According to Sociology II, the belief that sociological research can be in any way separated from political and social action and its consequences is not only deluded, it is deliberately self-deceiving, and therefore an ideology, as we are using this term.

To the Bay of Pigs: the Involved Life
of an Activist

For many young sociologists, the explosive failure of Project Camelot at last blew Sociology I's "value-neutral" stance right out of the water. The fall of Camelot was accompanied by renewed interest and further development of the work of a sociologist who had been teaching and writing throughout the 1940s and 1950s side-by-side with the leading Functionalists at Columbia University in New York (and who was coincidentally my first instructor in undergraduate sociology).

C. Wright Mills had never subscribed to the value neutrality doctrine of his professionally dominant colleagues.* When Mills died of a heart attack at the age

---

*It is said that he paid personally for this in terms of academic advancement and opportunity to teach graduate students, but the following account is disputed by others: "Though the most widely-read sociologist outside the academic world, Mills was barred by his university from training graduate students, for fear that he would raise up others in his image." And, more generally and vaguely put: "As an anti-stereotype, Mills quite naturally was disqualified, unrecognized, and degraded, especially when he touched upon forbidden themes, or failed to make criticisms more or less pleasing to the governing elite, or firmly implanted in the North American conscience a problem as serious as Cuba" (see Nicolaus, 1971; Casanova, 1965; Mills, 1963).

of forty-five in 1959, sociology lost its greatest Activist of the time, and I personally mourned the death of the most exciting and inspirational professor of my undergraduate career. Often, Mills would arrive on campus on a Harley Davidson motorbike, wearing a black leather jacket. He lived intensely, irreverently, and with passionate commitment to the two elements that for him comprised the backbone of social health—reason and freedom.

His published work also contained this passion and intensity. It endures because of its continuing relevance to the social diseases plaguing us. Mills' openly biased exposé of the cozy relations between top men in the supposedly separate and countervailing power institutions in the United States, *The Power Elite* (1956), and his evocation of the plight of the nation's self-blinded, nonunionized working class of "happy robots," *White Collar* (1951), were fierce challenges to Sociology I's consensus theory of a classless social order.

Listen Yankee: The Revolution in Cuba (1960) and *The Causes of World War III* (1958) were even more strident warnings to the powers that be in the United States that their uses and abuses of power in the world social system were exacerbating our universal illness to the point where fatal consequences could be predicted unless drastic changes were made.

It was his involvement in the Cuban situation that marked the termination of Mills' turbulent, and relatively short, career. Mills argued in *Listen Yankee* that the Cuban revolution was a move toward fulfillment of the genuine aspirations of the masses of the Cuban people, and that the values espoused by the Castro government were the same values of democratic participation, human rights, and social equality that are proclaimed by the American government, and deeply held by the American people. The blight of tyrannical rule and gangsterism represented by Battista had been lifted from Cuban society by the revolution. Should not the American government and people welcome Cuba into the circle of free nations, since we too fought a revolution to free ourselves from tyranny?

This was not to be. The policy of the U.S. government appeared to favor military dictatorships over successful revolutions. Mills lobbied feverishly in Washington to change his government's mind about Cuba, but the invasion at the Bay of Pigs, designed to overthrow Castro and restore the exiled conservative businessmen to power, went forward with CIA support and participation. Some say it was this that broke C. Wright Mills'. heart. Clinically, however, it is medical fact that he died of a long-standing coronary condition.

The resurgence of Activist sociology after his death would have warmed Mills' heart, however. Not only was he personally honored by colleagues (as in the publication in 1965 of *The New Sociology: Essays in Social Science and Social Theory in Honor of C. Wright Mills*), but a number of volumes on and of "radical sociology," "critical sociology," and "living sociology" appeared, making Sociology II much more a part of the acceptable mainstream of sociological research and teaching in universities and colleges (see Horowitz, 1971; Hansen 1976; Weinstein, 1974).

❦❦❦

AN INNER VOICE

It sounds like, whether value neutral or value engaged, doing sociology may be harmful to your health. Surely these are exaggerated examples, but just as sure, there's danger here. Especially for an Activist. You have to go up against the big guys, the establishment, to do any Sociology II-type research. A lot like investigative reporting in journalism. Like the guy in Arizona who got blown up in his car.

At this point, the analogy between the Activist sociologist and the medical scientist or physician really begins to break down. After all, everybody wants the doctor to succeed, and when he discovers a disease and cures it,

he gets nothing but praise, honor and rewards from the whole society. But the Activist sociologist discovers and proves that the social disease benefits certain parties, at least in the short run, and that the illness is caused or prolonged by the privileged elite. So he gets nothing but harassment, disapproval, and dismissal from the only members of the society who have the power to reward anybody. And the more successful he is in medical terms, the more dangerous he is seen to be by the elites, and the more trouble he gets himself into. I knew Activism would get you into trouble!

❦❦❦❦❦❦❦❦❦❦❦❦❦❦❦❦❦❦❦❦❦❦❦❦❦❦❦ ❦❦❦❦❦❦❦❦❦❦❦❦❦❦❦❦❦❦❦❦❦❦❦❦❦❦❦❦

Don Juan's Truth: One Rebirth of a Naturalist

In the same mode as our earlier Naturalist's discovery of an argot, Carlos Castaneda found himself looking into himself when he tried to study the cultural practices of the Yaqui Indians of Mexico.

The total, painfully self-aware involvement of Castaneda in his research is dramatically evident in every line of his published work, now totalling four best-selling volumes (Castaneda, 1968, 1969, 1971, 1974). I have had no personal contact with this exemplar of one extreme of sociological involvement, as I had with Mills and Hopper as an undergraduate and graduate student. Yet I feel as if I have known him personally for a long time, because Carlos Castaneda the person is so intimately *in,* and so inextricably *is,* the data of his scientific research.

Castaneda's story might not appear to be analogous to that of the other two scholars because Hopper and Mills are dead, and the manner and timing of their deaths were important parts of their stories. Castaneda, on the other hand, is alive and well and living in (as of last reports) Los Angeles. But the Carlos Castaneda who went into the line of inquiry that produced his four books, as well as his M.A. and Ph.D. degrees at U.C.L.A., died and passed out of existence just as certainly as Rex Hopper and C. Wright Mills did, or so we are asked to believe. The Carlos Castaneda living now is a different being, totally transmuted, born again into a different reality.

One might also quibble that Castaneda's attempt to understand the ways of an exotic culture is really anthropology, not sociology. But Castaneda's reports and insights transcend disciplinary boundaries. Castaneda started out to make an anthropological field report, but he wound up as a totally involved Naturalist exploring the limits of what can be accepted as truth in any culture or in any society, Castaneda intended to report on the native pharmacology of psychotropic herbs by questioning a knowledgeable Yaqui Indian sorcerer, an informant given the cover name don Juan. Instead, he was taken on as a sort of sorcerer's apprentice.

In demonstrating the effects of different psychotropic herbs, don Juan administered the drugs to his pupil and taught him how to "see" what is to a Westerner supernatural realities through them. Then don Juan taught his pupil to see these realities without drugs. He taught Castaneda to see the equal and cumulative validity of alternative realities at will, convincing him that Western scientific rationality is not the only path to truth in this multiple world we inhabit.

What Castaneda describes then, is not the pharmacology of Yaqui culture; it is not even really "what don Juan's reality is like, and how it differs from scientific reality." Rather, Castaneda is describing the many different ways and means one can see and create truth in social interaction. (In this case, the interaction is primarily between Castaneda and don Juan.) That is why Castaneda is an exemplary Naturalist sociologist.

Castaneda gives vivid reports of painful experiences with don Juan. As his taken-for-granted conceptions of what is factual, what is real, and what is illusion, myth, and magic are systematically broken down, and new cognitive avenues are opened up, Castaneda is wrenched with doubts, fears, and confusion. He is no longer basically *comfortable* in the rational world of U.C.L.A. when he returns from the desert, any more than he was comfortable as the struggling and confused pupil of don Juan. Mental anguish in all environments can be the lot of the sociological Naturalist. To *see*, clearly and unmistakably, how artificially contrived are all of the tenets of reality by which we live, and to be involved in the passionate study of precisely that kind of artifice, that mode of contrivance, is to abandon comfort.

This form of genuine involvement in multiple realities, reporting one's own participation in the creation and transformation of one's own and others' experience of the world, is the epitome of sociological Naturalism. Quite clearly in the case of Carlos Castaneda, it is also a dizzying, sometimes terrifying, life experience. Castaneda reports continued doubts, torments, fears of losing his mind, guilt feelings, and anxieties. Is it a denial of his rational scientific background for him to "see" another truth as truth? Is it a betrayal of his now closest friend don Juan to report this experience to a skeptical world?

Castaneda's report is a painful alternation between worlds. At one point he identifies himself most seriously as don Juan's disciple, and at another as a social scientist reporting on his experience, and then back again. He suffers the agony of self-doubt and the loss of his taken-for-granted certainty, security, and familiarity with the "real" world.

His reportage falls short of the Naturalist's ideal in one important respect, however. Castaneda fails to tell us how he came to see the "truth" of Western, scientific rationality in the first place, before he went looking for don Juan.

There is a further objectivity-subjectivity problem with Castaneda's work. Many critics doubt that the interaction between Castaneda and an actual person named don Juan ever took place. It is speculated that Castaneda dreamed the whole thing up. While this would do Castaneda credit as a literary and imaginative genius, it would certainly disqualify his reports as sociology.

This problem, however, is not restricted to Castaneda. It is endemic to all Naturalist sociology, and to all forms of description based on participant observation in sociology and anthropology. Unlike a reaction between two chemicals in a beaker in a chemist's laboratory, social interactions can never be replicated, the observations of one scientist cannot be confirmed by the observations of other scientists. Every observer's report is subjective in the sense that only that observer was there in that position at that time. Our only warrant for the accuracy or believability of his report is that, based on our assumption of Schutz's "reciprocity of perspectives," we take the observer's word for it, and assume that if we ourselves had been there we would have seen the same things. If we refuse to take Castaneda's word that he and don Juan did what they did, we cannot read his reports as factual accounts, but only as a literary creation. If we wish to take his word for it, if we can find no good reason not to, we can read his reports as factual accounts of an extraordinary set of experiences. In Naturalistic sociology, for good or for ill, there is no stronger warrant for believing any description of social interaction.

Sociological Naturalism awaits the reports of even more daring explorers. The Naturalist who can give us a descriptive account of how he or she became the apprentice, then the disciple, and finally a "true believer" in the unique, magically constructed truth seen and constructed by his or her *parents,* will open many more doors to the mysteries of our various social realities. This trailbreaker will probably pay heavily for the achievement, however, in the form of precarious mental health. Is it worth risking one's sanity to find out how the world was made "normal" for us all?

IN SUM

Of course most sociologists, whether practitioners of Sociology I, II, or III, do not suffer the extremes of involvement depicted in these three cases. In each and every case of a sociological study, however, the inevitable line of connections presents itself, and can be seen by the careful reader-between-the-lines, even if it is not made explicit by the sociologist writing the report. The sociologist starts with a social problem, a "puzzle" of social life. Using one particular brand of sociological theory and method, the inquirer transforms this puzzle into a sociological problem, a theoretically consequential question that can be studied empirically. The social problem thereby chosen, and the manner in which it has been translated into a sociological problem, casts the sociologist into a particular relationship with the subject matter, a particular form of personal sociological involvement.

In my personal view, the question for the sociologist is not involvement or noninvolvement; it is what kind of involvement, and is this involvement conscious, intentional, and clearly stated in the work, or is it suppressed and denied. The reader, however, may want to argue the other side.

Thus the sociologist's *self* is always crucially involved in the creation of sociological truth, the self that is always inextricably tied up in relationship, interaction, involvement with other selves in society—the social self. For this reason we move, in the next chapter, into the first concrete "puzzle" of social life observed and analyzed by our three sociologies—the problem of the self and others.

DOING SOCIOLOGY

Begin a sociological clipping file *to be maintained cumulatively throughout the term. At least three times a week, clip out and affix into an album-style file book a story from your daily city or town newspaper. Refer to these stories in class discussions, and as "data" in compiling group and individual research reports. Each week you should file at least one story relevant to the concerns of each of Sociologies I, II, and III, as explained below.*

Every clipping filed, to be useful for any form of future reference, must have attached to it the following two types of information:

a. A reference: The clipping must have the name of the newspaper from which it was taken, the date of that day's issue, and the page from which this clipping came.

b. Relevance criteria by which you selected this story: Write above the clipping itself your title for it: "Soc. I: Example of a social fact," "Soc. II: Combatants in the arena identified," or "Soc. III: Disputed identities," and the like. Below the clipping, write a full three-sentence paragraph explaining why you chose this story as evidence of a social problem relevant to the sociological problems of Sociology I, II, or III.

The Truth in the Newspaper: It is undeniably the case that everything that appears in the daily newspapers, from the ads to the front page news stories to the wedding announcements, is a distortion of reality, a journalistic confabulation of the facts. It is also the case that everything in the newspaper is the truth. The way to resolve this apparent paradox is to ask, the truth about what?

If we start from the perspective of Sociology III, we can say with some certainty that what we find in the newspaper is the truth about how journalists organize the world for their readers. As a cub reporter myself (on the staff of a New York metropolitan daily for four years) I was taught by my editorial supervisors just how to distort what I observed in the field so that it would shape up into an acceptable news story. Even without this training, however, the intelligent reader can find, in almost any news story, clear evidence of how "journalistic social reality" is constructed and sustained.

For instance, it is common knowledge that the standard pattern for writing a news story is the "inverted pyramid" form. This means that in general a news story will contain the most important information in the first paragraph, with the less significant detail making up the rest. Read the first and last paragraphs of half a dozen news stories comparatively and ask yourself, what kinds of things do journalists assume are "more important" than what other kinds of things? What might be a set of criteria for putting items of information toward the top or the bottom of a news story?

And what about everything that does not appear in the paper? What are the criteria that make some events "news" and others business as usual? As the course progresses, I would suggest that the student search each week for the news story that best exemplifies some similar principle of news reporting, which also synchronizes with the topic being studied. This would be the week's clipping file entry under "Sociology III."

For instance, the current topic might be "modes of involvement." The journalistic equivalent would be "styles of attribution." Every full-fledged news story contains not only information and analysis about events in the social world, but a carefully constructed answer to the question, "Who says so?" The answer to this is the story's "attribution." Unless it is an editorial, the writers of news items can not appear to "say so" themselves. The source of the information must be an official one, or a named participant in the event described. Clip an article that shows attribution clearly, underline those parts of it that do so, and write a short explanation of just how attribution is made in this story. In class discussion, try to discover how many different styles of attribution the class as a whole has collected and identified.

A second form of truth to be found in the newspaper consists of symptoms, indicators that, when read from the perspective of Sociology II, reveal the existence and sometimes the location of underlying social illness. One answer to the question, "What makes an event newsworthy," is that there is conflict involved. Some kind of struggle is taking place that breaks out into a reportable instance of violence, or legal action, or confrontation. The eye of the Activist sociologist is focused on such symptomatic reports, through which he reads the truth about the social arena. This week, in line with our sociological topic, choose an article to file under Sociology II that identifies the collector, reporter, or publisher of news as a major combatant in the social struggle, and that gives evidence of a symptom of the underlying struggle toward or away from justice and freedom of information. Look for a conflict of involvement in journalism.

Finally, the daily newspaper is the major transmission belt by which "social facts" as perceived by Sociology I are passed on from the officials who collect and compile them to the public at large. The Functionalist sociologist will of course "read through" the presentation of a social fact in the newspaper to its significance as a sociological fact. Let every article clipped under the heading of Sociology I be primarily about a rate of some kind, that is reportedly rising, falling, steady, or just reportable. It is then the task of the collector of such articles to determine and state in the paragraph beneath it, what is the larger significance of this rate in the social system as a whole? Each week, try to relate the factual content of the chosen clipping to the sociological topic under consideration.

This continuing exercise is designed to provide the student with practice in translating social problems, as presented in newspaper accounts, into sociological problems in the three styles of sociology. Keeping an adequate, cumulatively interesting, and informative clipping file is the student sociologist's problem.

The Self and Others; Puzzles of Social Identity

3

AN INNER VOICE

Who am I? Am I the self my parents created genetically and molded through training— the patterned self further shaped and controlled by the push and pull of society's rewards and punishments? Or am I the self I have painfully begun to forge on the anvil of history, the hard-won self still struggling to *breathe free and make its own mark on society? Or yet again, am I the self that simultaneously reflects the demands and opportunities of the immediate social situation I am in, and creatively helps to construct and shape that very same determinative situation?*

In this chapter we shall carry the question of the involvement of the sociologist's self in the social puzzles studied to its logical and socially general conclusions—to the problem of the self-in-society, society-in-the-self, and sometimes, the self *versus* society. Three quite distinct images of the social self will be outlined through the lenses of sociologies I, II, and III. The topic of the social self can also be seen as the puzzle of social identity and social identification, and the problems that arise in the relationship between the self and society can be seen as the roots of social order, the core of social justice, or the essence of social meaning. Several key sociological concepts must be introduced in order to develop this topic. The student is asked to become familiar with these concepts so that they may be taken for granted as commonly understood terms of reference in further topical inquiries. The main concepts to be grappled with are: *the social role; class consciousness; membership; socialization; repression;* and *labelling.*

Society is a paradox. The relations between individual men and women and their societies are contradictory and full of conflict, and yet display a remarkable orderliness and predictability.

Consider the obvious fact that each of us is predominantly a creature of society's making. In addition to their genetic makeup, each person reflects the culture and the social position in which they were taught how to be the person they are. For example, the language one speaks is an important part of one's culture, and the vocabulary, accent, and speech pattern one uses is a product of the region, the ethnic group, and the social class in which one has been brought up. Yet how one speaks is considered to be one of the most unique characteristics of each individual.

Consider next the equally obvious fact that whatever "society" or "culture" is, it cannot exist in and of itself, outside of the society-sustaining and culture-creating actions and interpretations of individuals. Through the organized and organizing procedures we have developed for the mutual generation, recognition, and communication of facts, we *make* the society that teaches us to be selves, and we make and remake the culture we are taught. Each person, in concert with others, is free to remake the social world in his or her own image; yet everyone's actions are determined and constrained by the social world.

These are the multiple contradictions in the relationship between the self and society. Our three sociologies focus on this topic in different ways. Each sociology emphasizes one of the cardinal points in the puzzle, and clarifies that point only to obscure the others. With all three lenses in hand, the informed sociological viewer can confront the paradoxes and contradictions in all their vividness. The socially constrained self, the socially conflicted self, the socially constructed self—three versions of the social reality of the self, or of social identity.

◆◆

FOUNDING FATHERS

Emile Durkheim on Self in Society—Society in Self

Durkheim is the strongest proponent of the Functionalist idea that the demands and requirements of the social system penetrate the individual, and cause him to act as an instrument or agent of the system, even though he feels he is an autonomous being.

"Society . . . gives us the sensation of a perpetual dependence. Since it has a nature which is peculiar to itself and different from our individual nature, it pursues ends which are likewise special to it; but, as it cannot attain them except through our intermediacy, it imperiously demands our aid. It requires that, forgetful of our own interests, we make ourselves its servitors, and it submits us to every sort of inconvenience, privation, and sacrifice, without which social life would be impossible. . . . the collective force is not entirely outside of us; it does not act upon us wholly from without; but rather, since society cannot exist except in and through individual consciousness, this force must also penetrate us and organize itself within us; it thus becomes an integral part of our being and by that very fact is elevated and magnified." (Durkheim, 1912, pp. 206—210)

◆◆

THE SOCIAL SELF AS A TOPIC

Through the lens of each of our three sociologies, we shall view the social self as a sociological topic. For centuries, thinkers have considered personal identity a profound puzzle of the human condition. The philosopher, the poet, the dramatist, the novelist, the psychiatrist, the theologian—each has a fully developed technique for defining the problem and methods for dealing with it. For the sociologist, the self is a particularly relevant topic for sociological inquiry. The sociologist's eye is always focused on the *relational* aspects of personal identity, or the origins of the self. How is the person identified in relation to other societal members, how is the person identified *by* them, and how does the person act out, struggle with, or create an identity *for* them?

The Self in the System

Sociology I perceives the social self as a crucial part of the social system as a whole, and describes the self's dependence on, and penetration by, the social system (compare the quotation from Durkheim immediately above). Sociology I concerns itself with the *relational* aspects of self-identity, thus making it a sociological topic. The key concepts in this theory are *social role* and *socialization*. A person's place in the system at any particular time, combined with the social tasks that person is expected to perform, is that person's *social role.* The process by which a person is trained to perform particular social roles is called *socialization.*

The ways in which the actions of individuals are determined by the social system, and can therefore be predicted, is the concern of the Functionalist. For the Functionalists, social identity is a question of whether a person's place in the system corresponds with that person's self-image.

Central to the Functionalist image of social life as a systematically integrated whole is the idea that people are part of society only insofar as they fulfill the expectations of others. Social roles represent sets of requirements that the social system makes of individual members. In making these demands on its members, the system gives to each individual a set of roles that, taken together, serves that individual as a social identity, a recognizable self.

★★★

LEADING LIGHTS

Talcott Parsons on the Social System and the Personality System

Contemporary Functionalist Talcott Parsons, taking his cue from Durkheim, further elabo- *rates on the penetration of the individual by the social system. The self is a system in it-*

self, Parsons says, the personality system, which operates as a subsystem of the social system. Through the process of socialization, the values and rules that are integrated into the personality system are brought into line with, and made functioning parts of, the social system.

"The major functional problem concerning the social system's relation to the personality system involves learning, developing, and maintaining through the life cycle adequate motivation for participating in socially val-

ued and controlled patterns of action. [Let us identify such patterns for the moment as "roles."]

"Reciprocally, a society must also adequately satisfy or reward its members through such patterns of action, if it is continually to draw upon their performances for its functioning as a system. This relationship constitutes "socialization," the whole complex of processes by which persons become members of the societal community and maintain that status." (Parsons, 1966)

★★★

Of course, each person in society is called upon, from time to time, to perform several different roles. Over the course of a lifetime, one might be required to perform properly the roles of dependent infant, young learner, apprentice, industrial producer, senior master of an art or trade, retiree, and once again dependent, infantile oldster. At any one period in one's life, multiple role demands are likely to overlap—employee, consumer, citizen, spouse, parent, friend, juror, borrower, congregant, etc.—each role a mask to be worn at different times of the day or on different days of the week. Taken together, all of the socially required roles any person performs, has performed in the past, and is likely to be called upon to perform in the future, comprise that person's composite social self. The social self consists, from the perspective of Sociology I, of the multiplicity of role-demands that the system makes upon the person.

We can compare this role playing to the requirements for playing a specific position in a baseball game, say, first baseman. The first baseman must perform his first-basemanly duties properly in order for his team as a whole to function in competition with the other team, and ultimately in order for baseball as a system to function at all.

The role requirements of first baseman can be described independently of any particular player who might be assigned by the coach to play first base. It is in this sense that Sociology I presents the role as something independent of the role player. Whoever it is that plays first base, however, must be fully integrated into the role of first baseman, so that the actions that he performs on behalf of the systematic functioning of the team can be taken as swiftly and unselfconsciously as if they were "second nature." This captures the Functionalist idea that the person's social self *is* that person's social roles.

It should also be noted that any first baseman, aside from his performance of this role, has many other roles to play, both on and off the baseball diamond. He will also play batter, perhaps team rookie, veteran, or clown, team captain or team rebel, and maybe leading sex-object for the fans. Off the field, he may play the roles of husband, father, friend, entrepreneur, citizen, etc. Taken all together, this collection of roles defines the player's social self, and his overall position in the social system.

Social systems operate most smoothly and efficiently just as teams win ball games, when incumbents of roles identify most completely with their roles— when people learn to require and expect of themselves just what the social system requires and expects. The social system is best served when the role incumbent performs, naturally and without internal resistance, the tasks the system has assigned. Role incumbency and proper role performance is thus every person's most pressing social obligation, and the social system contains elaborate mechanisms to ensure that members learn, and are continuously motivated, to play their roles properly. As a result, the people who live up to their various roles are the most well adjusted, mentally sound, and self-satisfied of society's members. This is the member's just reward for giving to the system what it most vitally needs. In other words, people are trained to give their *selves* to society; in return, the society grants to its cooperative members an integrated, balanced, and healthy social self.

The social system does more than just train its members to comply with its role demands by rewarding and punishing behavior. Through socialization, society causes its members to *internalize* its demands and expectations. This is the process by which the "penetration" of the individual by society (Durkheim) actually takes place.

From infancy, we are taught to model ourselves on others who are properly performing their roles. As children, we learn how to be parents by watching and admiring our own parents' actions toward us. As we grow into adults, we identify with and internalize the expectations of our peers, our school teachers, our employers and fellow workers, and all our other fellow role performers with whom we interact, or who are held up to us as models to learn from and follow.

Socialization is Sociology I's name for the complex, life-long process by which a person absorbs the relevant elements of the social system into that person's own *self,* and at the same time, is absorbed into the system, and transformed into a social self. The result of this process for the self, as Durkheim and Parsons pointed out, is that the system dominates the person thoroughly, but not wholly from without. The totality of system domination lies in the fact that the system penetrates the person, is internalized, and *becomes* the person. Therefore even those actions and choices that might appear to us to be self-directed are in fact system determined. Thus, there can be no fundamental conflict between the self and the system, because they are merely two facets of the same thing.

The Self in the Struggle

By contrast, looking through the lens of Sociology II, the self in society presents a much less peaceful picture. If one sees society as a system of injustices perpetrated by a small elite on a large number of underdogs, then the self appears as a living, healthy, social entity only when it is consciously and forcefully involved in conflict with the dominant forces of the system. The self only comes alive in struggle; it is lost or deadened the minute it stops fighting back against the process of "socialization."

Activist sociology approaches the topic of the self in society through the concepts of *class consciousness* (and its corollary, false consciousness) and *repression*. "How can men and women determine the course of history in their own interests, and reshape their societies to suit their true selves?" is the operative question for Activists. The problem for the social self is thus to throw off an oppressive society's propaganda, to find one's true self and begin to act effectively in the pursuit of one's real self-interests.

In order to freely act on the stage of history, each person must become fully conscious of his social self and of his situation within the larger historical context. He must discover what course or direction is in his own best interest. The Activist sociologist insists that the fully conscious self will always discover that the most important feature of our historical situation, the most crucial fact of personal identity, and the minimum requirement for realizing the self's own interests, is a particular kind of consciousness that is traditionally called, after Karl Marx, class consciousness.

Class consciousness is an awareness on the part of all individuals that they are members of a collectivity that is in fact formed up on one side or the other of the great social battle. This membership makes each of us, whether we like it or not, a combatant in the struggle between warring groups and warring principles in society.

The combatant who is unable to distinguish which side he or she is on is obviously unable to act very effectively in the battle, and that is the importance to the self of class consciousness. But the combatant who fights for the enemy without knowing it is an even worse threat to fellow class members. The unknowing collaborator with the opposition is suffering from what Activist sociology calls *false consciousness*. The task of the Activist is to alert and educate each person to their true situation, to fight false consciousness and help the person correctly identify with the oppressed masses with which he belongs.

It is assumed that everyone will generally act in the furtherance of their own interests, insofar as they can be clearly seen. Only if a person consciously and intentionally identifies with a social class will that person act to further the class's interests; only insofar as men and women act consciously to improve the situation of their class do they participate actively in the long march toward justice and freedom. Finally, only insofar as a person participates in this struggle does a truly human social self emerge.

The Functionalist view of the self as a bundle of internalized roles, seeking approval by conforming to the expectations of others, is rejected and strongly criticized by many sociologists. In a famous essay (Wrong, 1961), Dennis Wrong argues that this picture of the self in social interaction is incomplete and misleading. What is lacking is a discussion of the conflicting elements within each self, and the conflict raging between each self and the society in which it is involved. This critique leads to the edge of the Activist position on the self in society, that the self must be won through struggle against social repression and oppression (see also Stein, 1960).

In answer to the Functionalist assertion that socialization is a benign and helpful process of adjustment, Sociology II counters that the process of socialization is rather a form of social *repression* (see Marcuse, 1955). Through repressive socialization, the elite prevent the rest of us from discovering or realizing our true selves. Because they control the media of communication, the educational system, and most other organized means of expression, social elites have the power to teach us to delude ourselves about our real needs, our real interests, and our real identities. Such self-delusion, inculcated through mass propagandizing, leads us to deny our own best impulses as human beings, to deny our true natures, to deny even the evidence of our senses. Self-denial based on self-delusion—that is the meaning of repression.

Viewed through the Activist lens, social roles are false identities foisted on powerless people to keep them powerless, and even to engage them in the task of keeping themselves powerless. The role of the housewife, for instance, is an instrument to keep women from taking on their rightful shares of power and responsibility in society. Social propaganda spreads such delusions as the idea of the natural incapacity of women to perform more responsible jobs, and their natural aptitude for the tasks involved in motherhood and housewifery. Such propaganda leads women to deny their own abilities, and to deny their frustrations and dissatisfaction with the housewife role.

But that which has been repressed has the potential to return, to be once again freely *expressed.* The struggle to achieve, to realize, to express, and to fulfill one's true self in society requires that each individual fight back *against the roles* society imposes. The Activist sociologist engages in this struggle on behalf of the oppressed by identifying those roles or elements of roles that are repressive, by linking that repression with the elites who benefit from it, and by holding up as a goal a positive, healthy image of the self in a just society.

The Self in the Situation

To recapitulate: For Sociology I, the social self acts as a functioning part of the system by fulfilling social roles. The mechanism that insures the proper performance of roles is socialization. For Sociology II, the authentic, healthy social self is to be found in class consciousness and action on behalf of the individual's class and, therefore, in its own interests. The mechanism of repression leads the masses to deny their true selves and act in the interests of society's power elites.

Sociological Naturalists approach this topic by observing that *membership* is an integral feature of social life. Social participants are everywhere identified by each other as members of some category, class, type, or group. The particular membership that is used to identify a participant in a specific social occasion could be called that participant's situationally assigned self. But we must remember, as Naturalists, that we cannot decide *for* others what is their true self. We are strictly limited to what we can observe about social life. From the perspective of Sociology III, then, social identity is a passing series of situationally assigned memberships, and the mechanism through which these memberships come to be be assigned or achieved is a complex process called *labelling*.

Naturalist sociology is interested in observing the interactions through which social selves are created, identified, and modified for the purposes at hand of social participants. The Naturalist focus has traditionally been on the construction of selves in social interactions, beginning, perhaps, with philosopher George Herbert Mead.

❖❖❖❖❖❖❖❖❖❖❖❖❖❖❖❖❖❖❖❖❖❖❖❖❖❖❖❖❖❖❖❖❖❖❖❖❖❖

FOUNDING FATHERS

George Herbert Mead on the Construction of Self

Mead observed the give and take of social interaction and concluded that the self is not a preordained entity but an interpretation of one's experience that is formed over the course of social interaction.

"The self is something which has a development; it is not initially there at birth but arises in the process of social experience and activity, that is, develops in the given individual as a result of his relations to that process as a whole and to other individuals within that process. . . ."

"The self, as that which can be an object to itself, is essentially a social structure, and it arises in social experience. After a self has arisen, it in a certain sense provides for itself its social experiences, and so we can conceive of an absolutely solitary self. But it is impossible to conceive of a self arising outside of social experience."

Much of what Mead had to say about the self indicates that he thought of it as a single entity for each individual, a lifelong self inherently continuous and homogeneous. Yet there was a glimmer, even in Mead, of the idea of the multiple, situational, flexible selves observed by today's Naturalists:

"We are one thing to one man and another thing to another. There are parts of the self which exist only for the self in relationship to itself. We divide ourselves up in all sorts of different selves with reference to our acquaintances. We discuss politics with one and religion with another. There are all sorts of different selves answering to all sorts of different social reactions. It is the social process itself that is responsible for the appearance of the self; it is not there as a self apart from this type of experience." (Mead, 1934)

❖❖❖❖❖❖❖❖❖❖❖❖❖❖❖❖❖❖❖❖❖❖❖❖❖❖❖❖❖❖❖❖❖❖❖❖❖❖

The idea that the self is an "interpretation of one's experience" is a key departure from the Functionalist notion of the self as an instrument of the system. The self of Sociology III is a created self, partly created by the actor himself and partly created in interaction with one's fellows in society. It is also never a hard-

and-fast reality, but an interpretation that is continually in transformation and re-formulation.

Each individual participant in social interaction is given a situational identity, but not by "the system" in the abstract, nor by any unseen forces or processes, either in history or in society. The person can be observed being *nominated,* by others or by him or herself, to perform the appropriate self for the occasion at hand. For instance, a student in one of my classes brought in the following description of a scene she had observed in a park:

> A three-foot-tall person ran over toward a six-foot-tall person and said, "Daddy, I fell off the swing." The larger person picked up the smaller one and appeared to comfort it.

First let us note that the apparent child was observed nominating the apparent adult as "the Daddy." Given that all we know, and all we can ever know, about these two persons is contained in the reported observation, we cannot possibly say whether the child was the child of that adult, or whether the adult was that child's guardian, or babysitter, or a complete stranger. In other words, everything we can know or infer about the social identities of these two persons lies implicit in the label "Daddy" that we observed one of them assigning to the other, and in the apparent response to that label observed in the ensuing interaction.

This tiny case-example contains in miniature all the essential elements of the labelling process. First of all, "Daddy" is a good example of a social identity label because it provides an identification for a social participant that is a membership in some social type, category, or classification. The child "memberships" the adult in a family relationship by choosing a category that is linked to other categories, such as "mommy," "baby," "sister," "brother," etc. To be identified by the label on any one of these categories is to be offered membership in the collection, "family." Secondly, the label is associated, in the child's statement, with a clear and distinctive description of the situation at hand, the occasion upon which this label is to be taken as appropriate and meaningful, in saying, "I fell off the swing." Such a statement of the situation, preceded by the label "Daddy . . ." in some sense calls for an appropriate response from the participant so addressed. What the Naturalist can observe is that in picking up and comforting the child, the adult also implicitly accepted the label "Daddy."

The labelling process always includes the actions of both parties to the transaction—the one who labels and the one who is offered or assigned the label. To label someone with whom you are interacting is also very often to assign them a temporary or situational role task, a part to play in the ongoing drama of the interactive occasion. Moreover, a label does not automatically stick to the person to whom it has been assigned. A process of negotiation can be observed in many social situations through which the person who is offered a label rejects it, alters it, or throws it back at the labeller, rather than act according to the implied script. For instance, you are introduced by your host to another guest by the use of your most formal title (The host offers to label you "Professor Smith"). You don't want to play that formal a part on this occasion, at least not in relationship to the other guest to whom you are being introduced. So your next line, after the host has introduced you both, is to offer the guest another label. ("Just call me Smitty.") You have thereby erased the host's label and substituted one of your own. The other guest, of course, has the option of rejecting your label for yourself, and thereby rejecting the style of interaction you are offering, by some such line as, "Let's stick with Professor Smith, if you don't mind."

There is a growing Naturalist literature on labelling and categorization as interactive social processes resulting in the situational construction of the social self. (See Sacks, 1974.) One important point to remember is that the Naturalist sociologist provides no guidelines for deciding which of the many identities we present ourselves in is the real self; nor is the person seen as merely an instrument or an expression of the system. Instead, there are as many selves as a person may present to others in interaction, and each is equally authentic or equally fabricated. The self-identity that emerges on any scene of interaction is the product of the mutual construction of identities worked out by all the participants.

Naturalists are interested in seeing how selves are constructed in social interaction, and therefore in the methods and procedures social participants use to identify one another. Sacks focuses on one rather universal technique of identification, the verbal application of membership categories like the use of "Daddy" in the example cited above.

> This process thus consists of "Any collection of membership categories, containing at least a category, which may be applied to some population containing at least a member, so as to provide, by the use of some rules of application, for the pairing of at least a population member and a categorization device member. A device is then a collection plus rules of application. . . .
> "An instance of a categorization device is the one called 'sex'; its collection is the two categories (male, female)." (Sacks, 1974)

Using any one of these devices, Sacks points out, a member can make "adequate reference" to any other member, that is, for all situational intents and purposes, *identify* the other.

The idea of the social role, in this perspective, is reduced to simply one more kind of label that can be assigned to any person for the situationally defined purposes of identifying that person. "Housewife," then, is the label a woman might assign herself when asked her occupation by a census-taker, or it might be used by a public agency to label all females not otherwise classifiable as single or employed outside the home. The situation of labelling is what determines the use of this label more than anything else, and the potential for negotiating an acceptable identity has just begun with the utterance or writing of that label as an offered identification. How do social participants ward off or erase unwanted labels? How much of the power of bureaucratic organizations in this society inheres in their power to label individuals whether they want those labels or not? These are some of the questions Naturalists pose in their research.

THE SHOCKING EXPERIMENTS
OF DOCTOR MILGRAM

The person who, with inner conviction, loathes stealing, killing, and assault may find himself performing these acts with relative ease when commanded by authority. (Milgram, 1974)

Working at Yale University from 1960 through 1963, Stanley Milgram presented hundreds of experimental subjects with the following dilemma: You are asked by a scientist to administer electrical shocks of increasing severity to another subject, the "victim," by pulling a series of levers on a "shock board." Even as the victim screams in agony and pleads for you to stop, the experimenter orders you to increase the voltage. The experiment is conducted under various conditions (you can see the victim, or only hear him, the experimenter is in the room with you giving orders, or only ordering you by telephone). Do you obey, or do you refuse to continue with the experiment?

Under all of the experimental conditions, more than half of the subjects obeyed, and went all the way to the highest voltage on the shock board. In subsequent interviews, these obedient subjects assured the researcher that they really believed the shock was real, and that the victim experienced pain. (Of course, the "victim" was not another experimental subject, but a professional actor who convincingly faked being progressively electrocuted.)

Why? What caused these ordinary individuals to behave so savagely, with such calm inhumanity, toward another person? Dr. Milgram himself was shocked, he writes, by the large percentage of subjects who were totally obedient to his inhuman commands. What these experiments centrally reveal, according to Milgram, is ". . . the capacity for man to abandon his humanity, indeed, the inevitability that he does so, as he merges his unique personality into larger institutional structures." (P. 188.)

Dr. Milgram's book provides a full account of the experiments, the subjects' later reactions to them, the attacks on his work by critics of all persuasions when he released his experimental findings during the 1960s, and Milgram's defenses against these critical attacks. The presentation is full enough so that the question of the social self can be analyzed from all three sociological perspectives using the evidence provided in this one source.

Interestingly enough, in trying to answer all of his critics, Milgram himself provides explanations for the behavior of his experimental subjects from all three of our sociological perspectives. Without apparent acknowledgment of the self-contradiction involved, Milgram claims that persons who pulled the top levers on the shock board were exemplars of the socialized self, of the repressed, dehumanized self, *and* of the situational self.

Beginning in the mode of Sociology I, Milgram the Functionalist detaches himself from the moral issues involved in such research, and claims that his goal is merely to discover the causes of human behavior in general. He discovers in these experiments that most people will obey orders when the orders are given by a duly constituted authority, and will do so without much reflection on the right and wrong of what they are ordered to do. He explains his subjects' submission to authority as a product of their past socialization. They have been socialized so that they have internalized the rules of social obedience, internalized them and thus turned them into their own individual motivations. The obedient subjects were simply behaving as any socialized self must behave, according to the social system's programming. From this Functionalist perspective, the penetration of individual selves by the demands of the system as exemplified in these experiments is the necessary requisite for social order.

Apparently stung by criticism from the left that accused him of being in league with totalitarianism, Milgram argues in this book that he is really, and has all along been, a moral diagnostician of the sick social system in which we live. He accepts critics' label of his work as "The Eichman Experiments." His experiments revealed to Americans that what happened in Nazi Germany when too many persons unquestioningly obeyed orders *can* happen here. Milgram's experiments, he now explains, were demonstrations of what Hannah Arendt has called "the banality of evil," or in Milgram's words, " . . . the ordinary and routine destruction carried out by everyday people following orders" in an overly dominant social system.

> The importation and enslavement of millions of black people, the destruction of the American Indian population, the internment of Japanese Americans, the use of napalm against civilians in Vietnam, all are harsh policies that originated in the authority of a democratic nation, and were responded to with the expected obedience. In each case, voices of morality were raised against the action in question, but the typical response of the common man was to obey orders. [P. 180]

By warning us that we, too, have the capacity to abandon our humanity, Milgram is trying to encourage us to reassert our true selves against the persistent authoritarianism of the system. We must learn to judge for ourselves the moral implications of commands handed down by those in power, and learn to disobey. Milgram cites and quotes a letter from one of his former students who claimed to have learned the importance of moral disobedience from the experiments, and went on to refuse to serve in the Vietnamese war. This is Milgram the Activist, advocate for the self-directed moral self against the system.

In yet a third explanatory mode, Milgram abandons both the invisible process of socialization and a repressive authority system as the causes of subject's shocking behavior in the laboratory. Here he explains the obedient behavior as a response to situational factors. Milgram the Naturalist observes the experimental situation as a social occasion in which "each person respects the definition of the situation presented by the other, and in this way avoids conflict, embarrassment, and awkward disruption of social exchange." (P. 152.)

The contradictions involved in these experiments and evident in all three of Milgram's explanatory modes reveal Stanley Milgram to be a fully human social scientist, just as they make this work as a whole a marvelous presentation of the multiform puzzle of the self in society.

Problems in Sociology I

The obedience experiments were carried out using the methods, imagery, rationale, and view of science characteristic of Sociology I, Functionalist sociology. In this mode, Milgram could assume that the behavior he observed in his laboratory was the expression of internalized role playing on the part of fully socialized selves. The experimenter took on the role of the authority figure, and the obedient subjects automatically responded in the role of subordinate. Let us look at just three of the many logical problems and contradictions involved in this analysis.

First there is the puzzle of the double meaning of "role playing" in an experimental laboratory situation such as this one. The subject was asked or cued in to play the role of obedient subordinate by the researcher, but not until after the same subject had been asked to play the role of "experimental subject" in a research project. Which of these roles is the genuine part of the subject's socialized self, and which of them is the subject living up to in obeying the experimenter's commands? Can the conditions of "real life" ever be simulated in a sociologist's laboratory when subjects are always aware that the immediate context is a laboratory experiment?

Second is the problem of representativeness. The logic of the experiment demands that these particular subjects be taken to represent, if not all of humanity, at least the kinds of people prevalent in and produced by the particular social system from which they are drawn, that they are in some important sense a sample of the population at large. But can it ever be said that people who are willing to become subjects in a laboratory experiment are representative of everyone in the social system? Especially in a case like the Milgram experiments, the problem of self-selection severely distorts any possibility for generalization from the results. All of Milgram's subjects already indicated their willingness to "obey" in important respects by giving themselves over to the experimenters for the purposes of scientific research. What can the results of experiments on such subjects have to say about those who would not subject themselves to experiments of any kind?

The third problem is perhaps the most logically profound—the *tautology* common to much Functionalist research. The causes and effects being studied through these experiments are essentially "socialization" and "obedience to authority," respectively. That is, Milgram observes obedience to authority in the laboratory, and explains its causes by referral to the socialization process. But it should be clear to any reader that "socialization" and "obedience to authority" come very close to being one and the same thing! How then can one be considered the cause of the other?

Problems in Sociology II

Shocked by the unresisting, immoral obedience of his subjects, Milgram blames society for producing such attenuated selves, and warns of the dire consequences we can expect of such a diseased system. But this second analysis, introducing the moral element in a forthright way, still accepts the system-determined self of Sociology I, and allows the subjects, and by extension the rest of us, no ground on which to take an antisystem stand, no room to fight back within the tight causal nexus of system and self.

What Milgram apparently can't see, because he fails to adopt the value reflexivity required by Sociology II, is that *he* created the evil in his laboratory, and brought out the very worst in his subjects, which is only one part of their potential as human beings. The Activist would by and large reject any such laboratory experimentation because there are enough evils to be found in the real world, without creating new ones in the lab. It is the Activist's task to alert us to these naturally occurring evils, and then to call forth the best in us to struggle against them.

High on the list of such evils to be exposed and fought by Activist sociologists would be the very type of exploitation and dehumanization represented by Milgram's experimental program. The authority of supposedly "value-free" or objective social science is one more propaganda tool that serves the interests of the power elite in our society. Because of the sanctity of science, people tend to believe anything the social scientist says about humanity. Experiments like Milgram's always seem to find that the injustices in our society have their roots in the victims of injustice. It is human nature, or the system that benefits us all, or the oppressed person's willingness to obey orders because of his internalized obedience, that oppresses us, *not* the beneficiaries of the injustice, the wielders of power, the privileged elite.

Milgram might vainly hope that his experimental findings will teach us to begin to disobey, but the entire theoretical and methodological network into which he has entwined his subjects merely deepens their oppression. His subjects come to deny their own experience, and to believe they have brought their powerlessness upon themselves.

Problems in Sociology III

By introducing a situational explanation for his subjects' obedient behavior, Milgram has unknowingly allowed under his tent the nose of an extremely critical camel. If the situation in the laboratory is what called forth the subjects' responses, then the situation in Milgram's office later called forth those same subjects' avowals that they had really believed in the pain of the actor-victim, and so neither Milgram nor anyone else can ever know what the subjects believed or experienced when they pulled the levers. If we can't know whether they really believed in the harmful effects of their actions, we also can't know much about the nature of their "obedience"—whether it was morally indefensible, or an expression of their true selves, or even the result of their socialization.

Looking through the Naturalist's lens, we see an additional problem in the experiments. Is the self an organic whole? Milgram assumes that the self that is presented in response to the experimental situation reveals or represents the "obedience" of the *whole* self. What if we are really loose collections of fragmentary, situationally created selves? What if there is really nothing behind the collection of masks of identity each of us wears on occasion? Couldn't any of us then give Milgram whatever self he seemed to want from us, without revealing anything about our "true" selves?

Sociology III demands an even deeper reflexivity than that of the Activist perspective. It demands awareness of the *mutuality* of perspectives created in interaction, including the mutuality of perspectives between the social scientist and the "subjects," and of the *negotiated* nature of all social realities. A true Naturalist study of what happened in the lab would look most carefully at the elements of the situation set up by Milgram as well as the social meanings he and his assistants unintentionally may have given off. Milgram negotiated a reality with each subject. Therefore the other side of Milgram's own situational explanation needs to be carefully examined: "Each person respects the definition of the situation presented by the other . . ."

Milgram was one party to the laboratory exchange with each subject. He accepted and respected the subjects' definitions of the situation, in each case a construction and a fabrication, just as his own was. But he took their presented definitions (calling them "responses") to be scientific evidence of their inner states, their prior conditioning, or their readiness to obey, even while he was fully aware that his own presentation to them was a conscious deception. In other words, just as most of us are most of the time, Milgram was deceived by his own deceptions.

And therein lies the full paradox of the scientific study of the social self.

AN INNER VOICE

I wonder how I would have reacted in Milgram's laboratory. Would I have pulled the switch on the victim, all the way to top voltage, when the experimenter ordered me to? And if I did, would it be because I've been programmed by the system to do as I am told? Could I then turn around and criticize this society for being so authoritarian that I have no moral will left to resist? Or would I just be playing the game, presenting a self in the laboratory that is no essential part of "me" but just the subject-self they expect in the lab and therefore get? If I'm always presenting masks to others, where's the me behind the mask? This needs straightening out; more for me in the long run of my life, than just for a sociology course!

─────────── DOING SOCIOLOGY ───────────

A JOURNAL OF THE SOCIAL SELF   Beginning with this assignment period, keep a daily journal for the remainder of the course along with your newspaper clipping file. The last bit of reflection and writing before retiring for the night is ideal for making that day's journal entry. Each entry need be no longer than a paragraph, though some will seem to insist, themselves, on running much longer.

Reflect back on the events and experiences of the day just past. Choose, in your mind's eye, one scene of social interaction in which you participated, and which illustrates the point you wish to make about your own social self in interaction. Describe that scene as briefly but as completely as possible.

Label the entry as being illustrative of Sociology I, II, or III. For I, choose scenes in which you can see yourself acting out the roles you have been routinely socialized to enact, the times you can see yourself conforming to the system's needs. For II, describe instances where you have fought back or at least wanted to fight back against the imposition of roles and role demands, times when you have actively struggled to build an independent, more fully realized, self. For III, describe the ways in which you and your fellow interactants have established identities on the spot, or examples of the sticking on, the peeling off, and the negotiation of labels.

Your journal entries are of course your private property, a collection of written information only you have any absolute right to read. Keep it generally private, but choose those items or extracts that you wish to share with the class when they become relevant to class discussion, or when they are useful as illustrative material in a term paper or essay.

A Naturalist would say that the keeping of this journal is an instrument for building a social self as well as recording, measuring, and analyzing it. Some students will find that the pleasure and value of keeping this journal is encouragement enough to continue it long after termination of the course.

How to Get Yourself Involved Sociologically

4

Five research projects designed for the introductory sociology course and use-tested by students in my classes and those of several of my colleagues are presented here, along with some analysis of their usefulness, limitations, and possibilities. These research projects are intended to substitute for the standard "methods" chapter found in most introductory social science texts. Having students carry out their own projects will give them first-hand experience with sociological methods. In addition, doing these projects should serve to concretize the broad theoretical introduction of the first three chapters, and prepare students for the more topical sociological research in chapters to come.

The student will also note that instructions for conducting these projects and even suggestions on how to evaluate students' performance are not reserved for an instructor's manual. It is a basic intention of this text to reduce or eliminate the gap between professionals and laymen in sociology; in this case, this means reducing the gap between the instructor and the student.

This chapter gives students a chance to reflect back on the preceding chapters and prepare for those to follow by taking an experiential excursus into sociological methods. Students will review the preceding material by successively *doing* the three distinct sociologies outlined in Chapter 1; in doing research in the three sociological modes they will to some degree *experience* the kinds of interaction between researcher and subject matter discussed in Chapter 2; and, if they are carefully self-observant over the course of their involvements in these projects, they will be more clearly aware of their own social selves in action, as described in Chapter 3. At the same time, participation in the research projects will inevitably make them begin focusing outward on the real worlds of the social system. Project work introduces the student to facets of social reality to be taken up in successive chapters, and in addition begins to get sociology *out of the book,* even out of the classroom, and into the real social world.

WHY DO THE PROJECTS?

For the past ten years, I have had my introductory sociology students carry out many different kinds of "special assignments" —something other than the standard essay, term paper, or report. In doing this I have been trying to follow the general guideline that student efforts ought to come to some better end than a mere letter grade, and further, that students ought to come to grips with realities outside the classroom. Some of these projects have worked out splendidly and others were flops, but each was a memorable experience for everyone involved. We were experimenting, dealing with the unpredictable world outside the classroom, capitalizing even on our mistakes. The world outside the classroom often meant the entire university community, or even the entire municipal area surrounding it. It became a standard alibi for about three years for students at the university, when arrested for performing some prank, to claim, "I was just doing a project for Professor Boughey's sociology class." This is not to be encouraged, of course, and none of the projects proposed here could conceivably lead to such a situation. The point, however, is that there is always some danger in allowing sociology to leak out of the classroom and the library, to become a part of real social participants' lives.

I have always found that the benefits far outweighed the dangers. What one *does* is always a better lesson, more deeply learned and longer remembered, than what one reads, hears in a lecture, or sees on a screen. As potent teaching-learning tools, the projects I have assigned have all been designed to move participants toward the following goals:

- To immerse students in the total experience of one or another form of sociological theorizing, research, and action, so that they come, for a while, to live in the project.
- To have students suffer the consequences of doing each kind of sociology, and of being, if only temporarily, that kind of sociologist. It cannot be emphasized too strongly how important this aspect is. The complete cycle of sociological research activity must be experienced in order for the nature of each kind of sociological work to be fully comprehended. The end of that cycle is when the work one has done in the social world comes back, in one way or another, to affect the researcher's life.
- To maximize student choice in the selection and development of specific research topics and ideas, so that the topical direction in which the research proceeds is the responsibility of the students themselves. This aspect adds reality, relevance, and an atmosphere of freedom and democratic decision making to the learning environment of the class, all of which, again, increase the experiential potency of the projects.
- To introduce students to sociological methods as tools for solving research problems, rather than as a disembodied "methodology." There need not be anything mysterious or dull about methods. If the student is confronted meaningfully at the introductory level with the range of practical problems that a methodology is designed to solve, the ground will have been prepared for a future course in social science methods per se.

While on the subject of methods, we should take care we do not fall into the trap of reification. In this instance, the danger would be to conceive as an immutable fact a special relationship between one set of methods and one mode of sociology. Functionalists have been known to use all of the techniques proposed here, as have Activists and Naturalists. The association of particular methods with particular sociologies is intended only to typify the activity and experience involved in a particular sociological perspective.

Some of the activities that have been assigned in past courses have met one or another of the criteria stated above, but failed in others. Some have met all of the criteria, but in doing so have caused so much trouble for both "town" and "gown" that I dare not propose them to others. The reasonably successful but not too troublesome remnant is presented here as a list of suggested options to be assigned or not by the class instructor, along with some evaluative comments on how they worked in my classes.

GENERAL RULES FOR GROUP PROJECTS

Each project is expected to take approximately four weeks of work by a student research group—work over and above the normal routine of reading course assignments and attending lectures. Each instructor will have to work out with the class the grading credit merited by this amount of work, as compared to that granted to examinations and individual essays or reports. In my classes it has evened out at 10 percent of the course grade for each project, with either three or four of the projects assigned for any one course. Up to 40 percent of a student's course grade could thus depend on his or her performance in the research project group.

Sections of introductory sociology classes are usually large, yet group work seldom succeeds in groups of more than ten members. (Plato's *Symposium* apparently managed with twelve to fourteen, but as I understand it, at least two or three of those young Greeks were there just for decoration.)

I have insisted on group work for these projects in order to provide students with some relief from the scholarly isolation and overly individualistic competition they suffer during most of their academic careers. In addition, the aim is to set up some concretely real problems of small-scale social organization—the organization of work in the project group—which can later be analyzed sociologically, as in Project E, below. Bureaucratic contingencies will differ from school to school, but in the universities in which I have taught these projects, I have been able to substitute the project research groups, their meetings, and their consultations with the instructor and teaching assistants for the regularly scheduled tutorials or seminar groups.

The suggested projects, then, are workable after the class has broken itself down into ten-member research groups that will remain together throughout the term. Transfers from one group to another must be clearly outlawed from the start. Members who select each other as fellow group members will have to cope with each other for the term.

One class session might be fruitfully devoted to deciding democratically how the class ought to group itself into tens, and then to carrying out this plan.

From then on, the group must meet on its own time and at its own selected place, probably at least weekly. It chooses its own leader or leaders and makes its own rules. The only imposition of outside authority is the project assignment and the deadline set by the instructor. Everything else that goes on in the group is its own business. The group must come up with its own means for meeting the deadline with a first-class project.

The group chooses a specific topic for each project assignment, divides up the labor, and carries out the research and research presentation. At the end, the instructor grades the finished project, and all ten members of the group receive this grade. Group grading tends to make members feel a sense of responsibility toward each other and toward their group. There is bound to be some sense of unfairness involved, hence the proportion of any individual's grade coming from group work should never exceed 40 percent. The reality sense brought into group work by the group grade, in my estimation, far outweighs the sense of individual unfairness sometimes experienced.

One further note about group work. If the instructor assigns Project E, each group will be required to keep careful records of its interactive history from group formation to the end of the term. Therefore, a record-keeper should be chosen at the first group meeting, and motivated to keep good records throughout.

The instructor and the teaching assistants will make themselves available throughout the week for consultation with groups or group representatives. Problems concerning group organization, the cooperation of members, or the methods and contingencies of research projects should be brought to these outside authorities whenever necessary.

The key point to remember is that the adviser may give information and advice, but never direction and control.

THE PROJECTS

Project A. Social Injustice Research

Assignment: Your group must investigate a "ripoff" whose victims and perpetrators are to be found in the local community of the university or college and its municipal surroundings, an instance of some organization, group, or individual that is systematically taking advantage of some class of people or of "we the people" as a whole. You must decide in advance that the ripoff is wrong, by your group's agreed upon moral standards, and that it adds another bit to the general quantity of social injustice in your society. Then you must satisfy yourselves, through documented research, that there really is such a ripoff, that it really is an injustice, that some people really do suffer from it and others profit. The second task is to decide theoretically how this localized ripoff is connected with larger issues of social injustice. Finally, the crux of the assignment is—do something about it. The most effective and available action for ripoff researchers to take is pub-

lic exposure of the ripoff, its perpetrators, and its victims. Therefore each group must present its documentation to the available public media, and work with media representatives to shape this information into a publishable or broadcastable story. The project is only complete and deserving of a course grade when the printed news story has been presented as a clipping to the class and instructor, or when the radio or television broadcast of the story has been scheduled, announced to the class and instructor, and viewed or heard by all. Whether or not the ripoff is ended or cured by media exposure cannot be controlled by the research group in this kind of project. What counts is the media exposure itself, and it is this that will be graded by the instructor.

In past trials, the announcement and explanation of this assignment to the class has been met with shocked disbelief by most students. Initially, no one believes it can be done. By the deadline date, however, every research group has in fact accomplished the impossible, and relief and pride predominate. By deadline date there are also a number of public controversies going on in the community as well, in the newspapers, over radio and on television, putting the students in the center of the social arena, and in various kinds of trouble as well.

All of these extreme emotional stimuli taken together make up a salutory shock treatment to engage the class in the full experience of doing and suffering sociological research, of one particular sort. That is why I find it the ideal first project for the research groups to attempt. Tempered by fire, the students enter subsequent projects without fear.

Success usually comes after a topic of reasonable size and scope has been selected, and after, through a division of labor in the group, one or more individuals have been assigned exclusively to the task of contacting and working with the media representatives. The newspaper or broadcasting station concerned will guide the research group as to limits of liability, acceptable documentation, and even the intricacies of method, as well as on the newsworthiness of the project.

Choosing a Ripoff.   Members of each research group bring to their first meeting enormous stores of information about the surrounding social communities, as well as untapped reservoirs of ingenuity. The ripoff to be researched ought to emerge as the result of long and intensive discussion, in the form of "brainstorming" within the group. Some one or more group members should have personal knowledge of the alleged ripoff, and the group as a whole must agree that this is the ripoff to study, that it is researchable within the time limits, and that all members agree it is a wrong in the community that needs to be exposed and possibly righted.

In one successful instance, one group member recalled during the brainstorming session that he had noticed a strange pattern in municipal tree-planting when he worked as a laborer for the city the previous summer. It seemed that the city workers had two different species of sapling supplied to them. Both were maples, but one was a longer lasting, more beautifully leafed, and twice as expensive species of maple than the other. He didn't remember exactly how the word had come down, but as he recalled it, he and his fellow workers were always planting the cheaper maples in front of houses in poorer neighborhoods, and the more expensive, fancier trees in front of the more expensive, fancier houses. And, he remembered, each householder was billed exactly the same amount, per tree, by the city for the planting.

As soon as he had stated it, all other options seemed to fade away into insignificance. The members of the group came to rapid consensus that this was their topic for Project A, and the group was ready to begin serious research and documentation on the case of the "Maple Tree Ripoff." How the research was done will be considered in the next subsection.

Another group contained two members who discovered only through the brainstorming session that they shared the same problem, and were victims of what the group came to see as an as yet unpublicized injustice. Both members were partners in couple relationships, and both of these couples had decided to live together rather than get married. But neither couple could find an apartment to rent anywhere in the university area. It seemed to them that landlords in the area systematically refused to rent to unmarried couples, and that this was a form of discrimination. The group agreed, if it could be documented that such discrimination occurred, that this was indeed a social injustice. Thus the "Living Together" project was born.

In similar fashion, the following research-action topics were launched: "The Unisex Haircut Ripoff" group set out to document and expose the fact that at a half-dozen haircutting parlors in the city that advertised unisex hairstyling for both men and women, women were routinely charged more, often 100 percent more, than men for exactly the same hairstyle, at exactly the same hair length, and for exactly the same amount of time and attention spent by the staff. "The Car Repair Ripoff" group decided to attack the discrepancy between estimates and charges for the same automobile repairs by different repair shops and garages, discrepancies amounting to up to 400 percent difference. "The Poor Man's Food Ripoff" group attempted to prove that supermarket branches of the same parent chains charge significantly higher prices for the same staple items in lower income areas that in higher income areas of the municipality. "The Health Food Ripoff" group diagnosed as a ripoff-sized social illness the alleged fact that much of what appears on health-food store shelves is just repackaged foodstuffs from the nonhealth supermarkets, marked up to double and triple the price because it comes in brown bags with penciled labels. The "Cold Weather Anti-Freeze Ripoff" group decided to try to discover and expose the real reasons anti-freeze prices went up to six times their former levels as cold weather approached, on the grounds that there was a shortage of supplies, after which it turned out that there was plenty to go around after all.

Documenting a Ripoff.   Each topic chosen under Project A demands its own unique combination of methods for gathering information, documenting, and proving the social injustice or ripoff, and finally reforming the illness through media exposure. There is no general formula, no cut-and-dried method or set of "cookie cutter" standards, that would unify and standardize the research process for every topic. In consultation with the instructor and teaching assistants, the groups researching the topics described above found the following collections of methods satisfactory; perhaps they will prove helpful for your research group:

Both the "Maple Tree Ripoff" and the "The Poor Man's Food Ripoff" were cases of the rich gaining an unfair advantage over the poor through the actions of a powerful agency—in the first instance the municipal government, in the second the huge supermarket chains. The first thing needing to be established in both cases was the absolute consistency of the advantage. Can it be said that the cheap trees are planted only in poorer neighborhoods, and the expensive trees only in rich neighborhoods? Is it the case that poor people always pay more at their local supermarkets than rich people pay at theirs?

The "Maple Tree" group consulted real estate agents, and procured a real estate map of the city, showing the exact "market boundaries" between blocks of houses at varying price ranges. They then drove, in pairs, down every residential street in the city and noted the type of tree planted along the curb. Comparing a tree-type street map with their real estate value map, the group found some blurring and overlap in the areas near the middle of the housing price spread, but, at both extremes, the correlation was perfect. Thus, they could report with a fair degree of certainty that in front of the most expensive houses in the city, municipal tree planters had placed only the more expensive species of maple, and in front of the least valuable houses in the city, municipal tree planters had placed only the cheaper trees. This represented the major "finding" of the research group's visual survey. As far as the group was concerned, this was enough to establish an injustice. But more research, using different methods, was required of them by the media representatives they contacted in order to expose it, as we shall discuss in the next subsection on media exposure.

The supermarket survey required first of all an income map of the city. Students put together a map of census tracts with income data from the census bureau dug up in the library; then they located chain supermarkets that had branches in both poorer and richer census tracts. A shopping list of some twenty-five staple items, giving brand name and quantity where possible, was then made up, and individual members of the group priced the twenty-five item list in each of twenty stores on the same day—two stores per student per survey day—in order to equalize variations in prices that might be explained by specials on different days of the week. All told, the student researchers priced twenty-five items in sixty supermarkets, representing six different chains.

The group found variation between the total prices for the twenty-five items from store to store within the same chain as high as 20 percent, but, as in the maple tree example, the differences between prices in census tracts in the middle income range were slight and varied in both directions. This group also decided that its strongest argument could be made in terms of the differences between prices in the very wealthy suburban neighborhoods and the very poorest of inner city districts. Using the results from only twenty supermarkets, the research group could report that prices in the supermarkets in rich neighborhoods were lower, and often as much as one-fifth lower, than prices in the supermarkets in poor neighborhoods. They could also say that this price difference existed within the same supermarket chains, though in smaller percentages.

The group developed a number of plausible explanations for this clear case of social injustice. Perhaps the rich have more clout, are able to bring pressure to bear on supermarket chains and store managers, whereas the poor are powerless, and can only shut up and put up with whatever they are given. Perhaps businessmen who run the chains assume the rich are smarter than the poor, wiser shoppers who have to be catered to in pricing policy, whereas the poor are just dumb consumers who buy what they need blindly, whatever the price, until their money is mysteriously gone. In any case, it looked to the group like a clear case of exploitation. Once again it took the guidance of media representatives to force the research group to ask the question Why? over again, and to try to answer it through further research.

The "Living Together" project and the "Unisex Haircut Ripoff" had in common an alleged discriminatory treatment of different types of consumers by sellers. In both cases, *controlled comparisons* were required in order to compile convincing information to make the case. Couples who admitted they were just "living together" attempted to sign up for advertised apartments; when they were refused, usually on the grounds that the apartment was taken, a "married" couple, wearing wedding rings, would attempt to make the same rental. The research group managed to compile twenty-two such pairings, which proved to be adequate proof of landlord discrimination against unmarried couples to make it a front-page issue in the local daily. The haircut study required a male and female pair of researchers, their hair of equal length to start with, to go to the same salon and order the same cut from the pictures on the wall, then compare the prices charged. This twelve-member group managed thus to investigate six parlors, and their evidence was adequate for a large feature display in two bi-weekly papers plus a short note in the daily press.

The "Car Repair" group straightforwardly took three automobiles with a variety of dents and defects to some twenty different repair shops, large and small, throughout the city for estimates on the cost of repairs. They then compiled and reported the price differences for the same repairs, garage by garage, giving names and addresses. Their aim was to warn consumers about "highballing" repair shops through the media, in hopes that the offenders would mend their ways to recover lost business. Similarly, the "Health Food" group purchased common foodstuffs packaged in brown paper bags in health food stores, then bought identical items at the local supermarket and compared prices, ounce for ounce. They reported the discrepancies in the press, again naming the offending stores.

The Anti-Freeze group collected news stories about reported shortages of anti-freeze before the first winter cold spell, and documented the rising prices being charged by service stations per gallon of the precious stuff, until anti-freeze reached six times its previous price. Then they surveyed distributors to find that all had adequate supplies, and no one seemed to know where the story about shortages had ever come from. An oil company executive, who had been quoted in earlier stories about upcoming shortages, denied to group members that he had ever claimed such a thing. Altogether, the group's information added up to a history of a consumer ripoff by the oil companies, and several newspapers were glad to publish it.

Publicly Exposing a Ripoff.   In any project of the sociological Activist orientation, research must be directed by ultimate goals, the *action* the researcher wants to take with regard to the social issue or illness that has been diagnosed. In this case the mode of action is public exposure of a ripoff through the media, and the group grade depends entirely on the instructor's evaluation of the media report that results from the group's work. Therefore each group must think hard from the start about exactly how their research activities will achieve media coverage. Coverage, by broadcast or in the press, must meet the deadline date for the project, and evaluation of the group's work will depend on their success in getting widespread, prominent exposure of the ripoff. This means publication in the most widely read papers or broadcast over the major network stations, as well as good coverage in those media. A front-page, two-column story in the largest daily ranks above a page 15 two-inch note in the suburban weekly, and ten minutes of air time on the network "issues" program ranks above a one-minute spot on local cable TV.

One generally successful group strategy has been to select one or more group members to work exclusively on media coverage from the start of the project. All class members, of course, having begun and kept up clipping files as assigned in Chapter 2, will now be familiar with the kinds of issues that can become news stories. Each research group's "media experts," however, will have to equip themselves more thoroughly with information and contacts. As soon as the ripoff is chosen by the group, the media experts should begin to make personal contacts with newspaper reporters, radio and television news staffers, and public affairs programs staff.

Let the media staffers know as soon as possible what the group will be researching, what it hopes to prove, and what methods it intends to use to make its case. Media professionals are always looking for stories, and are generally glad to have a story, plus ten unpaid hardworking "legmen," dumped into their laps. They will become methodological guides for the group, indicating the kinds of things they can and cannot say in print or on the air, how much proof is proof enough to publish, and where the researchers might tread on dangerous or legally objectionable grounds.

If the big daily paper or the network broadcasting station isn't interested in the group's project, then the media contacts must move quickly to establish a working relationship with the weekly papers, the suburban press, or the local stations.

At any level, however, the group's relationship with the media should remain a partnership between autonomous coequals. The group must decide for itself whether and to what degree it wishes to take the advice of media representatives. Certainly the group must resist any pressure to mute or divert the activism of the project, the genuine public exposure of an injustice.

But some necessary compromises of the group's activist fervor will actually deepen and strengthen the project. For instance, in the "Maple Tree Ripoff" case, a reporter for the city's leading daily newspaper agreed to try to get the story published, but insisted that the group interview municipal officials to get a rounded picture. At first the group resisted, arguing that their case was complete and unassailable—there were the trees, and there was the correlation between poor neighborhoods and cheap trees, so why give the politicians a chance to cover up before the ripoff is exposed? But the reporter prevailed, and the group questioned the parks commissioner, the commissioner of public works, and finally the parks superintendent down the line who was called by his superiors "responsible for overseeing street tree plantings." These officials denied any economic discrimination in tree planting, told the students they were wasting their time with this research, but also confirmed that the more expensive trees last longer, and are planted in neighborhoods that already have expensive trees to "match" existing plantings. The whole story, including the back-tracking denials by officials, made a fine front-page box (set aside for stories of unusual interest) in the daily paper, got a by-line for the reporter, and was picked up by international news wires for newspapers and radio news broadcasts all over the world.

Multiple coverage is something to be expected, even hoped for, by many research groups who are successful in exposing a ripoff through one media outlet. If the story is picked up by other media outlets and republicized, the group should get additional credit from the instructor for their continuing success. The "Unisex Haircut" story, for instance, was first rejected by the large daily papers, then printed, with photographs of students displaying new haircuts, in two suburban weeklies. Two television stations then contacted members of the research group and asked them to appear on daytime talk-variety shows to explain their odd research project. A week later, a radio show called up representatives of the group and asked them to be interviewed over the telephone on an evening network broadcast. The "Health Food" group first appeared on a local cable TV station's local issues program, as a group, and explained to the interviewer what they had found out about health food store prices. The story was only then picked up by a daily newspaper, which reported mainly what the students had said on the TV show.

The newspaper editor covering the supermarket price project insisted that managers of supermarket chains be asked why prices differed in different stores of the chain in different economic areas. Some explained that prices varied from day to day, which the students countered by pointing out that all the comparisons were done on the same day. Others placed the responsibility on individual store managers who, they said, had some discretion on the pricing of individual items. This, the students answered, still doesn't account for the consistency of higher prices in lower-income neighborhoods. Finally, one chain executive admitted that shoppers in the better-off suburban neighborhoods are more mobile, having cars, than are inner-city buyers, and therefore prices must be more competitive in the former areas than in the latter. All of these explanations and the students' answers became part of the story, which the newspaper ran in full despite the threat to its advertising revenue from supermarket chains.

This is all part of the continuing involvement one may experience as a participant in an Activist research project. Interviewers ask tough questions, public officials or company officials reply to attacks upon them or their organizations by maligning the students involved or the university or college, and in any number of ways, researchers find themselves "called to account."

The instructor, of course, will have to stand ready to back up the student research groups when they are attacked, justifying the research projects as a learning experience worth the troubles they cost. The student participants are never involved in breaking laws in collecting their information, and the newspapers and broadcasting stations are legally responsible for what they allow to be published or broadcast, so there are really no serious repercussions to worry about. The class as a whole and individual students by themselves just have to be ready to stand up to the flack they might provoke from the powers that be.

Cautions.   The student should not assume that by doing Project A one has become a full-fledged Activist sociologist. This is just a mild form of social involvement, with many safeguards built in against the researcher really getting hurt.

Most sociological. Activists would reject such activities as "band-aid" social reformism, treating the most superficial symptoms without getting at the underlying causes of social injustice, and thereby perhaps even serving to cover up the true disease. Some would even say that such piecemeal reform does more harm than good, because it tends to *legitimate* (to make something appear to be right and proper) the oppressive system by making it appear flexible, self-correcting, open to positive change, etc. A full-fledged Activist would identify the media organizations themselves as parts of the oppressive system, ruled by publishers and station owners who are members or hired hands of the power elite. Anything they would allow to be published in their propaganda organs, therefore, could not be a true exposure of social injustice, but must be a more subtle cover up.

Project A is just a sweetened taste of true sociological Activism, which requires a full and deep commitment to revolutionary change, and which demands that the participant place the active self wholly within the large-scale arena of human history. True commitment regularly costs Activists dearly in terms of career, money, reputation, even at times beatings and jail terms. Compare the minor risks of Project A with the risks a true Activist is subjected to in the struggle against apartheid in South Africa, for instance.

Project B. Research into Routines and Rules

Assignment: Your group must choose a recurring scene of routine social interaction as your observational target—for instance, a bus stop, a supermarket checkout counter, a tavern or pub, a coffee counter, a subway coach, a library reading room, etc.—a scene that can be observed naturalistically by the group, over and over again. Group members will have to participate as natural interactants in the scene while observing it, so choose a scene that normally contains more than a dozen participants, and that your group's members can naturally participate in. Observe and take notes on everything you see each session. In successive group meetings, note in particular what you have been able to observe to happen again. Repeat the observation at least three times, and often enough so that you can compile, as a group, a list of at least ten "rules" of behavior for the particular scene of interaction you have been observing. Consider a form of action or behavior to be governed by a "rule" if it occurs just that way every time, and it appears to the group to be a characteristic and necessary form of action for this scene to take place smoothly and normally. Try to imagine your alleged "rule" being violated by behavior that is just the opposite in some sense. Would this violation disrupt the standard scene? If you think it would, put this "rule" on your group's list.

Having compiled the list of ten rules for proper behavior in your chosen scene of interaction, you must next write a script for a little playlet, an enactment of the scene you have observed with its ten rules of behavior. Write parts for all group members, and plan a performance before your sociology class. The group's research presentation for Project B will be this performance before the class. The enactment should take no longer than fifteen minutes. Ten minutes is usually enough. The goal of the performance is to reproduce, before the class, the standard scene your group has been observing, with special emphasis on the ten rules of behavior you have been able to observe within that scene. The class is asked to try to spot the rules you are enacting for them, and to write them down while watching you perform. The instructor will evaluate the performance as an intelligent presentation of the group's observational and analytical work.

The post-performance phase of each group's presentation will provide further lessons for all. The instructor will elicit from the audience the rules they have written down during the performance, and placing these on the blackboard, compare the list with the original list supplied by the performing group.

Once again the group is thrust into action in unfamiliar territory. You are being asked to behave like strangers, or tourists, in a world of standard social routines that is so familiar to you that you take its contours for granted. You will have to force yourself to see it with new eyes. In the past I have found that research groups enjoy this project very much, once they have gotten over this feeling of awkwardness. The results have been highly successful from the instructor's point of view as well, especially when the following procedures are followed.

Choosing a Scene.   Once again those projects have been most successful that have taken the end product of the research project into account from the very beginning. For Project B, the end product is the performance, so choose a scene of publicly observable interaction that could conceivably be reproduced in the space available at the front of your sociology classroom.

One of the most amusing and insightful examples was the work of a research group that focused on behavior in elevators in large business and public buildings. The only props necessary for the performance were a chalk-line elevator-sized box drawn on the floor, a "down" and "up" button drawn on the blackboard and a narrator, whose only lines were "doors open" and "doors close." A second memorable choice was the greeting area at the international arrivals gate of the nearby major airport. The door into the classroom served as the final gate through which passengers come when they have cleared immigration, customs, baggage pick up, and the rest, while their friends and relatives crowd, crane, complain, and finally, one group at a time, explode into the standard forms of greeting as "their" arrival comes through the door.

The scene will also have to be observed by the group as a portion of the scene's natural participants, so it should be a scene in which group members feel comfortable, and in which an additional ten college students would not particularly stand out or look out of place.

Some past choices that filled this criterion well were the observation of weekend drink-and-dance tavern behavior by a group who just attended week after week as a group out drinking and dancing; the rush-hour subway project in which the ten-member research group couldn't have been less conspicuous; observation of "queueing" on the sidewalks outside movie theatres, and the "hanging around the shopping plaza" group who just joined the throngs of youths who so casually, yet so artfully, do their thing of an evening around the mall.

Other scenes that have been successfully participated in, observed, and then reproduced in classroom playlets include the short-order restaurant; the urban "mini-park"; the art gallery; the bus ride to work; the supermarket checkout; the library reading room; a section of the stands at the "big game"; inside the movie theatre; and many others. Hopefully you will find this list suggestive, and in further brainstorming sessions, will come up with a good choice for your group.

Participant Observation.   The basic method used in Project B is *participant observation,* and it has a long and respected history as a method in the social sciences. There is much that could be said about doing sociology with this particular methodology, but here we wish only to discuss it fully enough so that students doing Project B will be adequately equipped to do the job, and fully aware of what they are doing when they use this method.

From the standpoint of Naturalist sociology, the term "participant observation" is redundant, because you cannot be a participant in social interaction without making careful observations on what is going on around you so that you can guide your own actions appropriately, and you cannot observe naturally occurring social interaction without being, at the same time, some kind of a participant (even if your participating role is artificially reduced to that of "the outside observer"). "Objective" observation is always impossible in social science because of this dual involvement: the observer, as a participant him or herself, must experience that which is observed to some degree *subjectively* because it concerns and affects every participant; conversely, the very presence and participation of the observer "changes" the event in some way. Thus, the observer to some unknown degree *creates* what is observed. However, relatively accurate and nonbiased observation and recording of social interaction is possible, and, from the Naturalist perspective, quite adequate as scientific evidence or "data."

One way to avoid the bias that can be a part of the observer's inevitable subjectivity is to choose topics for investigation that nobody cares much about in moral or political terms. This means the complete reversal of the Activist type of research focus developed in Project A. Project B thus avoids observer bias by avoiding controversial issues, adopting the Naturalist interest in the most commonplace, everyday forms of social interaction.

In order to achieve a high degree of accuracy of observation, Project B requires that a number of different observers observe the same scene at the same time. The group's description of what happened will then be reduced to what all ten observers can agree did happen, what everyone saw and understood as the action. Individual distortions can then be somewhat filtered out, and the remaining description can at least claim a high degree of inter-observer corroboration.

The research group must decide upon a strategy for participant observation once they have chosen their observational scene. Should group members stick physically together, and interact mainly with each other as a group, or should they disperse among the crowd and act like strangers to each other? Is the scene naturally a collection of groups, or is it an amalgam of individuals? How long should group members participate and observe before withdrawing for a meeting to discuss and record what was seen? Do participants of this scene naturally come and go as they please, or do people regularly stay for set time segments? The observational strategy chosen, in other words, should fit the scene to be observed.

What is it that is to be observed by the participating research group? Assume your group has chosen a scene, decided on a strategy, has now entered the scene for the first time, and is successfully mingling and participating. What should the members look at, and what should they be looking for? Each of you has been in this scene before, as an ordinary participant, and of course you have watched the others and therefore observed the scene with your everyday eyes. Now it is necessary to alter your focus a bit, to try on slightly new eyes. Watch the *actions* of the other participants in the scene as if they were *performances* written down in a script. Try to imagine how the script would be written. Try to think of a label for the action you are watching, a title for that set of lines and stage directions. For instance, here is a fellow participant before me at the "hanging around the shopping plaza" scene. I think I'll call what he's doing "lounging," or better, "doing a lounge." Now, how would the stage directions in the script read for an actor to faithfully reproduce this "lounge"? I'll have to note down in my mind all the small actions, postures, and expressions that I can observe going into the composite action he's doing, his "lounge."

There are innumerable actions going on all the time, in any scene. Which actions should the group observe carefully, and later try to describe as scripted performances? The answer to this question will have to be revised several times as the group observes, discusses, and observes the scene again. The actions to be watched most carefully will be those that the group comes to recognize as the typical actions that particularly characterize this scene and that can be used to express the basic rules of behavior for this scene. In other words, the choice of actions to be zeroed in on will develop as part of the group's analysis of the scene and its bounding rules.

Rule Analysis.   The development of a list of ten rules characterizing the behavior appropriate for the group's chosen scene will best be achieved through a process of alternation between observation and analysis. You don't have to know for sure why the rule is being followed, or even how it is enforced, in order to see recurrent actions as rule bound. For instance, during its first observational session, the research group looking at "elevator behavior" noticed a few striking features of the scene. It appeared that everyone stood for the whole ride facing front and looking straight ahead or slightly upwards at the lighted floor numbers. The group decided to observe again the next time more carefully, to see if indeed it could be said that two rules of elevator riding are, "Stand facing the front of the car," and "Don't look anywhere but straight ahead or up at the numbers." Their repeated observations confirmed that, with very few exceptions, this was the rule in elevator riding, and they had the first two items of their list. "If you speak at all, lower your voice and direct it only to your intended listener"; "Move to the rear of the car to let new arrivals in, even if this means you have to push back up through everyone to get off at an early stop"; "Women are to be politely allowed to enter the car before men, and then rudely crushed into the back of the car by the same men"; "When you are crushed into the back of the car by others larger than yourself, don't say anything about it at the time, but on your way off, you may express outrage and indignity"; "Passengers getting off have the right of way over passengers staying on and over passengers getting on, and may express this right of way by saying (sometimes self-righteously) 'excuse me,' "; "Bodily contact with other passengers is to be avoided strenuously, until the crush of passengers makes it unavoidable"; "When bodily contact has become unavoidable, women shall cover their breasts with their forearms and men shall avoid any contact with anyone with their hands"; "Whether waiting for the elevator or riding it, do not trust anyone else to have pushed your button already. Even if it is lighted, make sure to push your button again yourself." That concluded this excellent project's list of ten.

The sense in which we are calling these statements "rules" is simply that "as a rule" this is the way we have observed participants to behave during repeated occurrances of this kind of situation or scene.

It is extremely helpful, both in observing a rule, and in portraying the rule, if explicit *violations* of alleged rules can be observed, and sanctioning, or corrective actions can be seen to follow the violations. Watch carefully the actions of young children, foreigners, or other novitiates into the culture, and the reactions of others to their unknowing violations. The elevator observers, for instance, were fortunate enough to see a child refuse to move to the rear of the car when new arrivals were getting on. The child's mother pulled him by the arm and said, "Come on, move to the back with me." The child shook the mother off and said, "But we're getting off next stop and we'll have to push all the way up front again." The mother pulled him back, this time successfully, and said, still in the hushed voice appropriate for elevator conversation, "I know, but you move to the back anyway."

This conversation gave the observers the full complexity of the rule. It also indicates an interesting feature of many of the rule-like behaviors to be observed in social scenes—the rules do not always dictate the most sensible course of action, and as a matter of fact often fly in the face of reason. That is why the rules cannot be intellectually deduced from the theoretical analysis of any social situation—their enforcement and violation have to be empirically observed.

Scripting the Scene.   Now that you have derived from repeated observational sessions a list of ten rules for behavior that you think characterize the scene, you must translate this list into an enactable script. This entails weaving together your ten rules and their violation and correction into a continuous story line of between ten and fifteen minutes duration. The script should include parts for all ten of your group members to play, and for each part, dialogue and stage directions have to be written. Once written, the script should be copied so that each performer has one in hand, and the whole playlet should be rehearsed by the group.

Remember that the script has two sometimes contrasting goals. You want to point up the rules you are portraying very clearly, so that the audience, the rest of the class, can actually write down your original list of ten rules just from watching the playlet. At the same time, the performance should reproduce, as naturalistically as possible, the scene as you originally observed it. Thus dual goal can be approached most successfully by observing the following methodological dictum: *Try to make it possible for your audience to observe the rules in action in the same way in which you originally observed them, by presenting to the audience the same actions that the naturally occurring scene presented to you.*

Performance and Post-Performance Analysis.   I have found it practical to dedicate a one-hour class session to the performance and analysis of two group projects at the maximum, calculating ten to fifteen minutes for performance and an equal amount of time for class discussion of each performance. It has always seemed that it would be better if we could have afforded a whole hour for each performance and the ensuing discussion, because so much of interest comes up in the wake of each performance.

The group performs, while the class notes down the ten rules it appears to be enacting on stage. Then the group's representative hands the instructor the group's original list of ten rules, and the instructor reads them out or puts them on the blackboard, asking for each one how many members of the audience "got" that one. The number of people who identified each one is an indicator of how successful the performance was in getting across each rule. But something very strange and interesting is now left over. Each of the students in the audience has a list before him or her of ten rules observed in the group's performance. But for each student, only a portion of the list matches the list given by the group. The instructor then asks for additional rules written down by audience members. In some cases, the additional rules have made up a list of over one hundred. And all of them were there to be observed in the group's performance! Why and how this should be the case is the topic for the ensuing discussion.

Cautions.   Use the post-performance discussions to avoid another kind of reification—reification involved in thinking of "rules" as real things. The fact that behavior *can be described* as rule-bound does not warrant the assumption that rules are there, in the behavior, or that rules as things-in-themselves dictate or govern the behavior. The observations, the performances, and the observation of the performances all merely indicate that "rule-bound" is one way we describe the behavior of our fellow humans.

A full-fledged Naturalist sociology would call Project B an exercise in the creation of rules as fictions by which to communicate the meaning of what the research groups observed to others, and the further creation of rules by the audiences as a way of making sense out of what they saw on the classroom stage.

Project B fails to go all the way toward Sociology III's requirement of reflexivity in social science—the intensive focus on what we, as observers and analysts, are doing when we observe and analyze. How is it that group members were able to choose a scene as distinct from other scenes to observe in the first place? What distinguishes one type of social scene from another for us as participants? What skills do we use and what assumptions do we rely on in order to "see" one collection of interactions as a repeated enactment of the "same" scene over again? How do we matter-of-factly single out an "action" from the welter of experience surrounding each of us in any social encounter? How do we manage to assume that what that other person's action signified to me, the observer, was in any way the same thing that action meant or was intended to mean by him or her, the actor?

These are but a few of the deep questions left unanswered by Project B that must be asked if one is to attempt seriously a Naturalist sociology.

Project C. The Social Facts about Census Tracts

Assignment: Your group will choose or be assigned a single, specific census tract within your geographic area. Using the most recent census materials available in your library, plus information available in the files of your local police department, physical and mental health institutions, political party headquarters, governmental offices, church organizations, chamber of commerce, welfare and social service organizations, and any other organized body of information you may find useful, answer the following questions about your census tract:

1. *What is the population of your census tract?*
2. *How many persons per square mile reside in it, compared to national, state, and local municipal averages?*
3. *What is the per capita or per family income of your tract, compared to national, state, and local municipal averages?*
4. *What is the rate of violent crime in your tract, compared to local rates, the state rate, the national rate?*
5. *What is the suicide rate in your tract, compared to other places?*
6. *What is the unemployment rate in your tract, compared to other places?*
7. *What is the average level of education completed by residents of your tract, compared with local, state, and national averages?*
8. *What is the average length of residence in the same house or apartment in your tract as compared to local, state, and national averages?*
9. *What proportion of the people in your tract are on welfare or social assistance programs compared to proportions elsewhere?*
10. *What is the age distribution of the residents of your tract as compared to national, state, and local age distributions?*

Having compiled these comparative social facts, your group will now construct a report on the Sociological Profile of your tract. Part One of the report will simply report the social facts in some kind of logical order; Part Two will discuss the most interesting connections your group has been able to make between the various social facts, especially any causal relationships you think might exist between any of the facts. Further, can you characterize this census tract as representative of a particular sector, part, or subset of the society as a whole?

Finally, make enough copies of your report so that you can distribute one copy to each other research group in the class.

The instructor and teaching assistants will have to be especially helpful with advice and counseling on Project C, because the availability of information will vary greatly in different localities. Each of the questions needs to be interpreted according to local standards and availability of information. In general, choose the interpretation that fits the information most easily available. Even then, however, don't assume that the facts "speak for themselves." Each research group has to decide what to make of population size and distribution, income averages, and the rest of the various rates. The question at hand in writing the final report is, given these preinterpreted facts, what can we reasonably say about the social contours of that piece of the social system found within the boundaries of this census tract?

The project becomes most interesting after it has been handed in and graded, when the copies of the reports are distributed to all the research groups, and class discussions can focus on comparisons between the various census tracts in the local area that have been studied. Now the class is talking about a sample of census tracts from the surrounding population area as a whole. What can be reasonably said about this entire area as a subsection of the state or national social system as a whole?

Further, the information collected in answer to these ten questions will provide recurrent illustration of the general statements to be made in each of the ensuing chapters of this text.

Project D. Theorizing about System Requisites

Assignment: Your group will draw up a "social constitution" that makes adequate provision for the constitution of a complete social system, or society, in ten subsections. The society you are hypothetically founding on the basis of this constitution must be designed to survive over three successive generations as a cohesive system, that is, it must perpetuate itself. What are the ten necessary conditions, the ten functional requisites, for the organization and continued operation of a social system?

Again, provide every other research group with a copy of your list, and hold class discussions on the similarities and discrepancies between them.

This is the second project in the mode of Sociology I, or Functionalist sociology, but unlike Project C, which dealt exclusively with social facts, Project D deals exclusively with social theory, or social theorizing. "Armchair theorizing" about the basic conditions necessary for social organization is one of the favorite pastimes, and sometimes the serious professional business, of Functionalist sociologists. The criteria for doing this well are the logical cohesion, the generality, and the completeness of the theoretical statements made.

It might not be a bad idea to begin your constitution with a preamble, beginning, "We hold these truths to be self-evident . . ." In it, state a few of the principles of human nature that the members of your group agree are self-evident truths, and that will underlie, as assumptions, the construction of your ten necessary requisites or preconditions for the construction of a stable society.

Successful interpretations of what a "requisite" or a "precondition" might be have varied greatly in past attempts, and hopefully will vary further in future run-throughs of Project D. Some groups have come up with elaborated, justified lists of the ten basic *rules* needing to be instituted for a viable society, some of these in "Thou shalt not . . ." format. Others have listed and explained the ten crucial *roles* that must be rewarded and manned for any society to survive. Still others have outlined the ten essential *relationships* that must be established and maintained for the social order to remain integrated and functioning over time. The ten necessary organizations, the ten essential institutions, or the ten basic activities are other possibilities to be explored.

The intellectual creativity of your group will get its best chance to shine through in doing this project, and instructors will be hard pressed to find reasonable ways to give less than top marks to all of the groups doing project D.

Project E. Research Group Research

Assignment: Compile and write up a "natural history" of your research group's life as a social entity, from the day of its formation up to now, or, if projections can be made, to the day of its dissolution at the end of the course. Analyze the dynamics of your group's interaction that led to its successes and failures, its strengths and weaknesses, and compare it with other research groups in the class. If your group had the course to do over again, what changes would you make in the way the group is organized? What have been the major motivational problems in getting individual members to carry out group-required tasks? How much of the group's success or failure can be accounted for by the particular individuals who made up the group, and how much by the form of organization and the mode of interaction of the group as a whole? What changes in individual behavior were observed to be the result of group pressure? How have the issues of distributive and collective justice affected the group's social life?

These are just some of the questions your group essay might come to grips with. Reflect upon your experience as a group. Analyze the records of group action and group problems you have kept. Theorize about how your group might have worked if certain organizational changes had been made.

Then, make enough copies of your report to distribute to the other research groups. Compare notes.

Project E calls for the combined use of methods and modes of analysis involved in all three sociologies. The issue of social justice in the group, with regard to group grades going to all group members, regardless of the individual's contribution or lack of it, is clearly the kind of issue at the heart of sociological Activism. The study of social interaction between involved participants, and the reflexive nature of the study itself, are part and parcel of sociological Naturalism. Finally, the question of the survival of the group, in terms of grades, the basic Functionalist question of what forms of social order are required for the best functioning of the social system, is of course at the center of Project E.

Many students have reported that Project E is the most totally involving of the research projects, and that group members seem to come out of the discussions in preparation for the writing of this project report either friends or enemies for life. Be prepared for a passionate examination of the basic sociological questions while doing this project. The two practical questions to be answered by the research report hide a minefield of hot issues: Why did we turn out to be the kind of group we are? and Why did this group do the kind of work it did?

DIMENSIONS OF SOCIAL REALITY

II

The projects presented in Chapter 4 will bring details of social life as seen through our three sociological lenses into sharp focus for the student. But what are the broad outlines of social reality that each sociology brings into view when one takes a longer and deeper view through its lens?

The social system, the social arena, and the social gallery each appear to be organized along three major dimensions when viewed from the appropriate sociological perspective. Wherever one looks, one can see the vertical organization of social life. The system has its chain of command and its hierarchy of responsibility; the arena is divided between oppressors and oppressed, top dogs and underdogs; and the gallery is full of exhibitions of put-downs and send-ups, of acts of superordination, subordination, and insubordination. The vertical dimension of social life, in other words, asks the question, how is society organized from top to bottom, from high life to low life?

Also present in every sociological view of social life is the temporal dimension. Time is a great and powerful organizer of our social lives, while at the same time, social events and social actions define what time shall mean to us. Societies move through history, and at the same time, history is nothing more than the compilation of social events. Sociological examination of the temporal dimension of social reality provides an interesting range of answers to the question, how do whole societies, as well as the everyday features of our social lives, change?

Finally, there is a third major dimension visible in social life when viewed with sociological eyes, the moral dimension. Everywhere in society we find lines drawn between good and evil, between the respectable people and the bad people, between the crooked and the straight. Sociologists focus on the differences and similarities between those people and actions considered correct in society, and those people and actions considered deviant. The study of deviance reveals the boundaries between the good and the bad in social life.

Three sociological versions of each of these dimensions are presented in the following three chapters. Chapter 5, "Deviance and Conformity: The Moral Boundaries of Social Life," introduces some of the diverse research on those members of society defined as social deviants, and tries to show how the particular view one takes of deviants reflects and shapes the image one has of society and of basic human nature. Chapter 6, "Stratification, Class, Hierarchy: The Vertical Organization of Social Life," emphasizes the serious differences between Activist and Functionalist views of the nature and causes of social hierarchy (the arrangement of groups of people in society one above the other), and then presents this author's idea of what a Natualist inquiry into the vertical dimension would show. Chapter 7, "Social Change: Evolution, Revolution, and the Search for Meaning in Time," contrasts Functionalist and Activist timetables for historical change in whole societies, and then takes a Naturalist look at the widespread social practice of constructing timetables.

Each of these chapters ends with a "Doing Sociology" section that may be assigned at the discretion of the instructor.

THREE MODES OF SOCIOLOGICAL ANALYSIS

Throughout the book, we will analyze facts, issues, and observations of social life. But for each of our three sociologies, the term analysis means something different. From the social system viewpoint of Sociology I, analysis means asking the question, "How do the parts make up the whole?" For an Activist, however, analysis means asking, "What is wrong with the patient, and how can it be cured?" In the hands of practitioners of Sociology III, analysis involves asking the question, "What is the meaningful structure of what we observe, and how may it be interpreted?"

Deviance and Conformity: The Moral Boundaries of Social Life

5

What is the difference between a mass murderer and a war hero? Lieutenant William Calley killed so many Vietnamese on the orders of his military superiors that he was tried and convicted for war crimes. Compare the assasin known only as "Carlos," or "The Fox." This figure is a hero to some, a mad-dog psychopath to others, and to still others, simply a man who is doing his job very well.

What is the difference between a common whore and a woman who "has loved, not wisely, but too well?" In the New Testament, Jesus is quoted as labelling prostitute Mary Magdalene the latter, and thereby saves her from stoning by the respectable people in town. In our own time, we read the confessed exploits of "The Happy Hooker," and wonder who could cast the first stone at Xaviera Hollander, while California prostitutes form a labor union (Hollander, 1972).

What is the difference, among the prisoners doing time in the same jail, between those who are there because they refused to fight in what they considered an immoral war, those who are there because they preferred getting high on marijuana to getting drunk on alcohol, those who are there because they preferred very young sex partners, and those who are there because they took someone's money or someone's life?

These differences, and the difference they make to our common social life, are the raw materials out of which the moral boundaries of society are constructed. For many of us, the line separating right from wrong, the good people from the bad, is much blurred today; the boundaries are unclear and appear to shift with the winds of fad and fashion. Why do some people deviate from, whereas most people conform to, the standard rules of right and wrong behavior in society? Do some members of society have the power to define their own behavior as right and proper, and the behavior of others as wrong and criminal? Are there really any standard rules to deviate from? These are some of the perplexing questions the sociological study of deviance attempts at least to clarify, if not fully answer.

Sociology cannot fully answer any of these questions because it is neither concerned nor qualified to decide what is right and what is wrong in human activity. Sociological inquiry is interested in how questions of right and wrong behavior relate people to one another and to their systems of interaction. The moral boundaries of society are to be found in these lines of relationship.

What these moral boundaries are, how they may be observed, and how they are created and sustained, are the questions about which the various sociologies differ strenuously. Society's moral boundaries may be seen, using the successive lenses of our three sociologies, as a multi-faceted phenomenon. In Sociology I, morality is the backbone and glue of the social system. In Sociology II, it becomes the battle line dividing the powerful from the powerless in the arena. Finally, Sociology III sees morality as a fundamental instrument used by everyone to sustain with each other the fiction of normality. For each of these insights, sociologists turn to the subworld of the social deviant. A strange discipline, that looks to the murky underworld of deviance for moral enlightenment!

WHO IS THE SOCIAL DEVIANT?

SOCIOLOGY I
The Deviant as Product of Defective Socialization

If the social system operated perfectly, it would turn out individuals who are perfectly adapted to their social roles, and it would provide social rewards adequate and appropriate to their faithful performance of these roles. This is the process that we referred to as *socialization*. Socialization is an essential part of the idea of society as a system. The products of a properly functioning socialization process are normal, conforming, socially acceptable, and socially approved selves.

When juvenile delinquents, habitual criminals, sexual perverts, drug addicts—in short, deviants—appear in an orderly, law-abiding society, we must assume that these people have been improperly or inadequately socialized. We must look to the process of socialization itself for the causes and cures of deviant behavior.

Properly socialized, individuals learn to perform their tasks and to identify themselves with their important social roles, in short, to conform without external restraints. When they do so, if the system is working properly, they are rewarded by social success and approval, both material and symbolic. These rewards continue the socialization process by confirming their identities, strengthening their loyalties to the system, and encouraging them to continue proper role performance.

But unfortunately, as every Functionalist recognizes, the social system never does operate perfectly. There is always some change going on, there are always strains developing between one component of the system and another. There is always some degree of slack, some lack of fit, between the ideal values of the system and the reality of its everyday operation. As a result of this chronic imperfection in the social machinery (which we shall take up further under "the causes of deviance"), the socialization process is also imperfect, both at the training end of the process and at the point where appropriate rewards and encouragements are supposed to accompany proper role performance. Some individuals are thus inadequately socialized—improperly trained, and inappropriately rewarded—in every social system. The consequence is that, in terms of the system's standards for right behavior, they consistently misbehave. Deviant persons are the system's failures.

Functionalist sociologists have made a continuous and consistent contribution to the public debate over the proper treatment of criminals and other offenders of public morality through their research into deviance (see, for example, Nettler, 1958—1959). By tracing the behavior of the deviant back to gaps or kinks in socialization, they have been able to show convincingly that it is the society that produces the offender. This constitutes an argument against the traditional punishment approach to deviants.

Punishment of deviants only makes sense if their nonconformity stems from their own wilfulness, if, knowing the difference between right and wrong, they freely choose to do wrong. But if individuals deviate primarily because they have been wrongly socialized, then society is at fault, not the deviants themselves. The proper treatment is thus of two kinds: *therapy,* to try to combat the ill effects of improper childhood socialization; or *rehabilitation,* to set right in the deviant's mind the proper relationships between behavior and rewards that have been misaligned by a skewed adult socialization.

The Functionalist identification of deviants as defective social products calls for the abolition of punishment and the institution of therapeutic and rehabilitation programs to *resocialize* deviants. Once deviants have learned how to conform and why, they will have internalized the standards of proper conduct accepted by the society at large, and they will simply cease to be deviants. The result is a more smoothly running social system.

SOCIOLOGY II
The Deviant as Victim, Hero, Political Activist

Activist sociologists look at this issue from the point of view of those who are defined and treated as deviants by the powers-that-be. Precisely because they are singled out by the establishment as wrongdoers, the "socially deviant" are seen by Activists as victims of social oppression and injustice. Taking, as always, the part of the underdog, Activists join the struggle on the side of the deviant.

The Activists reverse the sociological lens used by the Functionalists. In both perspectives, the deviant is the product of the social system. But instead of looking at this phenomenon from the point of view of the system and its needs, Activists side with the victim. From their point of view, it is not the deviant who has been insufficiently socialized and is therefore socially defective, it is the system that is sick.

Deviants may be regarded as social heros, refusing to conform to that which is unjust, unhealthy, and wrong about the system. Deviants in an oppressive capitalist system, for instance, could be seen as the leading anticapitalists, just as those defined and treated as deviants in a totalitarian socialist system might be seen as really the heros in the struggle for human rights and dignity against totalitarianism.

If society is an arena, in other words, deviance is not merely nonconforming or aberrant behavior, it is a political act.

★★★

LEADING LIGHTS

Horowitz and Liebowitz on the Deviant as Political Dissenter

Irving Louis Horowitz and Martin Liebowitz argue for the view of the deviant as political dissenter (see Horowitz, 1974). The "conflict model of deviance" that they propose focuses the sociologist's attention on the political conflicts between the controllers and the controlled in society. Deviants then are sim- *ply those members of society whose behavior has been forbidden, and who are struggling in more or less organized ways against society's controls, and in the long run, against the controllers' right and power to control them at all.*

★★★

The Activist can often intervene in favor of the underdog by helping to organize groups of deviants into more effective political' units. Horowitz and Liebowitz cite sociologist Richard A. Cloward's trail-blazing work in organizing welfare recipients so that they might struggle more effectively against the restrictive and demeaning rules and regulations of welfare authorities and welfare organizations (see Cloward and Elman, 1966).

Activists also find themselves involved in the struggle of unorganized groups of deviants to become aware of themselves as political combatants. As examples of such deviants, Horowitz and Liebowitz cite the vandals, arsonists, and rioters in recent black ghetto disturbances who are beginning to define themselves as political guerrillas; juvenile delinquent gangs, such as Chicago's Blackstone Rangers in the 1960s, which negotiated with the Chicago police and other civic agencies as a self-proclaimed organizing force in the black community; Hell's Angels and other more or less permanent motorcycle gangs; members of the gay liberation movement; and even drug addicts trying to wrest control over their lives and their habits from the authorities, as in the Synanon organization in California.

Another category of deviants emerged from the antiwar and civil rights struggles of the 1960s. Fully aware of the political struggles into which they are entering, this new class of deviants comes mainly from white, middle-class backgrounds. They have consciously become deviant in the eyes of the authorities in order to defy and reject a social system they perceive as basically unjust and inhumane.

Students became rebels by participating in illegal demonstrations; by evading the draft; by smoking marijuana and taking LSD; and by engaging freely and publicly in sexual activities. They also made a popular middle class sport out of shoplifting, deprived the telephone companies of millions in revenue by finding ingenious ways to make long distance calls toll-free, and discovered numberless devious paths to free food, free lodging, free entertainment. By other people's standards, the youth "counter-culture" in the 1960s was guilty of massive engagement in deviant behavior. The kids themselves called it "beating the system."

From the perspective of Activist sociology, deviants such as these need neither punishment, nor therapy-rehabilitation. All they need is a little help from their friends.

From this perspective, in fact, it is often the *conformist* who is seen as morally wrong, misguided, or needing rehabilitation, because this "straight" person is conforming to a destructive social system. It may also appear, upon close scrutiny of the available facts, that the biggest crooks and swindlers, and the most morally objectionable actions, are to be found at the top of society's power ladder. Thus those who are labelled "deviant" by society-at-large are simply those who are powerless to assert respectability, and powerless to impose labels of deviance on others. In an age that exposed the crookedness of former President Richard Nixon and Vice-President Spiro Agnew, and proved the top officials of the largest corporations guilty of multi-million-dollar bribery and other scandals, to continue to study petty thieves, vandals and pot smokers as social deviants is an absurdity.

SOCIOLOGY III
The Deviant as the Bearer of a Label

"The deviant is one to whom that label has successfully been applied; deviant behavior is behavior that people so label."(Becker, 1963, p. 9)

Naturalist sociology begins and ends with the image of social life as a vast gallery of exhibits, each one an observable scene of interaction that can be admired and examined in itself for its complex of created meanings, or analyzed in relation to other scenes, or to parts of other scenes, in order to see and wonder at broader and deeper meanings. The goal is a sense of understanding, and renewed admiration for the social art of even the least of our fellow humans.

From this perspective, the trouble with the definitions of deviance presented by Sociologies I and II is that one can't just straightforwardly observe a deviant doing deviant things. Somebody has first to identify the deviant as a deviant, and somebody has to identify deviant acts as deviant acts. Thus the behavior to observe for the Naturalist's gallery is an individual in the act of *pointing out* and *labelling* as deviant the acts of other individuals.

We have already examined some of the commonplace ways in which social participants verbally or otherwise assign one another labels of identity useful for the interactive situation at hand. Names, nicknames, roles, and epithets are offered through introductions, role assignments ("You play first base," or "I'll deal the cards") and other routine interactions. For Naturalist sociologists to study social deviance, they must first observe, record, and analyze interactive scenes in which participants assign roles of deviance.

★★★

LEADING LIGHTS

Thomas Scheff on Being Mentally Ill

In an almost classic study of the labelling process, Naturalist Thomas Scheff examined the official and unofficial situations in which people are labelled by others "mentally ill" (Scheff 1966).

Upon analysis of a great many such situations Scheff's study showed that there is a very poor "fit" between the labelling of certain actions as "abnormal" or "crazy" and the defining of persons performing these actions as mentally ill and in need of treatment. In other words, all kinds of "symptoms" lead to all kinds of "diagnoses," depending, it appears, on the situation in which the labelling takes place, and the relationship between the alleged deviant and the labeller. Relatives, friends, neighbors, and strangers all have their own laymen's methods for recognizing

and judging a person's actions as clues to his or her mental state. Once that person is steered into some kind of treatment, mental health officials and professionals have various psychiatric theories and official methods for eliciting from the potential patient the actions they will diagnose as the actions of a "sane" or "insane," mentally normal or mentally "deviant," person.

Because of the variations and discrepancies between all these lay and professional diagnoses, because of the lack of fit between actions recognized as mentally ill and persons diagnosed as mentally ill, all that one can say with consistency about persons who have been labelled "mentally ill," all that they have observably in common, is that they have been labelled mentally ill.

★★★

Remember, now, that we have also observed that the recipients of identity labels can either accept or reject those labels in the interactive situation. The labelling process, in other words, at least when it takes place between social equals, is often seen to be a process of *negotiation*. When the labels being handed out are deviant identities, however, we most often see an unequal relationship between the labeller and the labellee. It is those in positions of authority who label criminals, schizophrenics, drug addicts, prostitutes, and homosexuals as deviants, and those who receive these labels are seldom in any position to negotiate or reject them.

Here the Naturalist's observations confirm the claims of the Activists. "Deviants" are generally the powerless recipients of labels attached to them by the powerful. So we can amend Becker's answer to the question, "Who is the deviant?" to read "The deviant is the one who has been marked with a deviant label, usually by others more socially powerful."

●❍●●

AN INNER VOICE

All right, so I'm not a deviant, by any sociology's definition. I suppose my parents, teachers, friends, and the mass media "socialized" me pretty well. Here I am generally conforming, all the way into college, and getting pretty much the approval and rewards for it that I want and deserve, I guess.

Or is this conformity with its security what I really want? If the Activist picture is anywhere near the truth, I'm some kind of human deviant for conforming to the rules of this fouled up, corrupt social system we've got. Shouldn't I be out there with the resisters, the outsiders with enough guts and character to stand up to this lousy system and reject it?

On the other hand, again, I wouldn't really have to do very much to "become" a deviant. All it would take would be a shift in the social winds, and there could be powerful authorities painting their labels on me, and calling me "deviant." A chilling thought. For example, suppose all those people who have been driving big, gas-guzzling cars to conform to the standards of their neighbors were suddenly defined as energy-wasting social criminals, and the guy down the block who everybody said was weird because he insisted on driving his little bug becomes the social conformist. And who is now the social outsider, the smoker or the nonsmoker? And is the person who cheats on his income tax the deviant, or the person who doesn't cheat?*

●❍●❍●❍●❍●❍●❍●❍●❍●❍●❍●❍●❍●❍ ●❍●❍●❍●❍●❍●❍●❍●❍●❍●❍●❍●●

WHAT CAUSES DEVIANCE

Having outlined the nature of social deviance through our three sociological lenses, we can also consider in triple focus the possible explanations for its causes.

SOCIOLOGY I
Deviance as Consequence and Indicator of Anomie

Functionalist sociology looks at the larger picture of social organization whenever possible, so its focus on the deviant as a person who has been improperly socialized is only a prelude to its real aim—to measure and explain deviance as a feature of the social system as a whole. The Functionalist thus is primarily concerned with the incidence of deviant acts, a quantity that can be measured and monitored in its increases and decreases over time.

Deviance can thus be described in terms of the numbers and types of deviant persons prevalent in a particular society. But when Functionalists theorize on the causes of deviance in society, they no longer look to improper socialization of individuals as the "cause." Socialization may be the immediate mechanism that produces deviant personalities, but a deeper, more ultimate cause is sought for the incidence and nature of deviance as a whole. After all, what causes improper socialization?

Anomie is the Functionalist's candidate for the general cause of society-wide deviance. The Functionalist theory of the relationship between anomie and deviance could be simplistically stated as follows: "People break the rules when the rules break down." Anomie is the breakdown of stable rules in society.

◆◇

FOUNDING FATHERS

Emile Durkheim's Theory of Anomie as Cause of Suicide and Other Deviance

Durkheim introduced the term anomie, 'normlessness,' in his attempt to explain certain correlations with suicide rates. Divorced persons, for instance, have much higher suicide rates than those who are married. Suicide rates are high for people whose work organizations are undergoing rapid change, even when that change is, from everyone's viewpoint, for the better.

"To pursue a goal which is by definition unattainable is to condemn oneself to a state of perpetual unhappiness," Durkheim says. The unregulated life is impossible for men and women to live. When society is stable, a genuine regimen exists . . . which fixes with relative precision the maximum degree of ease of living to which each social class may legitimately aspire. . . . Under this pressure, each in his own sphere vaguely realizes the extreme limit set to his ambitions and aspires to nothing beyond. At least if he respects regulations and is docile to collective authority, that is, has a wholesome moral constitution, he feels that it is not well to ask more." (Durkheim, 1870)

But under unstable conditions, aspirations outstrip possibilities, passions are unbridled, the orderliness of society breaks down into the disorderliness of individual lives and plans. This disordered condition, both in society and in the person, is called anomie—the lack of rules, regulations, or normal standards to fit the situation.

According to Durkheim, suicide "results from man's activity's lacking regulation and his consequent sufferings." But much more than suicide results from this lack of regulation. Mental illness, crime, perversion, vice—all deviant acts—can be seen as "milder" symptoms of widespread social anomie.

◆◇

Anomie is thus that condition in society in which the commonly accepted rules for behavior no longer fit the practical situations people must cope with in their everyday lives. The things that large numbers of people have been trained to want and to strive for as children, for instance, could become unattainable or even undesirable goals by the time they are adults. Under conditions of rapid change in social systems, as in a social system whose major components are constantly out of alignment, such discrepancies emerge, and the rules no longer apply. This is anomie, and it is when anomie is rife that deviance increases dangerously.

Let us look at contemporary Functionalist Robert K. Merton's classic statement on the relationships between deviant action, deviance, and the American social system (Merton, 1949).

Social deviance, including crime, is defined as "behavior deviating from prescribed patterns of conduct" as a consequence and indication of anomie, or the breakdown of society's moral order. As Merton puts it, there occurs a disjuncture between cultural values and the situation of persons in roles or positions in the social structure.

"The social structure strains the cultural values, making action in accord with them readily possible for those occupying certain statuses within the society and difficult or impossible for others" (p. 163). This is how "some social structures exert a definite pressure upon certain persons in the society to engage in non-conforming rather than conforming conduct" (p. 132).

Merton proposes research into the specific factors that impel certain persons to break the cultural rules. This rule-breaking, he theorizes, is generally to be attributed to a breakdown in the normal relationship between the *goals* for action held up by the culture, and the *means* for achieving those goals made available by the social structure:

It is, indeed, my central hypothesis that aberrant behavior may be regarded sociologically as a symptom of dissociation between culturally prescribed aspirations and socially structured avenues for realizing these aspirations. [P. 134]

In American culture, where monetary success is widely valued, and many people are denied the legitimate means to monetary success, there is bound to be a great deal of deviance, though not all of the same type. The following typology, adapted from Merton (p. 140) shows the types of individual adaptation that can be made in a social system such as America's.

A Typology of Modes of Individual Adaptation

Modes of Adaptation	Culture Goals	Institutionalized Means
I. Conformist	accepts	accepts
II. Innovator	accepts	rejects
III. Ritualist	rejects	accepts
IV. Retreatist	rejects	rejects
V. Rebel	replaces	replaces

About "conformity" Merton has little to say. Most of the deviant behavior to be found in American social life, Merton expects, will be of the second type, "innovation." "This response occurs when the individual has assimilated the cultural emphasis upon the goal without equally internalizing the institutional norms governing ways and means for its attainment" (p. 144).

After acknowledging that those in the "upper economic strata" often use illegal or illicit means to success, and have a high unreported crime rate so that " . . . the official crime statistics uniformly showing higher rates in the lower strata are far from complete or. reliable" (p. 144), Merton nevertheless abruptly concludes that "the greatest pressures toward deviation are exerted upon the lower strata" (p. 144). Deviant adaptations such as organized vice, rackets, and crime are therefore rife among the poorer sectors of the working class. To sum up Merton's thesis,

> Of those located in the lower reaches of the social structure, the culture makes incompatible demands. On the one hand, they are asked to orient their conduct toward the prospect of large wealth—"Every man a king," said Marden and Carnegie and Long—and on the other, they are largely denied effective opportunities to do so institutionally. The consequence of this structural inconsistency is a high rate of deviant behavior. (P. 146)

The "ritualist" is the poor soul who obeys all the rules, follows all the prescription for success, continually fails, and yet "continues to abide almost compulsively by institutional norms." Merton finds this a fairly prevalent syndrome in American society, but it hardly qualifies as "genuinely deviant behavior" or "a social problem." Merton expects lower-middle-class Americans to form this adaptation. Today we might call this the "Archie Bunker syndrome."

"Retreatism," Merton's "Adaptation IV," comprises "some of the adaptive activities of psychotics, autists, parriahs, outcasts, vagrants, vagabonds, tramps, chronic drunkards and drug addicts" (p. 153). These are the people who have opted out of the culture and the social structure, and Merton expects this type to be least common of all.

"Rebellion" as an adaptation to frustrating social conditions is also given short shrift in Merton's analysis. He emphasizes the idea that the "new values" being substituted for the old make up just another social myth, around which new rebellions may be organized.

Notice, however, that in Merton's scheme, *everything but* "conformity" is labelled "social deviance," and conformity is described briefly in terms of middle class, upwardly striving, monetary success. If you play by the rules of American life, and win, you are a successful conformist. Otherwise you are a *loser* or deviant: if you win, but by breaking the rules, you are an *innovator*, and ultimately a loser, because your money can't buy you respectability; if you play by the rules but always lose, you are a *ritualist*; if you just refuse to play the game, you are a *retreatist*; and if you insist on changing the game altogether, you are a *rebel*, and still, of course, a loser.

The special form of anomie in American society outlined by Merton lies in the discrepancy between the goals of success inculcated in the population at large through socialization, and the means provided for reaching those success goals. Persons therefore suffer by being wrongly socialized into following rules that don't fit their situations, and that is why they practice deviance. The system suffers from its anomie with the high rates of deviance, and especially criminal deviance, that are characteristic of American society.

SOCIOLOGY II
Deviance as an Expression of Alienation

Merton's analysis of anomie in America leaves us with the picture of a breakdown of rule-following in society because there is disharmony between two structural parts of the system—the generalized value of monetary success, and the very limited means available to legitimately achieve that goal. By contrast, the Activist view of deviance in a society like the United States holds that deviance results from *alienation*—a disharmony or conflict between the social system and basic human nature.

❖◆❖

FOUNDING FATHERS
Karl Marx on Alienation in Capitalist Societies

Karl Marx introduced the concept of alienation as it is used by contemporary sociological Activists. (Let the student beware that this term is frequently misused by Functionalists and others as a synonym or equivalent for anomie, which it is not).

Marx criticized the development of capitalist societies, societies whose basic structure and values inhere solely in the ownership, production, profit from, and consumption of things with monetary value. This extreme concentration on money and objects of consumption was a direct threat, in Marx's view, to much more important human values. "The devaluation of the human world increases in direct relation with the increase in value of the world of things . . ."

The historical transition Marx observed, the change to the capitalist mode of production where the capitalist owns the tools, rakes off the profits, and controls the work life of the laborer, produces a situation where

" . . . the worker is related to the product of his labour as to an alien object. For it is clear on this presupposition that the more the worker expends himself in work the more powerful becomes the world of objects which he creates in the face of himself, the poorer he becomes in his inner life, and the less he belongs to himself . . ." (Marx, 1845, p. 245)

The nature of modern productivity in capitalist society therefore alienates people from their work, from the products of their labor, and ultimately, from themselves. When the manager or the owners of the corporation own you, you don't own yourself. The degree to which you are alienated is the portion of your life that does not belong to you. You are empty, and your existence is frustrated and meaningless. This alienated person is then likely to resort to deviant behavior as a way of reasserting ownership of the self.

❖◆❖

Deviance is thus the product of the system for the Activist just as it is for the Functionalist. But for the Activist, it is an unjust, dehumanizing social system that alienates most of its members, setting them off in opposition to itself, as its exploited victims. When they reassert themselves by any means that come to hand, they are branded deviants and further victimized. How much deviance there is to be found in a society is thus a measure of the degree of alienation—separation and conflict between basic interests—in that social system.

When the Activist enters into research on deviance, therefore, the focus of investigation is on what is wrong with the system, and its agencies and agents of control, rather than on what is wrong with the deviant.

For instance, sociologists Hans Toch, J. Douglas Grant, and Raymond T. Galvin set out to try to cure a social disease through sociological research (Toch, Grant, and Galvin, 1975). Police records often indicate that policemen "were required to use force" in interactions with the public, or "had to take violent steps" against citizens. These activist researchers diagnosed violent encounters between police and public as symptoms of a disease infecting the police force and tried to design research projects that would reduce the violence used by police, especially policemen who engaged in violence more often than others. If there were deviants to be studied here, they were not the "criminal elements," but the excessively violent policemen.

The authors identified the frequently violent policemen in a particular locality and engaged them as the expert observers and reporters in an ostensibly objective study of "violent encounters" between police and public. The research hypothesis was that if these policemen were made more aware of their own violent propensities through self-observation and reporting during their cooperation with the "research," they would become less violent in future encounters. The researchers would measure the success of their project solely in terms of actual reduction of police violence in the streets of the district.

To a limited degree, their cure worked, and their hypothesis was proven. During the year following the research study, police violence reported by victims among the public in this district showed a significant decrease. Temporarily at least, the citizens of this area experienced less alienation from the authorities, and possibly the police experienced less alienation from themselves.

★★

LEADING LIGHTS

Richard Quinney on Crime as the Result of Laws

Richard Quinney is another exemplar of Sociology II on the subject of deviance. Quinney (1970) utilizes the scientific apparatus, both theoretical and methodological, of both Functionalists and Naturalists in his book, The Social Reality of Crime. *He acknowledges the systemic interrelation of society's parts, emphasizing the conflictual aspects over the consensual ones, and he holds an essentially Functionalist theory of social integration, that coherence emerges out of the creative conflict of group interests.*

On the other hand, he observes social participants in the act of constructing social reality, just as Naturalists do, and therefore rejects the idea that social phenomena are merely the results of the push and pull of great social "forces." What identifies him clearly as an Activist, however, is the use to which he puts these perspectives.

Crime, according to Quinney, is entirely relative to the formulation and application of the law in any society. "It is formulated and administered by those segments of society which are able to incorporate their interests into the creation and interpretation of public policy. Rather than representing the institutional concerns of all segments of society, law secures the interests of particular segments, supporting one point of view at the expense of others." [P. 40] This is the Activist's diagnosis of the problem of crime in society.

Here is his program for cure: "The challenge for law of the future is that it creates an order providing fulfillment for individual values. . . . A new society is indeed coming: Can a law be created apart from private interests which assures individual fulfillment within a good society?" (P. 42)

★★

The quotations are only the briefest indication of the scope and depth of Quinney's work. But all of the book quoted from, and all the rest of Quinney's published work, is consistent with these proposals. He goes on to carry them through into detailed analysis of what is iniquitous about the formation and application of law in society, and how just legal systems could be erected.

Note that the interest here is not with the criminal, nor even focally with crime itself, but with the laws that define and "control" crime, and the system of legal change and administration.

SOCIOLOGY III
Deviance as the Product of the Situation of Counting Deviance

For the Functionalist, deviance is in the deviant, the product of inadequate socialization. For the Activist, deviance is in the system—in the police, in the legal system, in encrusted bureaucratic power systems—and the "deviant" is its victim and its most active opponent. For Sociology III, deviance only appears in the social *situation* in which it is discovered, and its nature and location depend entirely on who is doing the observation. What the Naturalist observes, in other words, is that "deviance" and "the deviant" are social meanings that are independent of observed acts and specific actors. Deviance, like beauty, is in the eye of the beholder.

Naturalists are concerned neither with the stresses and strains on the social system as indicated by varying rates of deviant acts, nor with the victimization of one social class by another. Their interest is in the social construction of moral meanings.

In this, the Naturalist agrees with the Activist that deviance labels are the crux of the issue, but more broadly. The Naturalist view is that all descriptions of behavior or of other people are morally tinged labels made up for the purpose at hand of the labelers. The determination of the meanings, moral and otherwise, of actions or of personal identities, is a matter of negotiation between social participants in particular situations.

The true Naturalist is satisfied if he or she can observe in fine detail the process by which some social participants identify certain actions and certain persons as violations or violators of any standard of conduct that may be invoked upon a particular occasion. In general, the Naturalist observes again and again, but each time with fresh insight into the phenomenon, that every identification of an action or a person as "wrong"—morally, legally, rationally, situationally or however—invokes a standard of "right" conduct, establishes it as the rule, and places all relevant participants on opposite sides of a moral boundary. Thus, what the Naturalists observe when they look into the question of social "deviance" is the building of moral boundaries. (Note that, in contrast, the Functionalist's notion of anomie associates deviance with the blurring and destruction of moral boundaries, while the Activist's idea of alienation implies the violation of *human* moral boundaries.)

The exhibits shown by the Naturalist in that part of social life's gallery marked "deviance" will therefore not be bizarre behavior held up for prurient, moral, or even scientific interest before a fascinated public of "straight" people. The Naturalist criticizes "conventional" sociology for doing just this sort of thing. (Conventional university courses on deviance have long been known by their contemptuous students as "the nuts and sluts course.") On the contrary, "deviance" exhibits presented by the Naturalists illustrate processes and methods by which social participants regularly form up the moral boundaries between any "them" and any "us."

Policemen were observed and questioned on their beats in two independent Naturalistic studies by Egon Bittner (1967) and Harvey Sacks (1972). They noted that in every situation in which the police officer observes "subjects," there are specific *normalities* of action or types of persons presumed, such that suspicious persons or actions can be identified by contrast. Policemen point out to the researcher that these actions or persons are "suspicious" *for this time at this place,* that is, situationally, *and* they are proud to point out, their potential criminality is noticeable only to a trained policeman's eye.

What these Naturalists observed is the artful way in which policemen construct on the spot a boundary between legally right and legally wrong conduct—an appropriate boundary for every new situation they confront. The general format for this boundary construction: "At this time of day or night, at this place on my beat, there should or should not be certain identifiable types of persons present. Given their presence, the people here now should or should not be performing certain recognizable types of actions. The actions we can see being performed in this defined situation reveal, display, or are attempts to hide certain intentions, or certain motivations."

By inventing and applying such formulae for the detection of wrongdoing, the policemen also establish the outlines of right action—what any upstanding, law-abiding citizen has a perfect right and obvious good reason to be doing here, now. It may also be pointed out that successful criminals appear to be well aware of such recognition formulae, because they are able to behave for police as if they were perfectly law abiding.

Naturalists maintain that any description or identification of deviance is thus situational, because no action can be described as right or wrong without reference to the time and place, the situation, of its occurrence. Think of any human action: there is some time, and some place, in the context of which this action is morally right from anyone's viewpoint ("Thou shalt not kill," except in self-defense, or in a just war, or as euthanasia, or in some other special circumstance). Similarly, any action one can think of, no matter how generally innocuous or appropriate, could be situated in a time and place where and when it would be irrefutably the wrong thing to do.

Further, deviance is situational from the Naturalist viewpoint because it is created by those who detect, describe, and account for deviance in social situations. The police define and thereby create criminal deviance, but so do newspapers create crime waves and social scientists and official record keepers crime rates. To note deviant behavior, deviant events, or deviant persons in a society is to point one's finger at certain things on one side of a definitional line and label them deviant. Deviance is created in the act of drawing the line.

The Naturalist's description of how policemen notice possibly criminal deviance is an exhibit of one of social life's many varieties of moral boundary construction. Others may take the underdog's viewpoint. Becker's (1963) description of how jazz musicians characterize and recognize "squares" is a classic case in point. Jazz musicians' audiences are said by the musicians to be made up predominantly of outsiders to their musical and social world. The squares not only fail to recognize "what's going on" in the music and in the social byplay of the jazzmen's world, they are also considered decidedly inferior human beings, morally, socially, and aesthetically. Jazz musicians are themselves considered deviant by many "straight" people, and this *mutual* finger pointing is what deviance is all about to Naturalists.

All the Naturalist's exhibits are thus instances of situational "finger pointing." They are variations on the theme of how we typify one another's behavior and thereby classify each other. The focus on deviance emphasizes the moral weighting in every typification and classification that we do.

❦❦❦

AN INNER VOICE

So, anomie, alienation, or the situation— which is the cause of social deviance? Once again, I guess we have to be satisfied with that cover-all answer, "It depends . . ." If I focus on the problem of order in the system, deviance represents the breaking down of the system of rules, or anomie. If I focus on the issue of human justice, deviance is the symptom of alienation. And if I focus on the interactive scenes in life's gallery where some people are labeled deviant by others, the only cause I can observe is the interactive occasion itself, the situation.

❦❦❦

WHAT ARE THE CONSEQUENCES OF DEVIANCE?

SOCIOLOGY I
Deviance Causes the Reintegration of the Moral Order

Deviance is the product of stresses, strains, and misalignments in the social system, but what is the reciprocal product of deviance? Interestingly enough, for Functionalists, while deviance is the consequence and symptom of trouble in the social order, deviance itself does not cause further trouble. In fact, it is highly beneficial to the social system. The function of deviance, Functionalists claim, is to reaffirm the moral order of society!

Deviance brings forth condemnation and punishment from the conforming elements in society. This has what one might call a "demonstration effect" on the members of society at large. In fact, the public drama produced by reactions to deviance serves as a major socializing force in society, a kind of moral education. By being taught, again and again, the price of nonconformity, most people are encouraged to continue to abide by society's rules and standards. In this way, the deviant mends the social order that was broken by the violation of its rules.

SOCIOLOGY II
Deviance Leads to Breakdown of the System and Revolution

From the Activist perspective, deviance is mainly a form of rebellion against an unjust, oppressive system, a reassertion of the deviant's self-ownership in the face of massive social alientation.

A significant increase in social deviance therefore, while it indicates that alienation and human suffering is on the increase, is a bellweather for historical movement toward massive, revolutionary change in the society. When more and more people, whether from courage or desperation, consistently break the rules set up by their oppressors, then revolution is soon to occur.

The Activists claim that Functionalists are totally wrong about the "demonstration effect" of deviance and its punishment. Seeing deviant behavior gives people the courage to try self-assertion themselves. The effect of the demonstration is thus to increase the rate of breakdown of the status quo, not to promote further conformity.

Deviance is merely the scattered, individual beginnings of social revolution. A buildup of individual rebellions will lead, at its peak, to the formation of organized revolutionary groups. Further, the increasingly oppressive counterreactions of the authorities to increasing deviance will cause larger segments of the population to sympathize with and finally join their fellows in rebellion. This is the basis for social revolution.

SOCIOLOGY III
Deviance Creates Social Meanings

All three sociologies come to the conclusion that deviance is constructive. Functionalists see the re-creation of the social order as a consequence of deviance. Activists see deviance as a form of rebellion against the established order, paving the way for the creation of a new social order. Naturalists see deviance, insofar as it is an observable phenomenon, as creating the basic social meanings of wrong and right behavior, thus giving us the moral boundaries by which we guide our lives.

Deviance as an observable phenomenon consists of those situations or social occasions on which some social participants point their fingers, negotiate identities, or lay on labels that indicate aberrant behavior. It is on these occasions that the moral boundaries of social life are created, set up like traffic barriers along a parade route to guide the marchers and watchers alike. Like moveable traffic barriers, these moral boundaries are temporary things, put into use for the occasion at hand, but available for use again on other occasions.

Frequently it can be observed that an immediate, practical social benefit accrues from the process of identifying deviance. Those who point their fingers at deviants simultaneously designate the rest of us as a group of acceptable, approved persons. The solidarity of the "in" group can be strengthened by creating a morally inferior out group.

The "demonstration effect" theorized by the Functionalists is probably also a valid part of what we see when we observe interactants teaching each other what right behavior is by pointing out and punishing wrong behavior. But Naturalistic observation cannot confirm the Functionalist theory that this represents a return to some formerly sustained level of social order and integration. The only integration, orderliness, and meaningfulness in social life that can be empirically demonstrated, is that which we can observe in naturally occurring interaction. Here we see orderliness and meaning emerging from the situation itself, apparently established anew each time such things as rules and standards are called into use.

Deviance is creative in the fullest, most immediate sense, then, from the viewpoint of the Naturalist. Without moral boundaries, an essential dimension of meaning would be absent from our lives; we would be just that much less certain of who we are and what we are doing. Pointing one's finger at deviant behavior, then, serves to add meaning to our actions and our situation. It gives us something we can cling to and feel certain about, saving us from the frightening abyss of meaninglessness.

SUMMARY

Let us return to the questions we posed at the beginning of this chapter, and try to answer them from the three contending sociological perspectives. Let us ask again, what is the difference between a mass murderer and a war hero?

Sociology I.   A properly socialized soldier obeys his orders. Conceivably, he might even overconform to the goal of killing the enemy. If Lieutenant Calley killed many Vietnamese civilians because he was following his orders, he is perhaps an overconformist. People in favor of this particular war would call him a war hero.

On the other hand, perhaps he was trying to gain credit as a good soldier by illicit means; that is, killing civilians and claiming they were enemy combatants, thereby increasing his "kill ratio." In that case, Calley is a dangerous war criminal who has been improperly trained as to the relations between means and goals in his society. Perhaps he can be resocialized in time.

Sociology II.   The preceding answer to the question is a typical Functionalist cop out. By feigning "objectivity," the Functionalist has evaded his responsibility as a human being to take a moral stand against such wholesale killing of innocents.

In a just social world, such massive killings of civilians would not take place. Thus the question is not one of the relation between means and goals, but of the moral condition of the society. Of course Calley was a war criminal, whether he was following orders or not. If the legal system fails to condemn him as a mass murderer, if it treats him leniently and largely supports him as a quasi-hero, then the system has openly condemned itself as criminal and murderous. In Viet Nam, the United States of America committed mass murder!

If we were to honestly follow out the Functionalist's theory of socialization on this type of issue, we would find that Calley was socialized only too well into the American way of death and destruction—that this system is rotten to the core, and will go on producing countless potential mass-murderers until it is radically changed—that is, fundamentally destroyed and rebuilt.

Sociology III.   As the answers given by Sociologies I and II illustrate, the difference between a war hero and a mass murderer is a question of whether he is one of us or one of them. Even a domestic urban terrorist, clearly a mass murderer to all civilized persons when he bombs a crowded cafe, is just as clearly a war hero to his fellow terrorists. The Functionalist speaks from the system's viewpoint, and therefore identifies as "ours" (war hero) all those who follow the rules, and as "theirs" (mass murderer), all those who break them, even when the rules are about proper and improper killings. The Activists stand on a self-created moral platform outside the system. Speaking on behalf of "mankind in general," they condemn as sick crimes all actions violating the rights of "us" (humanity), and as criminals the supporters and promulgators of antihuman systems ("them").

The Naturalists, too, participate willy nilly in all of these posturings, finger pointings, and cross-condemnations, as human beings enmeshed in the social world. But from time to time they take a step back from their own and others' society-creating activity in order to observe and describe it. The fact that Lieutenant Calley could be, and is, described passionately both as a war hero and as a mass murderer, both as a violator and as a chillingly proper product of his society's rules, is for the Naturalist one more fascinating exhibit of social life's wonders.

DOING SOCIOLOGY

You are invited to provide your own version of Functionalist, Activist, and Naturalist answers to the other two questions. If done in a class or seminar, be warned that this can turn into a disputatious exercise!

As a budding sociologist equipped with three sets of lenses, argue for and against all three perspectives on the questions:

What is the difference between a common whore and a woman who "has loved, not wisely, but too well"?

What is the difference, among the prisoners doing time in the same jail, between those who are there because they refused to fight in what they considered an immoral war, those who are there because they preferred getting high on marijuana to getting drunk on alcohol, those who are there because they preferred very young sex partners, and those who are there because they took someone's money or someone's life?

6

Stratification, Class, Hierarchy: The Vertical Organization of Social Life

A second basic dimension of social organization visible through each of sociology's lenses is the vertical organization of social relationships. The questions, "Who's on top, who is the underdog, who is in between, and what are their relationships with each other?" are an important element in every social encounter.

Social life is organized throughout in hierarchical form. That is, social relationships between individuals and between groups of persons are often, perhaps always, observable as relationships between superiors and inferiors. Equality in any relationship is an unattainable ideal. Consider even the limiting case of unborn identical twins. One of them is bound to be physically the "top dog," while the other bears the burden of oppression! And one of them must be born first, making him or her the oldest child.

These relationships themselves are of interest to all sociologists, but according to whether the social framework within which they are viewed is conceived as a system, as an arena, or as a gallery, the vertical dimension of social life takes on a very different reality. *Social stratification, class inequality,* and *superordination-subordination* are the key terms describing the vertical dimension in, respectively, Sociology I, Sociology II, and Sociology III.

That the social order appears to have a top and a bottom to it, with many steps in between, is for Functionalist sociologists natural, inevitable, and necessary. For Activists, inequality gives rise to most of the social injustices they are committed to putting right. For Naturalists, social hierarchy is a powerful set of social meanings that are constantly in the process of being made and remade by social participants in their day-to-day actions.

In looking at the vertical dimension of social organization, the three sociologies also perceive different social things to be hierarchically organized. The claim that each different sociological lens provides a view of a different social reality is here most emphatically demonstrated. For Sociology I, social hierarchy is an arrangement of more or less functionally important, more and less appropriately rewarded, social roles. For Sociology II, social hierarchy is the division of society into classes: the possessed and the possessing, the exploited and the exploiting, the dominated and the dominating. For Sociology III, what social hierarchy might come to mean in any particular situation of observable social interaction remains an open question. In each situation, meaning is created from acts of *superordination* or *subordination* and the participants' resultant experience of hierarchy. The aim of the Functionalist is to explain why unequal rewards are attached to different role tasks in society; the aim of the Activist is to expose and attack the iniquities of class; the aim of the Naturalist is to describe how social participants create and experience subordination and superordination in their social lives.

Let us first clarify our key terms, *stratification, class inequality,* and *superordination-subordination,* and then proceed with a full examination of the vertical dimension through three sociological lenses.

Stratification is the term used by Functionalists to describe social hierarchy in an intentionally value-neutral manner. A social system is *stratified* when different aggregations or collections of its population possess more or less of the social goods and the social advantages that the society has to distribute among them. Each of these aggregates can then be considered as a stratum, or layer, of the society. The intention to study social stratification announces an inquiry into how and why these differently situated aggregates are organized hierarchically, what kind of a system results from a particular pattern of layering, and what happens to the system as a whole structure if and when this pattern changes.

Class inequality is an admittedly biased term used by Activists to describe the major ways in which social injustice is created, maintained, or struggled against through social history. People are organized into hierarchical *classes* by their struggles to gain and hold on to the lion's share of material goods. War between the classes is a necessary social evil forced upon us by inequality in the distribution of society's resources.

Superordination and subordination are the Naturalist's observational terms for the interactions by which social participants can be seen to *do* social hierarchy. The ways in which people put each other down—subordination—and the ways in which people promote one another to higher standing than their own—superordination—create the vertical dimension of each social situation.

SOCIOLOGY I
The Necessity of Stratification

As seen through the Functionalist's lens, no social system could exist without the cooperation of most members in the performance of different essential tasks. At a minimum, some must nurture children and prepare food while others hunt and engage in war to protect the tribe. In more complex societies there are thousands of interdependent activities requiring ever greater specialization and differentiation. In modern societies, the interdependence required by industrial production and distribution, as well as the sheer *size* of our social units, calls for technological training and skill specialization in even greater measure—thus the continuous growth of post-secondary and post-graduate education and training in these systems.

The differentiation of social tasks is basically necessitated by the variety and interdependence of the social system's needs. Further, the performance of some tasks is more urgent for the maintenance of the system than the performance of others. For these key tasks, lengthy training and superior ability is required. A society will best thrive, therefore, if it fills its social roles in the following ways: There must be open pathways to positions of crucial responsibility for people of talent, initiative, and expertise. Members of the society must be motivated by the incentive of greater social rewards to develop their abilities and strive for the highest position they can achieve—the social role that makes the fullest use of their abilities. The incumbents of crucial roles must continue to receive relatively high social rewards to encourage them to perform those roles at a continuously high level.

Viewing the social system as a whole, distinct strata of role incumbents can be seen, layered one atop the other. By documenting and measuring the distribution of social rewards among the populace of any social system, Functionalists can draw a stratification profile of that society.

Stratification Profiles Theoretically, stratification profiles of social systems could range from a total hierarchy, where each member of the society occupies a separate rank above or below another—the profile being a straight vertical line, one unit wide—to total egalitarianism, where all members occupy the same rank—the profile being a straight horizontal line, one unit high. In fact, Functionalists do not find any examples, in past or present societies, of anything approaching either of these two extremes. Nevertheless, there is a wide range of profiles, from the "flat pyramid" (Figure A) profile where a large mass of peasants are ruled by a small, relatively undifferentiated elite

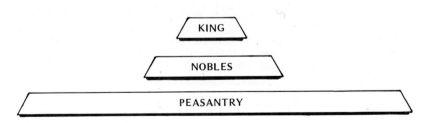

Figure A.   "Flat pyramid" stratification profile

to the "high pyramid" (Figure B) with many different ranks but consistently larger numbers as you move toward the bottom.

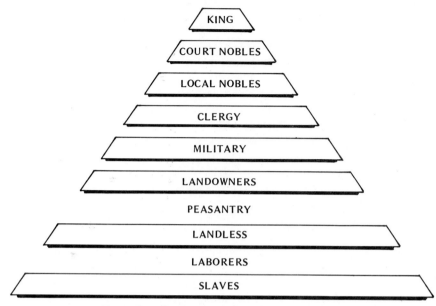

Figure B.   "High pyramid" stratification profile

Finally, there is the "diamond-shaped" profile (Figure C) with small numbers in the top ranks, very large numbers in the middle ranks, and a relatively small number in the lowest strata.

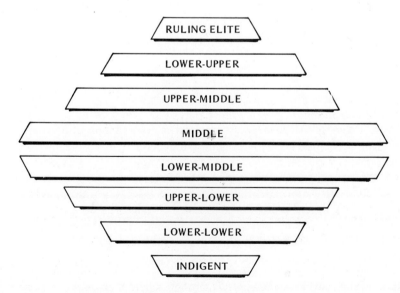

Figure C. "Diamond-shaped" stratification profile

Power, Prestige, and Property

The social system rewards those who perform their assigned role tasks in a variety of distinct ways. The differential distribution of these rewards in effect creates the stratification profile of the society, because it is the possession of these rewards that determines a member's rank in the social hierarchy, and the distribution of these rewards determines proportionately how many societal members will be positioned within each rank, and how many ranks, or strata, there shall be. Thus, the stratification profile can be seen as a profile of reward distribution in society, and any role's position in the hierarchy, its status rank, can be seen as a measure of the social rewards allocated to it by the social system.

What are the relevant social rewards that reflect and determine rank in a stratified society? Functionalist sociologists by and large agree that power, prestige, and property are the essential ingredients that go into the reward recipe associated with every social role, though each role has a different combination of these three. The hangman is feared because of his ultimate power over the condemned, but his prestige is very low, and the pay is not very good, either. The prestige of prophets, gurus, and saints is really all they've got going for them, since they are by definition powerless and by choice and commitment property-less. Finally, while some call girls may make considerable money, their power and prestige are notoriously low.

Property is used here to cover everything that can be construed as material social rewards, from gold bars in Swiss bank accounts to estates in Miami and California, to the devastating Wall Street question breathed among junior execs: "Are you makin' your age?" (translation: is your annual salary at least equal in thousands to the number of years since your birth?) to the inventory of resources required by the welfare department before it can decide whether a person qualifies for the ultimate degradation of receiving financial aid from the state. It can be measured fairly universally in dollars.

Power, while less tangible than material rewards, still has a solid, satisfying weight to it for those who wield and possess it, and an all-too-tangible feel for those who are subject to it. Social power is the likelihood that your commands will be obeyed by others, the difference between making decisions and carrying them out. Power is measured by some kind of combination of the number of others over whom you have control and the degree or seriousness of your control over them. The latter measure can range from the power of life and death to the awarding of a B+ rather than an A−.

Social power is more difficult to measure as a social reward than the dollar value of income and property, but to those who seek it and trade in it, the increments of more and less power are quite visible and calculable.

Least tangible of all is the social reward called *prestige*. This is the most purely social of the social rewards: whereas property can be categorized as economic and power can be classified political, prestige is *being looked up to* by certain numbers and certain types of other people, being *admired* by one's fellows.

The system of stratified social roles in a society is significantly shaped by the amount or degree of prestige attached exclusively to each role. The incumbent of this role then receives the admiration granted to it as his social reward. Of course any participant can enhance or degrade his own prestige-reward by performing his role exceptionally well or badly.

Sociologists have attempted to measure prestige as a social reward by asking large samples of the public how they rate various occupational roles in terms of desirability or admirability. From the answers to such questions Functionalist sociologists construct *prestige scales.*

★★

LEADING LIGHTS

"Occupational Prestige in the United States, 1925—1963"

In an article of the above title, Functionalists Robert W. Hodge, Paul M. Siegal, and Peter H. Rossi report on the sociological investigators who in 1947 and again in 1963 asked large numbers of United States citizens a set of questions about prestige. Both times, they got remarkably similar answers, indicating some stability in prestige ratings.

The respondents were given a list of ninety occupations and asked, "Please pick out the statement that best gives your own personal opinion of the general standing that such a job has: (1) Excellent standing; (2) Good standing; (3) Average standing; (4) Somewhat below average standing; (5) Poor standing; (6) I don't know where to place that one."

By translating the answers into rating scores for each occupational role, the sociologists constructed a prestige rating scale. Here is the 1963 rank ordering of ninety roles, with indications of actual scores and close-to-ties deleted:

1 U.S. Supreme Court justice
2 Physician
3 Nuclear physicist
4 Scientist
5 Government scientist
6 State governor
7 Federal cabinet member
8 College professor
9 Congressional representative
10 Chemist
11 Lawyer
12 Foreign service diplomat
13 Dentist
14 Architect
15 County judge
16 Psychologist
17 Minister
18 Member, board of directors of a large corporation
19 Mayor of a large city
20 Priest
21 Department head in state government
22 Civil engineer
23 Airline pilot
24 Banker
25 Biologist
26 Sociologist
27 Public school instructor
28 Regular army captain
29 Accountant for a large business
30 Public school teacher
31 Owner of a factory that employs about 100 people
32 Building contractor
33 Artist who paints pictures that are hung in galleries
34 Musician in a symphony orchestra
35 Author of novels
36 Economist
37 Official of an international labor union
38 Railroad engineer
39 Electrician
40 County agricultural agent

41 Owner-operator of a printing shop
42 Trained machinist
43 Farm owner and operator
44 Undertaker
45 Welfare worker for a city government
46 Newspaper columnist
47 Policeman
48 Reporter on a daily newspaper
49 Radio announcer
50 Bookkeeper
51 Tenant farmer—one who owns livestock and manages the farm.
52 Insurance agent
53 Carpenter
54 Manager of a small store
55 Local official of a labor union

56 Mail carrier
57 Railroad conductor
58 Travelling salesman for a wholesale concern
59 Plumber
60 Automobile repairman
61 Playground director
62 Barber
63 Machine operator in factory
64 Owner-operator, lunch-stand
65 Regular army corporal
66 Garage mechanic
67 Truck driver
68 Fisherman who owns his own boat
69 Clerk in a store
70 Milk route man
71 Streetcar motorman
72 Lumberjack
73 Restaurant cook

74 Singer in a nightclub
75 Filling station attendant
76 Dockworker
77 Railroad section hand
78 Night watchman
79 Coal miner
80 Restaurant waiter
81 Taxi driver
82 Farm hand
83 Janitor
84 Bartender
85 Clothes presser in a laundry
86 Soda fountain clerk
87 Sharecropper—one who owns no livestock or equipment and does not manage farm
88 Garbage collector
89 Street sweeper
90 Shoe shiner

Some degree of independence between the three forms of social reward is demonstrated by the fact that some roles with relatively low material rewards attached nevertheless rank consistently high on prestige ratings taken over long periods of time (for example, "Minister" (of a church) ranks just above "Member of the board of directors of a large corporation," ranking 17 out of 90). Others with high increments of power and/or material reward rank relatively low in prestige (for example, "Insurance agent" ranks 52, just below "Tenant farmer," and "Undertaker"

at 44 is below farmer, machinist, author, and musician). Nevertheless, it is generally the case that high and low quantities of these three social rewards go together. This consistency tends to have a reinforcing effect. For instance, a high salary tends to make an occupation impressive in the eyes of others, who will therefore also give it high prestige; money and prestige can be used as means for gaining and exercising power; and cyclicly, power can be used to accumulate more property. But these are all more or less serious distortions of the system of social rewards.

★★★

Recruitment and Mobility

The social system, if it is operating efficiently, rewards its role incumbents according to the importance of the contribution each makes toward the survival and smooth running of the system. Thus, if we assume that the United States is a fairly stable and reasonably efficient social system (no major revolutions and a high gross national product over several generations), the ranking of specific roles making up its stratification profile indicates the relative functional importance of those roles. Higher social rewards then can be seen as operating to assure that holders of crucial positions will be motivated to perform their roles most effectively.

Open and Closed Societies

There is a further function performed by the inequality of social rewards. The social system will run most efficiently if it is able to recruit the most capable and best trained of its members to take on the most important social roles. The offer of higher social rewards thus functions to assure effective social recruitment and to encourage capable individuals to undergo rigorous training and long years of education—*but,* these differential rewards can only have this effect if the social system's mobility pattern is open. Recruitment to all important roles must be on the basis of achievement.

The mobility pattern of a society is its stratification profile seen in cross section over time. From one generation to the next, what are the changes that go on in the stratification profile? Do lower strata disappear as all their members or all the children of their members move up to higher strata? Is there a cyclical circulation of members up and down the ranks, while the number and size of the strata remains the same?

In an open mobility pattern, great numbers of individuals experience movement both up and down the ranks. In a closed pattern, almost everyone retains the rank into which he was born for life, and one's children are born, and locked, into the same role as oneself. Historical and existent social systems are ranged along the continuum between totally open and totally closed mobility patterns.

The social mechanism that generates an open mobility pattern is called *recruitment by achievement,* and the mechanism that generates a closed mobility pattern is called *recruitment by ascription.* Ascription is the assignment of a role, along with its status and material rewards, to individuals according to fixed, ineradicable attributes they possess from birth. Recruitment by achievement, by contrast, is the awarding of roles and their rewards according to the abilities, training, and effort demonstrated by individuals in free and open competition.

In a closed system, an aristocracy of birth rules over a mass of lifelong slaves. Functionalism calls this a relatively inefficient recruitment system, not necessarily an immoral one. As social systems have become more open, and as more and more roles come to be assigned through achievement rather than by ascription, social systems have become not only more free and democratic, but more efficient and therefore more stable and capable of survival, as well. Therefore, as long as recruitment to higher ranking roles is open, granting greater rewards to some participants than to others is, in the long run, to the benefit of every member of society. Systematic inequality is thus not only a societal necessity, it is also a social good.

AN INNER VOICE

What about my social mobility and social status? Will my college degree move me up the ranking ladder? Sure, but only if I manage to get a job, a good job, and the job gives me occupational status. But how "open" is this society, really? Aren't there still a lot of ascribed traits in force, like "female," or "short," or "nonwhite," and don't these put most of us in something more like a caste system than a fair and free competition? Clearly this issue has many more sides to it.

SOCIOLOGY II
The Fatal Social Disease: Inequality

Power, prestige, and property—blandly called "social rewards" by Sociology I—are they not really the spoils of war? Rather than being routinely, systematically "allocated" to various roles and strata by "the system," aren't these scarce resources actually forcibly extracted from the masses to be consumed by the privileged few? "Stratification"—isn't that a typically antiseptic Functionalist word, a gauze bandage to hide the injuries done to humanity by social inequality?

Social justice and social health demand equality of power, prestige, and property: equal social and political power, in the form of rights and participation in decision making, for every member of society; dignity ("prestige" in the Functionalist's cheapened vocabulary) granted to every man, woman, and child without exception; and, last but not least, equal access to the material goods required to live a dignified, participative social life. By this standard, every form of social inequality is a deformation of true social justice, and a continuous detriment to social health.

Even if inequality of rewards were achieved in as benign a manner as that depicted by Sociology I, it would still be an illness needing to be cured. From the viewpoint of Activist sociology, however, "stratification" is not the reality of inequality at all. Sociology II sees class conflict everywhere in the social arena. Throughout recorded history the same struggle has been going on relentlessly; exploiting classes use every means to keep and expand their inordinate share of scarce resources, while the masses struggle just to survive, waiting for the next paroxysm of revolutionary violence to overthrow the hated masters. The identity of the elite and the size and location of the exploited class may change, the tactics and the language of the elite may vary, but the struggle is basically the same.

FOUNDING FATHERS

Karl Marx on the Class Struggle through History

*The following excerpts come from the Man-
ifesto of the Communist Party, written in the
mid-1800s and intended as an action-rousing
polemic. It does not represent the theory of
classes held by most contemporary Activists,
mainly because too much of Marx's analysis
and predictions have since been proven false
by history. But it does provide the
background, and still is true to the basic
thrust, of the Activist understanding of inequality. The names and locations of the
combatants have changed, but the class
struggle continues unabated.*

"The history of all hitherto existing society
is the history of class struggles.

"Freeman and slave, patrician and ple-
beian, lord and serf, guildmaster and jour-
neyman, in a word, oppressor and oppressed,
stood in constant opposition to one another,
carried on an uninterrupted, now hidden,
now open fight, a fight that each time ended,
either in a revolutionary re-constitution of
society at large, or in the common ruin of the
contending classes.

"The modern bourgeois* society that has
sprouted from the ruins of feudal society, has
not done away with class antagonisms. It
has but established new classes, new conditions of oppression, new forms of struggle in
place of the old ones.

"The bourgeoisie, wherever it has got the
upper hand, has put an end to all feudal pa-
triarchal, idyllic relations. It has pitilessly
torn asunder the motley feudal ties that
bound man to his "natural superiors," and
has left remaining no other nexus between
man and man than naked self-interest, than
callous "cash payment". . . .

"The bourgeoisie has stripped of its halo
every occupation hitherto honoured and

looked up to with reverent awe. It has con-
verted the physician, the lawyer, the priest,
the poet, the man of science, into its paid
wage-labourers . . . .

"The proletariat goes through various
stages of development. With its birth begins
its struggle with the bourgeoisie. At first the
contest is carried on by individual labourers,
then by the workpeople of a factory, then by
the operatives of one trade, in one locality,
against the individual bourgeois who directly
exploits them . . . .

"Now and then the workers are victorious,
but only for a time. The real fruit of their battles lies, not in the immediate result, but in
the ever expanding union of the workers.
This union is helped on by the improved
means of communication that are created by
modern industry, and that place the workers
of different localities in contact with one
another. . . .

"This organisation of the proletarians into
a class, and consequently into a political
party, is continually being upset again by the
competition between workers themselves.
But it ever rises up again, stronger, firmer,
mightier. . . .

"All previous historical movements were
movements of minorities, or in the interest of
minorities. The proletarian movement is the
self-conscious, independent movement of the
immense majority, in the interest of the immense majority. The proletariat, the lowest

---

*By bourgeoisie is meant the class of modern
Capitalists, owners of the means of social production
and employers of wage-labour. By proletariat, the
class of modern wage-labourers who, having no
means of production of their own, are reduced to selling their labour-power in order to live.

stratum of our present society, cannot stir, cannot raise itself up, without the whole superincumbent strata of official society being sprung into the air. . . .

"In depicting the most general phases of the development of the proletariat, we traced the more or less veiled civil war, raging within existing society, up to the point where that war breaks out into open revolution, and where the violent overthrow of the bourgeoisie, lays the foundation for the sway of the proletariat." (Marx, 1848, pp. 12—32).

◆◇

The Reality of Class

From the Activist's perspective, the reality of class and class conflict within a society like the United States is purposely disguised and clouded over by elites acting in their own interests with the aid and support, it would appear, of Functionalist sociologists. American society is made up of winners and losers in the class war, and the actual disparities between the rich and powerful and the poor and powerless grow larger year by year. Yet many Functionalists claim to see only "strata" of roles usefully sorted and rewarded according to their value to the social system, in an "open" society where everyone has a fair chance to succeed and no one will be allowed to starve to death.

The contemporary class struggle in America, seen through the lens of Sociology II, has both national and international components.

At home, the dominant class is the power elite, exposed to public view by Activist sociologists C. Wright Mills, William Domhoff, and others (Mills, 1956; Domhoff, 1967). This bourgeoisie is composed of the wealthiest families, the major corporate directors, top political leaders, and powerful military officers, who band together, through intermarriage and social hob-nobbing, to keep and exercise power.

Keeping the public in thrall through their control of the mass media, this elite operates behind the smoke screen illusions of democratic politics, free enterprise competition, and advancement by merit to maintain its status from generation to generation. The rest of us are divided into the great middle class, who are sated with material goods and brainwashed into thinking they have power and control; and the poor, who are convinced that they deserve their lowly fate because they have lost out in a fair and open competition.

While the mass media keeps our attention focused on the changes in governments, from Republican to Democratic and back again, the same military, industrial, and political leaders remain in power. Periodically, the attention of the public is turned toward the struggle between the United States' "free enterprise" system and "foreign ideologies" for control over one or another part of the world. This serves to further cloud over the society's internal contradictions. Of course, during the Vietnamese war, the reality of class at home came through despite the propaganda screen. It became clear that for some unknown reasons much larger proportions of blacks, Chicanos, and poor whites were killed in bat-tle than their better off white brothers.

But the attention of the masses cannot be focused on foreign relations too long, for then they might become aware of the reality of class conflict on a world scale. Such awareness is just what Activists are trying to promote. With the help of Activist scholars in many disciplines, as well as some journalists who declared themselves independent of the elite (see Hayden, 1972; Chomsky, 1970; Stone, 1967), the reality of class threatened to break through to mass consciousness over the course of the American war in Vietnam. Many Americans began to see themselves as duped agents of a rich corporate elite being sent out to kill im-poverished Asians so that corporate control over markets and raw materials in South Asia could be maintained, solely for the profit of those corporate elites. Perhaps the war was "ended" by the elite in order to prevent full dawning of this realization (see Hayden, 1972).

On a world scale, all citizens of mainly white, highly industrialized societies are members of a privileged elite (house-servants though most of us may be) when compared to the third-world masses we dominate and exploit, the two-thirds of the human brotherhood who are nonwhite and impoverished to the point of perpetual near-starvation. The relations between these two classes, the "first" and "second" worlds against the "third world," almost perfectly fits Marx's description of bourgeoisie versus proletariat.

It is the Activist's first task to expose the realities of the national and interna-tional class struggle. Activist sociology serves to document and demonstrate the paramount feature of class conflict in every aspect of social life.

The Activist approaches this task by tracing the symptoms of the disease back to the illness itself. Social issues can then be seen in their organic relation-ship to the underlying class struggle, which is kept hidden by those who benefit from social inequality. Let us look at two such major issues with both national and international relevance, racism and sexism.

Racism, National and International

Racism is a theory or doctrine that has been used, and continues to be used, to justify the exploitation of one category of human beings by another. Blacks are inherently inferior to whites, therefore their importation and use as slaves in America was only just. Likewise, the blacks' continued concentration at the bot-tom of the socioeconomic ladder in contemporary United States and the fact that most of the world's poor are nonwhite and most of the world's rich are white is a "natural" consequence of inherent inferiority or superiority.

Racism is the doctrine that visible physical characteristics can be used to categorize persons into subtypes of the human species. These subtypes or races represent pools of genetic materials whose differences, from race to race, account not only for physical characteristics but for differences in various capabilities, aptitudes, moral proclivities, dietary habits, and attitudes as well. Successive conferences of biological and social scientists called together by the United Nations have unanimously and indisputably settled the issue: a) It is not possible to distinguish any unambiguous or nonoverlapping physical characteristics to adequately place each into a racial grouping; every cultural group has its own historically formed mode of identifying persons as representative of types, none of them scientifically sound. b) There is no demonstrable connection between any genetic condition and any of the social attributes (e.g., intelligence, morality, perspicacity, or virility) claimed to be racially determined. c) Every difference found between the performance levels of different groups, however divided, can be demonstrated to be based on the different ways in which reputed members of these groups are treated by the agents and agencies of their society. Case closed? Not yet.

There are still "social scientists" in the U.S. and other Western nations performing statistical gymnastics to prove that black school children in the United States are genetically less intelligent than white children. Activist sociologists try to keep up with these claims to refute them, one by one. Some Activists even disrupt meetings and lectures at which these concocted "findings" are presented in order to prevent the spread of these false notions. Why?

The scientists who continue to try to prove genetic inferiority of nonwhites are seen by Activists as conscious or unconscious agents of the elites who rely on racist belief and racist action for the support of their power and privilege. Widespread, scientifically supported racism supports the entrenched elites in two major ways: a. What Functionalists call "prestige" is really the product of one of the elite group's main propaganda activities— *legitimation*. It is in the interest of the powerful that their occupation of higher-reward positions be seen by their underlings as *legitimate*. In the United States, it is the white, Anglo-Saxon Protestant minority that predominates in the upper reaches of the class structure; internationally, it is clearly the white Western elite that dominates the yellow, black, and brown masses. What better way to legitimate this strange hierarchy of colors than to prove scientifically that white people's genes are superior to nonwhites' genes? Then it is natural that whites find themselves on top of the ladder. They were just born into a superior race. Racism serves to legitimate the class structure.

b. The sowing of the seeds of racist belief serves another vital function for the power elite. At the bottom of the heap crowd the oppressed masses. Their chances for overthrowing their oppressors rest on one crucial fact—their large numbers. Their numbers can only count in the class struggle, however, if they are unified, if they achieve *solidarity* as a group.

One of the most important tactics used by the elites to prevent their overthrow by the masses, is to divide and conquer. Get the masses involved in conflict among themselves, and they will never form a unified opposition to the power elite. Racism serves this end by turning poor whites against poor blacks, even motivating poor blacks to kill even poorer Asians.

Sexism at Home and in the Marketplace

Another vicious doctrine that supports social inequality and aids in the exploitation of the masses by the power elite, again seen from the Activist's perspective, is *sexism*. Parallel to the doctrine of racism, sexism asserts that women are inherently inferior to men. This doctrine justifies the allocation of the "unimportant" tasks in society exclusively to women, while reserving the socially significant roles, with their attached honors and privileges, to men. The doctrine of inherent sexual inferiority is just as provably fallacious as that of racism, and it is the task of the Activist to demonstrate this fallacy and to join with women everywhere in their struggles to attain equality in society.

★★

LEADING LIGHTS

In the tradition of the above-quoted exposition of the class struggle in history by Marx, Dorothy Smith, an Activist as well as Naturalist sociologist, makes clear the connections between the allocation of the role of housewife to women in modern society and the interests of the corporate power elite (Smith, 1973).

The rise of corporate capitalism as the dominant economic system of the West, Smith says, also brought the division of the social world into public and private spheres. The home and family are defined as the private world, and political and economic activity is the public world, the world where history is made and important things get done. "The public sphere is that sphere in which 'history' is made. But the public sphere is also the sphere of male activity. Domestic activity becomes relegated to the private

sphere, and is mediated to the public sphere by men who move between both. Women have a place only in the private, domestic sphere. If history is viewed as an account of changes in human society, the reason women do not appear in history is because women's place has located them outside the public sphere where those changes are made to happen . . ."

In this form of social oppression, women become engaged in private service to their husbands. This oppression serves the interests of the corporate elite because middle-class men, as agents of the elite, must adopt a lifestyle that projects an image of legitimacy. Their wives are relegated to the role of support staff for sustaining this image. Women also organize the domestic consumption of corporately produced goods.

★★

Corporate capitalism oppresses women first by convincing us all that women are genetically incapable of performing the "important" productive roles in society, thus excluding half of the population from open competition for positions of power and high reward; then it assigns to these inferior beings a form of work that is not directly paid for, not recognized as a significant contribution, but which they must do because it is in their natures to do it—management of the household and care of young children.

To sum up, the vertical dimension of social life, viewed through the lens of Activist sociology, is characterized by domination and exploitation of the masses by the privileged elite. The oppressed classes struggle to overthrow their oppressors, and Activists lend their expertise to the struggle on the side of the oppressed. The special contribution of the Activist is to scientifically disprove the doctrines that legitimate the elites, such as sexism and racism, and to expose the connections between the social problems that appear at the surface of public life, and the underlying class struggle that produces them.

AN INNER VOICE

Am I exploited? If the corporate capitalist system is selling me goods I don't need, social roles that don't fit the true me, and the "rightness" of inequality, sexism, and racism, then I guess I am. But what if I don't buy any of this stuff? Does that make me part of the revolutionary proletariat? Can I be a rebel just by opting out of the system? I guess that's what the "beatniks" thought they were doing is the 1950s, and then the "hippies" in the sixties. But can I go along, get a good job, participate in the system's benefits, and still remain skeptical, making up my own mind about things? Can I be a rebel without rebelling?

SOCIOLOGY III
Doing Social Hierarchy

Naturalist sociologists seek an appreciation of the vertical dimension of social life in two major ways: by observing firsthand the actions of superordination and subordination that create social hierarchy in interactive situations, and by listening carefully to individuals defined as low, middle, or high in the social ranks as they describe their own experiences of living the hierarchy.

FOUNDING FATHERS
Georg Simmel on Superordination and Subordination as Cooperative Acts

German sociologist Georg Simmel introduced the idea of observing and analyzing acts of superordination and subordination in order to understand how verticality in social organization is established and sustained. It was Simmel's most striking observation that *every act of subordination requires a complementary act of superordination by the party subordinated; in other words, the underdog must cooperate with the oppressor or ruler in order for their respectively lower and higher rankings to occur.*

"The moral side of this analysis does not concern us here," Simmel wrote, "but only its sociological aspect. This aspect consists in the fact that interaction, that is, action which is mutually determined, action which *stems exclusively from personal origins, prevails even where it often is not noted. It exists even in those cases of superordination and subordination—and therefore makes even those cases societal forms—where according to popular notions the "coercion" by one party deprives the other of every spontaneity, and thus of every real "effect," or contribution to the process of interaction." (Simmel, 1908, p. 183)*

◆◆

The power of one person over another is therefore clearly not something "out there" in the objectifiable environment to be measured and counted, as Functionalists would have it, nor is it resident in the historically distant struggle between interest-defined classes, as the Activists depict it. Power is to be observed only in the interaction between the superordinate and the subordinate, the product of their mutual creation.

The creation of hierarchy is what the Naturalist observes in situations of interaction, just as the creation of deviance was observed in the preceding chapter. The social superior is he who is labelled and treated as the superordinate, and the social inferior is he who is labelled and treated as the subordinate, in specific social scenes.

In this manner, the Functionalist is *creating* a hierarchy of occupational roles when the Functionalist claims to be measuring or discovering such a hierarchy, and the Activist is *creating* a history of class struggle, while claiming to analyze and recount that history.

In one study, Erving Goffman participated in and carefully observed the interactive operation of a restaurant (Goffman, 1959). The swinging door separating the kitchen area from the dining room marked a striking disjuncture in the superordinate-subordinate behavior of waiters and waitresses. On the dining room side of the door, the restaurant employees carefully acted out their service roles with the customers. They treated the diners and their food with deference and respect, clearly and sometimes showily superordinating them, and subordinating themselves. The moment they passed through the swinging door into the kitchen area, however, their demeanor changed drastically. They caricatured and criticised the customers, treated the food with contempt, and in myriad other ways subordinated the diners, and superordinated themselves. Now, who was really of higher rank, and who lower? Who was the real exploiter, and who the exploited? Naturalists are not about to decide such matters for social participants. They are content to mount in society's intriguing gallery, under the heading "superordination-subordination," this fascinating two-faced exhibit.

Functionalists and Activists define in advance of their research where and in what form social hierarchy will be found—in the prestige ranking of occupational roles, or in the domination and exploitation, political or economic, of one social class by another. Through the Naturalist lens, by contrast, hierarchy is to be discovered, wherever and however it becomes observable in the interaction of people in social situations.

When described from the point of view of black or poor students, for instance (Kozol, 1970), the experience of schooling can be seen as primarily and predominantly one of subordination, of subjection to teachers from a strange culture and rules not made by or for one. (Contrast the Functionalist's view of it as "secondary socialization," of opportunity to acquire the knowledge and skills to equip one for the upward mobility journey to roles at higher strata.)

Even in white middle class schools, such as the kindergarten observed by Naturalist Harry L. Gracey (Gracey, 1972), what children can be observed to experience in school is in sharp contrast with a school district booklet's claim that "The most important benefit that your five-year-old will receive from kindergarten is the opportunity to live and grow happily and purposefully with others in a small society." This is also the Functionalist's ideal of the socialization process in schooling.

Gracey sums up his observations as follows:

> The children have learned to go through routines and to follow orders with unquestioning obedience, even when these make no sense to them. They have been disciplined to do as they are told by an authoritative person without significant protest. . . . The "living with others in a small society" which the school pamphlet tells parents is the most important thing the children will learn in kindergarten can now be seen in its operational meaning, which is learning to live by the routines imposed by the school. This learning appears to be the principal content of the student role.

Based on even more careful observation of the interactions between children and schoolteachers, Naturalist Robert W. Mackay (Mackay, 1974) asserts that all of what Functionalist sociology calls socialization is observably a series of superordinations and subordinations. What we see when we look at adult-child interactions, Mackay says, are "(a) the ways in which adults attribute incompetence to children and create situations for its manifestation, and (b) the structure of children's culture." The competence of children is evidenced in such feats as their ability to convince adults that they are being usefully taught by them when, in fact, they already know what it is the adult is trying to teach them. In other words, children can be observed to participate actively and competently in the process of superordinating adults.

One also comes to appreciate the competency of the powerless, the tremendously complex skills of coping when one is allocated neither power, nor prestige, nor property by the social system, in Naturalist Robert Coles' careful work (see Coles, 1967). Coles calls himself a psychologist, but I take the liberty to call his humane, open-handed reporting and analysis of what poor and powerless people, children as well as adults, said to him, Naturalist sociology. Coles respectfully listened to southern sharecroppers and northern slum dwellers, to migrant farmers and urban drifters, and recorded the artful ways poor and unimportant individuals learn to cope with an oppressive or neglectful society. His volumes—really, his respondents' volumes—stand tellingly as a Naturalist's depiction of the experiential realities of social hierarchy in the United States. Coles' human beings not only have a stature and a dignity that refutes any Functionalist classification of them as functionally unimportant, they also exhibit a clear consciousness of their situation, who their allies and who their true enemies are, that should make Activists pause and take new measure of the qualities of the "masses."

Sociological naturalist Elliot Liebow hung around and conversed for months with the unemployed "cornermen" who somehow generate meaningful lives on the streets of Washington, D.C. He reports, in *Tally's Corner* (Liebow, 1967), on the small-scale culture-building carried on by these men with no facilities or materials other than their wit, guile, and complicated humanity. Like James Agee's *Let Us Now Praise Famous Men* (1960), which presented heroic though commonplace survivors during the great depression, Liebow's book is a hymn of praise for the small favors that make even the least of us grandly, honorably, human.

Once we begin to carefully observe and listen to people in situations of social hierarchy; if we begin to develop a profound respect for the self-generated dignity of those without social honor and the strength, endurance, and resiliency of those without power; if we learn to respect creativity, ingenuity, good humor, and courage of those without property, it then becomes difficult for us to place people with any certainty in an objective ranking or social hierarchy. Who is superior, by any social criterion, the person who coasts to the top or the one who struggles heroically, day in and day out, just to survive with a minimum of dignity? But then, why should any sociologist decide who is at the top of which kind of hierarchy in society? Let the people decide that for themselves, in interaction, and let us, as Naturalist sociologists, simply listen in and observe how they superordinate and subordinate one another.

A common feature of the reported and observed experience of persons said by themselves and others to be at or near the bottom of the social hierarchy is *resentment,* an accumulating force of hateful sentiment building up over time, relentlessly, in the underclass.

Resentment is the accumulated consciousness of the unfairness of social inequality, given every man and woman's personal experience of the dignity, and hence the basic natural equality, of every human being.

Naturalists Richard Sennett and Jonathan Cobb have documented this resentment in a number of respectfully interviewed informants, members of what is called "the working class" in America. Sennett and Cobb's book, *The Hidden Injuries of Class* (Sennett, 1972), describes in detail, through the experience of its losing participants, the other side of the stratification hierarchy and recruitment system:

The terrible thing about class in our society is that it sets up a contest for dignity. If you are a working-class person, if you have had to spend year after year being treated by people of a higher class as though there probably is little unusual or special about you to catch their attention, if you resent this treatment, and yet feel also that it reflects something accurate about your own self-development, then to try to impugn the dignity of persons in a higher class becomes a real, if twisted, affirmation of your own claims for respect. Class, in terms of this book, class as a problem of day-to-day existence rather than as an abstraction, creates a hidden content in a wide variety of social issues, so that while people . . . seem to be fighting over general principles, they are in reality fighting for recognition from each other of their own worth. (P. 148)

What Naturalists are bound to discover about class and the experience of class, however, as they go on describing it in detail from various points of view, is that no matter how clearly they thought the phenomena had been seen and described, summed up and characterized, it is more complicated, still more mysterious than it was before the study began. An anecdote from my own experience that still haunts me will perhaps illustrate the point:

I was driving an old bread truck, painted over with colorful flowers and fitted out in back with bunk beds and camping kitchen, with a California license plate. I was wearing a beard and my jeans and a sweatshirt, driving through the streets of Brooklyn, New York, on my way to a friend's house on a Sunday afternoon. A ragged man wearing many suit jackets stood on a corner hawking fresh flowers by the bunch, and I stopped to buy one flower for a lady friend. He didn't want to sell me one flower, only a bunch, and we haggled, and he finally gave in when I told him I could only afford one flower. "So, how do you live?" he said to me as I took the flower and handed him the price in small coins. "In the truck," I said. "There's beds and stuff in the back." "No, no," he said, "I mean, you got this beard, and this crazy truck where you can sleep anywhere, pick up and go anytime someplace else, and you can't afford a whole bunch of flowers but you spent your last dime to buy one—so how do you live?" "Oh," I said, "Well, I teach some classes at the university and pick up a few bucks part time, you know." "No, no," he insisted, grabbing my sleeve so I couldn't leave, "I mean, I gotta be here every day to sell my stuff, I gotta get home for dinner, I *have* to do it, you know? So I mean, how do you live?" I pulled away, mumbled something about not knowing what he was talking about, and jumped into my truck. As I drove away, I could see the man in my rearview mirror. He was shaking his fist in the air. His face was bright red with anger. He yelled out after me, "How do you live, you son of a bitch!"

AN INNER VOICE

I've had experiences like that. Where you can't tell who's putting whom down, or who's on first, or what's up. I mean there are so many different possible totem poles that people can throw up all of a sudden and say, see this one, I'm on top and you're down there, or they can accuse you of holding yourself up on top of some hierarchy you weren't even aware of. Just look at dress on campus nowadays. You can't tell when it's going to be fashionable to be in a good suit and tie or some other straight outfit, and when the cycle is going to come around to grubbiest is snobbiest again. And even if you don't give a damn about clothes or who's on top on campus, you've got to wear something, and people will rank you by it just the same as if you were trying to make that particular impression. There are so many hierarchies in play all the time, you can't avoid them. Sexual hierarchies, academic hierarchies, athletic, economic, social clubs, even just height or attractiveness. It's a gallery all right, if you just take the time to observe it.

DOING SOCIOLOGY

Blue-eyed, Brown-eyed, Class War in the Classroom: This in-class project consists of a set of rules and regulations to be instituted and enforced by the instructor over the course of several hourly class sessions. The regulations can be kept in force while the normal business of the class takes place, and class discussions about the regulations and their consequences can be interspersed with this normal business.

First, the class shall be divided into the subclass of those having brown eyes, and the subclass of those having blue eyes. Those with green, grey, or other colored eyes shall be classified along with the brown-eyed group, since their eyes are, after all, nonblue. The seating arrangement of the class shall be altered for the duration of the project by having the blue-eyed group sit on one side of the classroom (preferably, the side closest to the doors) and the nonblue group on the other side, with an empty row of seats separating them up the middle.

Since any historical analysis of conquest and dominance in world society will show clearly that blue-eyed peoples have consistently won out and dominated over brown-eyed peoples, we shall assume that this social superiority has a genetic basis associated with eye color. Therefore the blue-eyed group in the class is genetically superior to the nonblue group. The following regulations merely institutionalize the rights and privileges naturally accruing to this genetic superiority.

1. In class discussion, or for any other purpose, only the blue-eyed students may raise their hands and be recognized by the instructor as the next speaker. Nonblue students, if they wish to speak, must ask and receive permission to speak from the selected representative of the blue-eyed group.
2. Only blue-eyed students may smoke or chew gum in class. On the other hand, nonblues are required to bring sufficient supplies of chewing gum and cigarettes with them to class so that they can supply blue-eyed students with gum or cigarettes when ordered to do so.

3. No brown-eyed student may leave the classroom to go to the next class, nor even leave his or her seat, until all blue-eyed students have packed up and left the room.
4. Before class begins, no brown-eyed student may enter the classroom until all blue-eyed students have gone in and are seated.
5. Brown-eyed students will make sufficient copies of their lecture notes for these class sessions so that they can supply every blue-eyed student with class notes. Blue-eyed students need not take any notes of their own during these class sessions, and should be duly critical of the quality of the notes handed them by nonblues.

Intermittent or concluding class discussions of this project experience might focus on the following questions:

1. Isn't it evident from the way they are behaving in this project that the non-blue-eyed students are inferior?
2. What are the evident superior qualities of the blue-eyed group?
3. How real are the antagonisms being felt in both directions by the two class subgroups toward each other?
4. Who is the actual creator of this conflict, and what interests does it serve?

Social Change: Evolution, Revolution, and the Search for Meaning in Time

7

Philosophers have long toyed with the fascinating mysteries generated by the interplay between the human experience of a stable world and the equally human experience of change over time. Looking in certain ways and at certain levels of reality, everything appears to be changing, so that "one cannot put his foot in the same river twice," not only because it is never again the same river water, but also because, given biological decay and the regeneration of cells, it is not even the same foot! Looking in other ways, at other levels, "The more things change, the more things remain the same," and "There is nothing new under the sun."

Change in time and constancy over time are basic contrasts in our experience of social life, as well as of natural objects. Relationships appear to begin, grow, develop, decline, and terminate over time, or to remain relatively stable, and the forms relationships take can be seen to change or remain continuous.

The picture of social reality we get when we take cross sections over various periods of time—into the past as well as into the future—make up the third primary dimension of social reality studied by sociologists. We have examined the moral boundaries of society, and we began to measure social verticality or hierarchy. Now it is time to look at society's *temporal dimension.*

This third dimension—social time or social change—is also of great interest to many other intellectual and scientific disciplines, and in a variety of ways to everyone in his everyday life. Time is a puzzle for the physicist because while he or she is trying to measure the continuity, the duration, and the periodicity of events in the universe out there, it is perfectly clear that what is actually being measured, all that can be directly measured, is the continuity, the duration, and the periodicity of human experience. Time is a problem for the man or woman in the street because it seems to be the most absolutely limited of commodities, so that even the richest and most powerful persons cannot increase the amount of it that is available to them by one second over the amount of time possessed each day by the down-and-out hobo. In what distinctive ways is it a puzzle or a problem for sociological inquiry?

The psychologist, to take one contrasting example, is concerned with changes going on in individuals over the course of their lifetimes. Growth, development, learning, maturation—these are processes of normal change associated with the psychological health of individual personalities. Fixation, regression, blockage, retardation, immaturity, infantilism are the abnormalities in personality-change patterns whose symptoms psychiatrists are called upon to cure. Transference, actualization, ego strengthening, re-adaptation, and coping are some of the forms of change brought about by successful psychotherapy. All of these are personality changes.

Social change, in comparison, concerns changes in social relationships. How have patterns of membership in any particular organization or society varied between Time 1 and Time 2? How have the relations between strata, between classes, or between symbols of authority and the deference paid them, altered from one decade, or one century, to another? What are the steps by which social systems progress, or are perceived to progress, from relations of feudal slave and master to relations of factory worker and manager? How do the relationships of group solidarity within a society appear to grow stronger over time, to decay slowly, or to fall apart rapidly? What can we learn from the history of social relationships that would allow us to predict their future directions of change and alteration?

These general sociological questions about social change can be seen reflected in more specific form in every sociological inquiry into social relationships. Social change thus is not merely one class of sociological subject matter, or one general topic in sociology, but, like social stratification, an underlying dimension of social life seen sociologically.

★★

LEADING LIGHTS

Robert M. MacIver on Continuity and Change in Social Relationships

American sociologist Robert MacIver had a great deal to say about social change. He saw change as the fundamental character of social life, with stability the problematic exception requiring explanation. Social stability for MacIver was at best a matter of continuity between successive changes.

"Social relationships are subject to an end-

less process of transformation, of growth and decay, of fusion and separation. Since they are all expressions of human nature, the social relationships of the present are found in germ at least in the past, and those of the past survive, if only as relics, in the present. . . ."

"The most significant social changes are

not those which bring an entirely new thing into being, but those which alter the relations of eternal or omnipresent or universal factors. The pattern is always changing but the threads endure. What is new is the emphasis, rather than the factor emphasized. Thus, for example, democracy is not a kind of rule—or a mode of life—wholly apart from oligarchy or dictatorship. The elements of all are present together—the difference is the degree of dominance of one over the other."

MacIver's productive career as a sociologist ideally illustrates the possibility that one sociologist could indeed make major contributions in the modes of all three of our con-

trasted sociologies. The statement quoted just below about change and continuity represents the Functionalist line on social evolution, which we will be following up shortly. But MacIver also produced careful Naturalist descriptions of ongoing social interaction along with its analysis, and also struggled through his work and in action for the cause of social justice through social change.

"Continuity, then, is an essential character of the evolutionary process. Continuity is the union of change and permanence, and when in this union we move in the direction of social differentiation we are following the road of evolution . . ." (MacIver, 1937)

★★★

What are the major differences between Functionalist, Activist, and Naturalist sociological views of social change? What are the different visions of the reality of change that are brought into view by peering through these three sociological lenses? I believe these differences may be most clearly seen in a comparison of the respective sociologies' treatment of the relationships between actual changes in social life over time, and the perception of those changes by variously situated social participants.

FUNCTIONALIST SOCIOLOGY
Perception Versus Reality of Social Change I

From the perspective of Sociology I, there is no doubt about the reality of social change. Change occurs, rapidly or slowly, catastrophically or only with all due haste, but change inevitably occurs.

The problem, as seen from the Functionalist viewpoint, is with people's perceptions of change. These perceptions are not always accurate, to understate the case. With regard to how things have changed in the past, how they are now changing in the present, and especially with regard to how things are likely to change in the future, people's perceptions of change are notoriously inaccurate.

The experimental logic of Functionalist sociological research makes the primary objective of the enterprise the improvement of the accuracy of social predictions. All Functionalist inquiry can be stated in the form *"If* certain changes occur, or are caused to occur, in one variable feature or factor of the social system, *then,* we hypothesize, certain reciprocal changes will occur in one or more other variable features or factors of the social system." It is through the experimental testing of such "If—then" hypotheses that the Functionalist establishes the necessary or causal relationships between system variables as scientific facts.

For instance, to refer once more to Durkheim's study of suicide, Durkheim's findings could be summed up in the following proposition: "If there is rapid change in a society or a sector of society such that the rules for behavior that people have learned no longer fit the situations in which they find themselves, then there will be a marked increase in the suicide rate, as well as the rates of other signs of personal distress, in that society or sector of society."

Functionalist sociological research, then, can serve to improve the accuracy of people's perceptions of change. They can become more certain about what things followed what in the past, and why, as well as make more accurate predictions about the future.

Functionalist theory holds that it is the *mis*perception of change that is at the root of many of society's social problems, because people who fail to perceive correctly the changes that are coming, and even those that have already come, cannot adapt themselves and their lives appropriately to the new social order. And it is precisely such maladaption that is the problem in such social problems as deviance and anomie.

Sociologists working within the system image of society have argued that technological change often exceeds the pace at which societal members can adjust their perceptual apparatus, leading to social upheaval and the breakdown of social order.

★★

LEADING LIGHTS

William F. Ogburn on the Theory of Cultural Lag

Ogburn theorized that the fundamental engine of dynamic change in society is technology. Progress, from manpower to horsepower to steampower, to electricity, jet propulsion and on into a future of nuclear power generation, has produced an ever-accelerating pattern of change in the way the social world operates (Ogburn, 1932). Technological invention and transformation changes the very landscape of our social lives, yet most of the time, most people cannot even see the changes going on around them, much less see their far-reaching consequences. People living in a nuclear age still perceive the world, and behave in their social relations, as if it were still the age of steam, iron, and wood.

The human changes required by these technological changes—adjustments in family life, organizational life, and social life in general—are constantly lagging behind the technological changes themselves, because of our generally poor perception of the implications of technical change. The gap between the rapid changes in technology and the much slower changes we are willing to make in our cultural and social arrangements is called cultural lag. *Ogburn attributes almost all of our modern social problems, such as divorce, juvenile delinquency, suicide, mental illness, intergroup hostility, and urban decay to this lag. To improve perceptions of technical change would make people better able to adapt themselves culturally to the demands of the future.*

★★

Functionalist studies of demographic change have shown that changes in population size and the consequences of such changes are not accurately perceived or foreseen by couples deciding to have babies, with obviously ruinous results for the social system. Autonomous social change overcomes those persons and systems that do not perceive it correctly and in time.

Sociology I attempts to predict change, and thus to improve social perceptions of change, by uncovering the hidden or latent consequences of superficially manifest social facts and trends. Functionalist and Naturalist sociologist Wilbert Moore, in his presidential address to the American Sociological Association in 1966, urged his colleagues to get more actively into the business of planning the future, constructing and building toward utopias, on the basis of predictive knowledge produced by sociology. "At the very least," he said,

> the sociologist can properly play the role of observer, including the observation of trends that permit him to be a prognosticator. And because he, the sociologist, is strong on relationships, he may claim some expert capacity to identify secondary and tertiary consequences of plans and programs initiated by others.

ACTIVIST SOCIOLOGY
Perception Versus Reality of Social Change II

Activists present the relationship between social change and the perception of change in a *dialectical* format. That is, each side of the equation is shown to influence or codetermine the other. Change is the central focus of Activism, but strangely enough, it is not considered as objective and concrete a phenomenon "out there" as it is to the Functionalists. The objectivity of change in the past, as *history,* is of course undisputed by Activists. In fact, they claim that Functionalists misperceive and ignore history. History, correctly perceived, is the history of class conflict, of violent revolutionary change or its brutal suppression by elites, and it has determined the conditions under which we are constrained to act in the present. But the *future* of social change is open, not mechanically determined by past and present realities, not a closed book simply needing to be read by more accurate Functionalist predictions. The future holds a number of potential changes waiting to be *made* by men and women who correctly perceive their possibilities and their interests.

Thus, for Activists, our perceptions of social change importantly determine what changes shall or shall not occur. False consciousness, the inability to perceive one's true position in the flow of history, and one's true interests in the potentialities of the future, can retard and distort the advancement of historical change toward universal social justice. By changing the perceptions of masses of people toward an authentic consciousness, or "consciousness raising," Activists hope to promote social change toward social health.

Making change toward greater social justice happen is the Activist's goal and task, and the primary instrument for making such change happen is the clarification of the perception of the masses of the people. The underclass needs a crystal-clear perception of social change—of what changes occurred in history to bring them to the situation in which they find themselves, and of what changes they must make in order to bring into being a future of freedom, reason, and justice.

Activists claim that the power elites of society are aware of the crucial role clear perception by the masses has to play in overthrowing their oppressors, because they do everything in their power to mystify the masses about the realities of social change. By demonstrating in scholarly fashion that "You never had it so good," by proclaiming a "revolution" every time a newly shaped soap box comes on the market, and in endless other ways, those who control mass media and education try to keep the blinders on the mass of the people. *Demystification* is therefore the Activist's key task.

NATURALIST SOCIOLOGY
Perception Versus Reality of Social Change III

For the Naturalist, perception is all. From the Functionalist viewpoint, social change is independent of perception of change, which is often incorrect perception. Through the Activist lens, we see a dialectical interaction between the perception of change and what changes can be made to occur. Looking through Naturalist eyes, the perception of social change *is* social change. The "reality" of social change can be stated only in the form of some social participant's perceptions of change, whether the perceiver be a sociologist, a government propagandist, or the proverbial man in the street. Social meanings are everywhere constructed with time-frames attached, and these temporal meanings always in one way or another concern social change or its defining opposite, social continuity. Social participants can be observed in the act of constructing histories for their present actions and relationships and scenarios for their future intentions, from the large scale of human destiny to the small scale of our last date and our next. The "reality" of social change remains an unknown and an unknowable to the Naturalist, but the observable, analyzable *perceptions* of change described by participants and used by them in their interactions abound for the Naturalist's bemused inspection.

It should also be remarked that the lack of change or social continuity and stability is just as much a matter of perceptions and interactive construction of meanings as change is. Change and nonchange are two moments in social time construction.

ৎৎৎ

AN INNER VOICE

The perception versus the reality of change. . . . Here's where my head begins to

spin. If I am really society's puppet, then the best I can do is try to predict which way the system is going to pull my strings next, and adjust myself to "future shock." On the other hand, if I'm out there struggling in the arena, I've got to decide on the basis of a realistic reading of history which way the boat can be steered, and which direction I want it to go, and then pull on my oar in that direction. Then again, if I put myself in a bemused Naturalist's position, I can simply amuse myself by watching from outside-inside, how I, along with the others, create the reality of change through our perceptions of change. Which way to go? Or could I try all three?

Having outlined the differences between the three sociological perspectives on change, we shall go more deeply into the complexity of social change as revealed and analyzed by these three sociologies. Depending on whether one sees social life as a system, an arena, or a gallery, different entities, different states of affairs, and different kinds of events are seen as "social change." There is a difference also in what such concepts as "history," "development," and "modernization" will come to mean, given our analytic perspective on these matters.

CHANGE IN THE SYSTEM

The social system adjusts itself internally in order to remain relatively stable in the face of changes thrust upon it from outside its boundaries. What counts as social change for Sociology I are these adjustments within the system—reactions to nonsocial changes such as ecological, technological, and biological events, or to the impingements of other social systems via war, economic or political domination, or cultural influence. Social systems and their component subsystems are continually adapting to change.

Some Functionalists see the process of adaptation as a fundamentally peaceful, orderly progression of mutual adjustments within a system whose members by and large agree on basic issues. Others consider it to be the push and tug between system components in conflict with one another, though the overall effect of this conflict is to interlock and solidify the pieces of the system as a generally orderly whole.

These two Functionalist views of adaptation to change are called the "consensus model" and the "conflict model" of the social system. There are sufficient differences between these two models that proponents of one or the other often claim to be doing altogether different sociologies; for our purposes in this text, there are sufficient similarities between the two models, and particularly between the two methods of model-building, for us to call them subvariants of Sociology I, the system-view.

Within a consensus or through conflict, change, in the form of mutual adaptation, or change in the relationships between system components, does measurably take place within the social system. At one time the religious component dominates the others in defining the values of the system; at a later time we find religion taking second or third place to science, or politics, or economic factors in determining system goals and values. The Functionalist asks, what has this internal shift in the functions performed by different components been in response to? What are the causes and systemic consequences of this major adaptation? If God is dead, who or what will now perform His role?

What Is History? I

Let us start with a very general definition: "History is the ordering of human events over time, from the past to the present and onward into the future." For Functionalist sociology, the relevant events making up the history of social systems fall into two major time frames.

The larger frame is the span of all recorded human activity, from the biological emergence of the human species beginning with its hominoid ape ancestors and on into the future. Within this span the relevant sociological events are the evolutionary beginnings and the successive transformations of different major types of social systems. Social change on this level is the historical evolution of societal structures.

The smaller time frame is the lifespan of any particular social system, or society. The history of a society begins with its formation as a systemic whole, and continues through its growth in size and complexity and the development of its internal structure, up to either its present state and future prospects or in some cases, to its termination as a society. Social change at the societal level is the process of *growth and development* of a social system over its historical life.

Early Functionalist theorists such as Auguste Comte depicted evolutionary social change as generally cumulative, progressive, and irreversible. That is, the events of human history were said to add up, over time, to concrete social facts that determine the potentialities and the limits of our present and our future as a social species (evolution is cumulative). Further, the direction or change in the overall pattern of systemic social life has been by and large "onward and upward," and throughout history, newer has always been better (evolution is progressive). Finally, there is no turning back to a simpler or a romanticized past, because we cannot undo societal evolution any more than we can or would wish to reverse biological evolution (evolution is irreversible). Even if it made sense to say that "we" were once unreflective, innocent apes, we are now unavoidably conscious and corrupted humans. Even if it made sense to say that "we" were once tribal brothers engaged in cooperative hunting and gathering, we are now irreversibly postindustrial competitors in nuclear blackmail and office politics.

Contemporary Functionalists, the "neo-evolutionists" such as Marshall D. Sahlins and E.R. Service (Sahlins, 1961), seriously modify this view of social evolution, particularly the "onward and upward" part. They allow that it is possible that the human race has lost a great deal even as it has gained through evolutionary change. The neo-evolutionists see social change through history as evolutionary growth and development for better or for worse. Like it or not, modern societies are more complex, more internally differentiated, and more technologically advanced than societies were in the past.

The growth and development of a society is its history, as seen through the Functionalist's lens, its progression through a series of stages or structural phases to the level of development, and the complexity of organization, that it possesses today. One developmental step leads causally to the next, so we can look to history to discover what has determined our present. Once we have established such determinative connections, we can begin to project from the present stage of the society into the probable future.

The United States has recently celebrated two hundred years of existence as an independent nation. Looking back over this bicentennial history, Functionalist sociologists might ask, what are the phases or stages of social structure through which this society has passed since its beginnings? What changes have there been in the relationships between the system's major structural components? How have relations between the individual and the society as a whole been altered and transformed? What new roles has this society required or expected its members to fulfill, and what old roles discarded or revised? Have the basic processes for selecting incumbents to fill key roles, and for training or socializing them into role competency been changed? What about the changing relationships between the values held by the system's members—their ideal society—and the always disillusioning realities they confront in their workaday lives—the actual society that must be lived in and coped with? And what have been the major causes or determinants of these changes? Looking ahead to the next fifty, or one hundred, or two hundred years of United States history, what are the prospects for the survival of this society as an ordered system? Can we project the past history of change into a prediction of the future probability of change? What forces, latent in the past and present relationships between the system's parts, will produce the manifest consequences that are the system's, and its individual members', future?

What Is Modernization? I

The fundamental course of social change from Functionalist sociology's viewpoint is the transition from traditional systems to modern systems—the process of *modernization* in society. Modernity and tradition are general names for all the various new ways of organizing social activities and relationships as opposed to all the various old ways in which they were once organized, and in some less developed societies, are still organized. A modernized society is one that has outgrown its time-honored traditions and has reorganized itself according to more rational, efficient, and scientific principles.

A modern society utilizes machinery wherever possible in place of human labor. It has a rational, nonarbitrary legal system. Its economy is a system of contractual, calculated exchange governed by principles of profit and loss rather than traditional obligations. Its dominant modes of thought and action are scientific and technical rather than religious or magical. Its productive roles are increasingly specialized and differentiated, so that the organization of work breaks each participant's job down into the smallest possible fragment of the whole integrated project for maximum productivity and efficiency.

The transition of any society from the traditional mode of organization to the modern mode is referred to as the process of *development*. The presence or absence of social change, or the relative speed or slowness of social change, is calculated and measured by Functionalist sociology in terms of a system's movement or failure to move toward the goal of further modernization. Different societies in the world today proceed at different paces in their development, with some systems, such as the United States, changing so rapidly as to become perhaps overdeveloped or postmodern in form, while others, such as tradition-bound India, remain almost stagnant, and certainly underdeveloped.

Functionalist sociology measures the process of development by the degree of *differentiation* of the parts and the functions of parts of social systems. The concept of differentiation

> describes the ways through which the main social functions or the major institutional spheres become disassociated from one another, attached to specialized collectivity and roles, and organized in relatively specific and autonomous symbolic and organizational frameworks within the confines of the same institutionalized system. (Eisenstadt, 1967)

Social change, then, is most importantly a question of changing the form of internal organization of a system. Specifically, it consists of the increasing differentiation and specialization of parts, or increasing organizational complexity. This idea is little different from the notions of evolutionary progress put forth by Auguste Comte.

The most commonly cited example of increasing differentiation is the transformation of the institution of the family and its functions. In traditional societies, the family is the over-arching institution, performing a host of social system functions within its all-embracing confines. As societies have developed and modernized, separate functions previously performed by and within the family have been successively differentiated, such as education, food production, crime control, religious practice, and medical care. Each of these functions is performed, in modern societies, by a separate, specialized institution, and the family is left with a small core of functions centering on reproduction, early child care, and emotional support. In the process, the traditional family group has been superceded by the modern "nuclear" family, consisting of only the married pair and their children.

When such changes occur with great speed and on a large scale, Functionalist theory identifies the resulting anomie as the cause of much human misery. But differentiation provides for the substitution of specialized, efficient institutions to perform the functions lost when traditional patterns break down in periods of rapid change. If old values and old roles disintegrate during developmental change, there arise new forms of integration to take their place. If traditional forms of community, or membership, of "the meaning of life" or of work and reward have been destroyed in the process of modernization, then Functionalist theories of social change direct our attention to their modern functional equivalents.

What we have lost in terms of our secure identity as members of the extended family and close-knit tribal community, we have gained in the form of multiple roles and freedom of social mobility in a complex, highly differentiated social system. What we have lost in terms of a rich symbolic life of magical and religious belief and ritual, we have gained in achieving mastery over nature and the certainties of modern scientific knowledge.

The Social Future.   A subcategory of Sociology I has emerged in the past two decades, called "Futurism." It merely extends the Functionalist emphasis on prediction into long-term projections of social trends. What will the social system be like in 1984? In 2000? In 2100? (Past this date lies the exclusive preserve of science fiction.)

A *projection* plots a line or a curve showing the pattern of change in some measurable unit that has been factually established from some point in the past up to the present, and carries that line on its probable course into the future. Futurists not only plot projections, they also speculate on the general societal consequences of a combination of probable trends, to try to outline a probable picture of social life at some future time. One major aim of this enterprise is to insulate us against what futurist Alvin Toffler calls "future shock" (Toffler, 1970)—the suffering entailed in confronting a series of ever more painful surprises.

Among futurists there are pronounced pessimists and optimists. The pessimists project exploding rates of population growth to a dismally overcrowded, underfed earth; the optimists project that fertility rates will decrease, keeping the world population at a density well within earth's life-support capacity. Pessimists warn that increasing urbanization of the world's population forebodes a future of ever more densely crowded, ever more unlivable cities; optimists project the predominance of "the wired city," an electronic communications network so efficient in the completion of economic and social transactions that the "city's" active particpants need not live or work in actual spatial proximity, but can be dispersed over large areas. Pessimists predict increasing feelings of uselessness and alienation among workers whose effort and skills will be rapidly replaced by automation and computerization; optimists herald the shortened work week as a prerequisite to expanded leisure time for all, leading to unprecedented opportunities for self-realization and the development of community.

The pessimists project that growing "third world" demands for their share of the material benefits of industrialization will run head on into the diminishing supply of nonrenewable resources needed to produce these goods, and bring increasing conflict and inevitable warfare among the nations. Optimists point to recent trends toward supranational organization and worldwide mass communications to predict the emergence of a global nation-state, where humanity overcomes nationalism, racism, and dog-eat-dog economic competition in time to realize our common interests and our common heritage as members of the human race. According to which sets of projections one puts one's faith in, we are now nearing the end, or just the beginning, of human society on this earth (Bell, 1972).

CHANGE IN THE ARENA

In the social arena, the Activist demands changes in the rules of the game, basic alterations in the structure of society's power contest such that the masses can win their fair share of scarce goods, and elites are forced to give up some of their entrenched privileges.

Redistribution of wealth, power, dignity, life chances is the only kind of change that counts. Those who have social privileges fight desperately to keep and enlarge them. Those who lack power, wealth, dignity, and the rest must fight to change the game of distribution itself if they are ever to win their fair share. That means the society's most basic rules, its very structure as a system, must be changed if social justice is to be advanced. What counts as change for the Activist is not the adaptation of system components within the system—*that* only serves to perpetuate the status quo. Ultimately, all that can count as change for the better is the overthrow of this system, and the erection of a new, and just, system.

For the Activist, history is not so much a set of abstract forces determining the social system's present state and future probabilities as it is the concrete set of circumstances in which we participate as social beings, within whose context we might find ourselves, and in which we must act. The Activist asks of history, "Who are we, who are our true ancestors and our likely descendants, and given our historical situation, what is to be done?"

The relevant events of history for the Activist are the massive, consequential actions of groups of people in their struggles to survive, to prosper, to realize their human potentialities, to achieve or to deny social justice. Systems of social interaction are seen to emerge, grow stronger, and decline over time in this view of history, but systems—economic, political, or cultural—are not the actors on history's stage. Systems of various kinds are merely the perceived consequences of people's more or less systematic actions when they come to grips with their historical situations. *People* are the actors, the makers of history.

To learn from history is to perceive the patterns of domination and rebellion that mark humanity's long struggle toward a just, egalitarian, humane society. From this perception of the past experience of human groups, the sociologist constructs a theory of how elite groups have come to dominate the masses and how those masses have generated among themselves the force and the organization to overthrow this domination.

In contrast to the Functionalist evolution of social systems, Activist history is the history of social *revolutions*. The Activist theory of history is developed not merely to predict future social structures, but to create the future. History is merely a prologue and a spur to action.

Revolution is the exact opposite of the main focus of attention of Functionalist sociology, the stability of the social system over time. Note the emphasis in the statement by MacIver quoted above on continuity. The Activist critique of Functionalist sociology states that Functionalists rewrite history for their own elitist, status quo purposes—to show the continuity and stability of all social systems, and therefore to demonstrate the natural, the necessary, inevitable character of our own social system. As Activists read history, the *discontinuities* stand out as the most significant events in the lives of societies, the disruptions of coercive stability and the formation of new forms of social organization through revolution.

★★

LEADING LIGHTS

Rex Hopper on the Four Phases of a Successful Revolution

Let us look at Rex Hopper's outline of the anatomy of revolutions to see what the Activist sociologist can make of a historical study of successful revolutions in the past.

A successful revolution has four major phases in its development, Hopper found (Hopper, 1950). The first phase occurs when members of the population begin to sense. that the established rules and values of the society no longer fit either the current situation or the raised aspirations of the people, and there is a great deal of social unrest, chaotic mob action, and other symptoms of unorganized dissatisfaction.

In the second phase, the unrest and dissatisfaction become organized into groups with much clearer goals in mind, opposition organizations led by two major types of revolutionary leader, both usually drawn from the intellectual class that once supported the powers that be. The two leader types are the prophet, who organizes the hopes and dreams of the dissatisfied masses by outlining the new utopia to be sought in the future, and the reformer, the street-level organizer who works toward specific, practical goals. In the third phase, the revolution actually begins. The leadership, the revolutionary aims, and the organization is formalized and consolidated. In the struggle between left and right wings of the revolutionary movement, the radicals win out. Finally, the revolutionary group takes over power and becomes the legal organization of the society. In this fourth phase, the radical and reformist elements are phased out once again, strong central administrators take over, and a new social order is established that combines elements of the old social order and those aspirations of the revolutionaries that can be practically instituted in a stable system.

★★

Looking at the U.S. bicentennial, the Activist wants to know, where is this society now on this continuum? Was the protest and rioting of the 1960s Phase One, and is the second phase now developing behind the scenes? Or is there no revolution developing within this society at all? Is it possible that revolutionary history has now shifted its locale to the world stage?

An Activist reading of history as class struggle would make it clear that we are now in an era of worldwide revolutionary struggle, with the third-world underclass pitted against the combined oppressors of the capitalist industrialized world *and* the socialist industrialized world, the Western and Soviet blocs.

In this revolutionary struggle, Hopper's Phase Two is well under way, with the war in Vietnam an early event in the emerging Phase Three—armed struggle. Suppose, because of historical, practical, economic, and political necessity, the United Nations should become the world government in fact as well as in an ideal sense, that it should hold the power of the state over all other nations at some point in the future. Then, project the democratic control over the United Nations now exerted by the third-world nations into that future. Would this not be Hopper's fourth phase?

In the postrevolutionary period to follow, the American Revolution would be celebrated as an early victory in the long struggle of the at last victorious colonized people of the earth over their colonizers, and the war in Vietnam would be equally celebrated as a victory of the colonized Vietnamese people over their French and U.S. oppressors. Busts of George Washington and Ho Chi Minh would stand side by side in the hall of revolutionary heroes.

What Is Modernization? II

Activist sociologists reject the Functionalist's view of social change wherein all necessary human social functions always are performed, albeit by changing institutional forms. The gains and potential gains of modernization of societies have been great, in their view, but the human losses have been extremely heavy, and they have not been made up or substituted for. A terrible human price has been paid for development, both by the developed peoples themselves, and even more so by those still undeveloped.

The Activist sees development in Western societies as terribly skewed. Technology and market productivity have been advanced at the expense of a just system of distribution, the wholeness of the person, a meaningful social and political community, and a livable physical environment.

The main beneficiaries have been the profiteering elites.

The Functionalist idea of evolutionary development of some modern societies as compared to the slow growth of other, more traditional societies, is, to the Activist, a mockery of historical truth. The rich and technologically privileged societies "developed" as a direct consequence of their imperialistic plunder of the third world colonial societies, and by means of their equally rapacious plunder of the nonrenewable resources of the earth itself. The one-third of the world's population living in developed societies is in the process of consuming and wasting virtually all of the earth's natural resources, while explaining that the paucity of food, clothing, and shelter left for the other two-thirds is the result of their underdevelopment.

To explain away how some nations got rich at the expense of others as "the process of modernization," or "differentiation," is, from the Activist's viewpoint, to be an apologist for the world elite in the name of "objective science."

The Functionalists distort history by focusing on internal processes in social systems, a view that makes it appear that Western industrialized nations have autonomously "developed," or pulled themselves up by the bootstraps. In fact, the historical reality has been a story of imperialist exploitation. The "underdeveloped" world were the victims of exploitation, not "slow developers," or victims of their own traditions. Modernization, for the Activist, is a synonym and a cover-word for exploitation, both externally through colonization, and internally through exploitation of workers.

Even within advanced societies, modernization has not been synonymous with human progress. Technological advancement, industrialization, and the breakdown of traditional group memberships, obligations, and values, have all had the primary effect of putting into the hands of the powerful elites ever more powerful instruments of control over the masses.

Mass production, mass communications, mass education, and mass organization of society characterize the modern as compared to the traditional world. "Differentiation" has meant mainly the fragmentation and thus alienation of the person. What is most ironic and most painful about these developments, from a sociological Activist's viewpoint, is that each of these new forms of social organization provides the potential for every human being on earth to develop to his or her full potential as a person.

The technology of mass production, harnessed to modern science, could provide the material means for a healthy and decent life for every man, woman, and child on earth, given a just system of distribution of the material goods produced in such massive, even excess, quantities. Instead, the gap between the rich and the poor of the world has steadily widened over the course of modernization, giving us the tragic paradox of massive surplus production of luxury goods in one part of the world and starvation and deprivation in another.

Nationalism, racism, and incessant warfare have all increased with the rise of modern communications and modern organizational efficiency. Social injustice on a scale and at an intensity never before experienced by the human race is the bitter fruit of modern development. The Activist asks, how can these modernized techniques of organization be turned against the elites? What should be the form and substance of the modern world's massive revolutionary struggle toward social justice for all? How can real change be made in society?

Damned If We Don't. The Activist picks and chooses from among the futurist's projects whatever he finds useful in his attempts to diagnose and cure social ills. In general, the Activist uses the pessimistic projections as warnings of what could happen if the people don't wake up, organize ourselves in the general interest, and fight for a decent future. The optimist's projections serve as goals and stimulants to action.

But the Activist rejects the idea that futurist projections are in any meaningful sense predictions of the future determined inexorably by the past. It is the present where history is made, according to Activists.

If we don't make the future what we want it to be by our conjoined actions today, then somebody else will, and our future will consist in living with the consequences of their actions, and our collective inaction.

CHANGE IN THE GALLERY

What counts as change for the Naturalist sociologist? Whatever people say is change, counts as change. The sections of the Naturalist's gallery of social life marked "social change" will not contain any instances of change per se. On the other hand, it should become increasingly filled with observed and recorded instances of social participants defining, creating, and thereby doing "social change" in their daily interactions. The Naturalist observes talk and action about change, or the lack of it, as a widespread social phenomenon. When people compare the "facts" about the past with the "facts" about the present in order to predict the future, the Naturalist asks, "What are they trying to do by making that comparison? Why have they selected certain "facts" and not others? What kind of a move is it in what kind of a game to talk about change like that?"

The Naturalist, in other words, witnesses "social-change talk," written as well as verbal, and in this talk perceives a crucial and universal process taking place—the creation of social time. Just as participants can be seen to erect the vertical boundaries of their social lives in their stratifying activities, they can also be observed to bound their actions and their social relationships in time by talking and acting with regard to "social change." References to change, to social history, or to the plans and possibilities of the future, will all make up the Naturalist's gallery of social change.

The Naturalist view of history has its roots in the writings of the humanists, who argued that history is the creation of historians who, in every age and in each society, construct an argument about the moral, political, or economic state of affairs of the present by rewriting past history. History then is a polemical instrument for debating where one's society now stands and where it ought to move next. It is a set of claims about the past designed to support arguments about the future.

As Naturalistic sociologists we can first perceive this practice closest to home, in the competing histories of social organization presented by contending sociologies. It would appear that those sociologists arguing for the uprooting and overthrow of a present unjust social order see and write history as the history of revolutions. It would also appear that those sociologists arguing for the reform and improvement of systemic efficiency see and write history as the history of social system growth and development. Both, it seems, claim to be striving for consistency with the "facts" of history.

On a smaller scale, Naturalists observe the creation and recreation of "histories" as an everyday occurrence in social interaction. When a married couple searches painfully for the causes of their present unhappiness in the sequence of "who did what to whom first," they are making history. Revisions of this history may take place freely up to the point where the decree of the divorce court concretizes the official history of the marriage in hard, cold print.

Historical commemorations, from candles on a birthday cake to the minutes of the last meeting, to the aforementioned U.S. bicentennial celebrations, abound in social life. These are all history-making actions, in a literal sense. Thus, families have histories, as do individuals, small groups, organizations, institutions, and nations. Through historicizing actions, all of these social entities are given historical reality and character, and their histories are sustained, passed on, revised, and used to win arguments.

Naturalists are concerned, on grand and small scales, not with the truth or accuracy of history, but with the competing claims of official and informal historians.

For instance, Naturalists are interested in the United States bicentennial insofar as it provides public opportunities to re-create the "facts" of United States history, especially in the form of political speechmaking. Electoral candidates may be observed in the act of history-making when each construes his own candidacy, and his own party's political philosophy, as the natural and historically necessary extension of the spirit of 1776. What the "founding fathers" really intended, what the significant events in American history really have been, and what they really mean, have been interpreted and reinterpreted anew in the campaign rhetoric of 1976. The use and abuse of history in this rhetoric is the focus of Naturalist interest.

What Is Modernization? III

The modernity of tradition is a theme that might best represent a sociological Naturalist's response to the theorizing of the Functionalists and the polemics of the Activists.

Neither the evolutionary nor the revolutionary rhetoric of sociologies I and II is convincing to the Naturalist, mainly because they are both pitched at such an abstract level, so far from the social experience of any actual human collectivity.

The basic question of what kinds of change, or how much change, can be considered an advancement of the human condition can only be answered directly from the standpoint of some specific humans, in some specific place and time, who are considering their past experience, their present situation, and their future alternatives. Then the question becomes, would it be most feasible and desirable to them to alter or retain certain features of their world?

★★★

LEADING LIGHTS

Peter Berger on Who Are the Change Experts

For example, in his critique of both Functionalist and Activist theories of and programs for modernization, which he labels "the myth of growth" and "the myth of revolution," respectively, Peter Berger takes a fully Naturalistic position. Neither development, nor revolution for that matter, "is something to be decided by experts, simply because there are no experts on the desirable goals of human life. Development is the desirable course to be taken by human beings in a particular situation. As far as possible,

therefore, they ought to participate in the fundamental choices to be made, choices that hinge not on technical expertise but on moral judgements. . . . To call for participation is to render 'cognitive respect' to all those who cannot claim the status of experts. . . . (This concept) is based on the understanding that every human being is in possession of a world of his own, and that nobody can interpret this world better (or more 'expertly') than he can himself." (Berger, 1974, p. 57)

★★★

Both Functionalists and Activists rely on the supposed superiority of "expert" analysis of other people's needs and prospects, whether it be scientific development experts whose science consists in knowing things about people they don't know themselves, or revolutionary experts who wish to relieve the masses of their "false consciousness" and give them the truth about history. The Naturalist begins from the premise that people know far more about themselves than any expert could ever hope to discover, and, by and large, what they don't know about themselves isn't true.

Studies of third world, or even primitive, social arrangements make sense to the Naturalist only when they focus on what we in the industrialized West can learn from these subjects. The process of modernization gives some of these studies a particular urgency— can we learn the strengths and richness of primitive forms of social organization before these forms have been completely eradicated by the bulldozers of modernization?

★★★

LEADING LIGHTS

Clarke and Hindley on the Contemporaneity of Primitives

A strong and fascinating case in point is The Challenge of the Primitives, a recent book by Englishmen Robin Clarke and Geoffrey Hindley that expands on the excellent field

work and analysis of many anthropologists. "This book, we hope," they write in their conclusion, "will be a handbook of alternatives drawn from the accumulated experience of other societies. *Its aim has been to suggest some ways in which denatured industrialized man might at last begin the trek back to social humanity" (Clarke, 1975, p. 348).*

Clarke and Hindley underscore the fact that primitive peoples, in their traditional modes of social organization and environmental exchange, have survived in relative peace with their fellows and with nature for millions of years. In contrast, civilized peoples have reached the thresholds of total war and exhaustion of the earth's resources in a mere few centuries.

There still survive some remnants of that long history of successful coping with the contingencies of nature, both human and environmental. Instead of relegating these cultures to a long dead past, the Naturalist views these "primitives" as what they in fact are—contemporaries who are living out very different life-styles from our own.

Hunters and gatherers, and even slash-and-burn farmers, eat better on the whole than we do. Clarke and Hindley point out that "millions more people die from starvation or its side-effects now than they did when all the world was a hunter and gatherer. However many justifications and qualifications one cares to heap on to this stark fact, the ultimate position remains unaltered: the world is worse fed now than it was in the days of our ancestors." (P. 31)

The rationality and economy of "swidden" (slash-and-burn) agriculture, the usefulness of herbal medicines and techniques for control of the autonomic nervous system that the primitive witch doctor combines, the effectiveness of premodern forms of population control (mainly sexual abstention and selective infanticide), and particularly the success of primitives in relating to nature and to their fellows, are all detailed in this handbook, making it a rich and perhaps even socially useful contribution to Naturalism's gallery of social change.

★★★

Basically, the Naturalist's position on modernization and similar concepts, is skepticism. The Naturalist will want to look more closely at their uses in social interaction. What are the advantages in characterizing social change as the transition to modernity, and who reaps them?

First, such theorizing is a handy device for organizing the complex universe of contending social realities into a monolithic unity—a monolith of time. Perhaps there is a kind of mental and emotional security to be derived from viewing all of humanity as a time-ordered unity. Then, those of our contemporaries whose basic views of the world are radically different from our own can be considered to be at an earlier stage of development than we. They cannot possibly challenge our present or our future if their first task is to catch up with us.

Second, this image of social time marching on provides automatic rebuke to those who may challenge the desirability of growth, automation, technical solutions to human problems, etc. These complaints are obviously absurd and inappropriate because they are *anachronistic*—out of step with the inevitability of developmental social change. A theory of change that supports the status quo? For the Naturalist, one more wonderful paradox in the human gallery.

Hopes and Fears

Naturalists observe that throughout recorded human history, futurism has played an important part in the organization of social reality. Prophets and oracles, soothsayers and science fiction writers have their most recent counterparts in the sociological futurists. Interestingly enough, they always seem to come in both varieties, pessimists and optimists, prophets of doom and damnation and prophets of a land of milk and honey.

Every cultural group, it appears, develops its own specialists in the production of believable, alternative myths about the future. At any particular time, then, our social future is the collective expression of our hopes and fears. Sociological Naturalism is dedicated to the description and analysis of those hopes and fears, and their modes of expression, as further clues to the character of this human collectivity.

How each social group predicts the future, and what this can tell us about the organization of its hopes and fears, is the Naturalist's topic of inquiry, upon which, however, little work has yet been done. I leave it to the futurists to predict whether futurism will become a well-documented and analyzed exhibit in the Naturalist's gallery.

AN INNER VOICE

I'd better pause, to review all of this in my mind. Each sociology's view of social change is a way of seeing time as a major dimension in social life. If I look at change through the lens of Functionalist sociology, I see the slow, steady evolution of social structure through eons of history, and I see the step-by-step development of my own society and the surrounding societies in the world, each at its own level of development, each moving at its own pace. Current events are just pebbles in the lake of social time, or perhaps a wide, slow river, whose currents move deep while the stability and relative tranquility of the surface is maintained over the long run of history.

If I look, now, through the lens of Activist sociology, I see again a river of time, whose course runs back to ancient times, but this river is running fast, and it is marked by

cateracts, massive waterfalls, and the turmoil of conflict and struggle. We are floating along this river in a fragile craft, and we have the power to change the course of our vessel, and perhaps even to join with others to change the course and the speed of the river itself. From the Activist study of history and our present social structure, we want to know, how far along is the next plunge into revolutionary cataclysm?

Yet again, if I look through the lens of Naturalist sociology, I see competing images of social time being constructed by Functionalists, by Activists, even by myself in my metaphor of the river. I see social participants everywhere giving meaning and significance to their actions, their lives, and their social commitments by framing these actions in time. This is how we all can be observed to do "social change."

—————— DOING SOCIOLOGY ——————

Predicting the Social Consequences of a Personal Change: *This project requires you to decide on a small change that you will make in your everyday routine, and predict the social consequences. You will then institute the change, observe the reactions of others in your personal social environment, and report back to the class on the success or failure of the original predictions.*

The first task is to choose a small personal change, a change whose consequences in your life are not likely to be either "trivial or tragic," in Wilbert Moore's terminology (Moore, 1965). That is, the change should not be so insignificant that no one with whom you interact will notice or care about it, nor should it be so drastic that your entire social life could be ruined by the reactions to it. The types of changes that students have made in past trials of this project, with generally satisfactory results, have included: changes in their standard of dress on campus, from normally casual, sloppy attire to something more formal and well groomed, or visa versa; change in their usual temporal organization of the day, from early rising—early retiring, to late rising and late retiring, or vice versa; change from being generally talkative to being generally taciturn or vice versa; and change from being private to being sociable, or vice versa. Of course, there is an endless variety of other possibilities to be invented.

THE INSTITUTIONAL ORGANIZATION OF SOCIAL LIFE

III

WHAT ARE SOCIAL INSTITUTIONS?

The word institution *has many connotations in the English language. It can be used to mean the establishment or the setting up of something; an already established law or custom; an organization like a hospital or an asylum; a building, such as a jail; or a set of rules or principals. Sociologists draw on all these diverse meanings when they define, describe, and analyze social institutions, but there is general agreement among all the sociologies that the term* social institution *will refer to a collection of established patterns of action integrated around a central theme.*

In Part I of this book, we have been introduced to the variety of sociological lenses through which the puzzles of social life may be viewed, and we have discovered some of the perils and pleasures of involvement in this multiple viewing. In Part II, we focused broadly, and trifocally, on three major dimensions along which social life can be seen to be organized. The moral, the vertical, and the temporal outlines of social organization are perhaps the most obvious features of the social landscape. Our focus in Part III requires only a small adjustment in the focal plane of our three lenses, because social institutions, too, are prominent features of the social landscape.

Of course, even when all three sociologies, Functionalist, Ac-

tivist, and Naturalist, have their lenses focused at the level of social institutions, and even if they all agree to define social institution as "a collection of established patterns of action integrated around a central theme," the social landscape takes on a drastically different configuration as each different lens is brought into use. There are three distinct realities to be discovered in answer to the question, how do social institutions organize social life?

The institutional organization of social life when viewed from the perspective of social life as the system, social life as the arena, and social life as the gallery is the subject of Chapter 8, "Institutions: System Components, Superstructures, Codes." Next, we shall focus on what everyone agrees is a major institution of social life in Chapter 9, "The Family." The institution of the family can itself be seen as a system, an arena, or a gallery, and since almost everybody has one, each student can check out the various sociological claims against his or her own personal experience of life in this institution. There are several other major institutional forms deserving of attention, but for reasons of brevity and economy, we close this section with only one more chapter, a comparative view of three related social institutions. Chapter 10 details "Three Arguments on Magic, Science and Religion." In this chapter, I argue that these three institutions share in the social organization of knowledge and belief, of what is held to be The Truth in any society.

Institutions: System Components, Superstructures, Codes

8

Viewed sociologically, a social institution is a collection of established patterns of action integrated around a central theme. The kinds of actions that sociologists consider *social* actions are those actions that persons perform toward one another, or with regard to one another—inter-actions. The fundamental forms of patterning found in social interactions lie in the organization or structuring of relationships. Thus a pattern of action can be seen in the typical ways in which a mother interacts with her child, a salesman with a customer, a doctor with a patient, a judge with a defendant, or a student with a teacher.

The institution of the family, for instance, may be seen to consist of the established, typical, patterned ways in which brothers and sisters, husbands and wives, parents and children, aunts, uncles, nephews, and nieces—in short, kin—relate to one another. Further, those patterned ways of interacting can be seen to define and establish the relationships and the relationship-identities family members have with one another. The boundaries implicit in kinship patterns of action also define the differences between the ways family members behave toward one another and the ways they behave toward nonfamily members.

The institution of the economy may be seen to consist of the established, typical, patterned ways in which buyers and sellers, practitioners and clients, employers and employees, producers and consumers, lenders and borrowers, landlords and tenants, and owners and managers behave toward and relate to one another. Similarly, the institution of language may be seen as the patterned relationships between speakers and hearers, writers and readers, liars and believers, questioners and answerers, callers and the called, and speechgivers and audiences. Other major social institutions recognized by sociologists—religion, the polity, law, education, sport, art, friendship, science, and magic—can be described in similar terms.

Once this rather cautious general description has been made, the various sociological definitions, observations, and analyses of social institutions begin to part company. We begin to see three different realities when we ask each of our three sociologies to answer in detail, "What are institutions made of?"; "How are social institutions related to one another?"; "How do institutions change?"; and "What are social institutions good for?"

WHAT ARE INSTITUTIONS MADE OF?

SOCIOLOGY I
Roles and Rules

From the Functionalist perspective, a social institution is an integrated collection of roles and the rules governing the performance of those roles in interrelation. The social rules governing religious behavior, for instance, define the roles of priest, congregant, novitiate, backslider, heretic, and agnostic, among others. These rules also specify the appropriate relationships between the incumbents of the institutional roles. Within the framework of each institution, a particular set of rewards and sanctions attach to proper or improper role performance. These act as constraints or reinforcements to insure proper performance of these roles. The fact that others understand the behavioral requirements of institutional roles leads them to expect certain behavior from role incumbents, and the expectations of others act as additional reinforcements of or constraints upon proper role performance.

Behavior in institutional settings thus takes on a predictable, routine form, and this, along with the interlocking coordination of the roles themselves, provides a certain internal cohesion and stability to the institution. In this way, each institutional subsystem is like a little system of its own, with its own boundaries, its own interlocking parts, and its own problems of maintaining order and stability over time.

The rules and roles making up institutions have both an external and an internal existence with regard to persons who relate and interact institutionally, according to Functionalist sociology. Externally, they are the abstract structures of values and facts, of "ought" and "is," that operate to constrain and guide the behavior of individuals in society. Internally, as Durkheim has taught (see the Founding Fathers excerpt in Chapter 3), the social system of rules and regulations penetrates the person through the process of socialization. Individuals internalize their appropriate institutional roles, along with the institutional rules regulating behavior in those roles, so that most of the time they behave automatically in the correct manner, without external constraints or rewards. Institutions therefore also exist inside the persons who behave in the institutionally appropriate manner; the rules and roles are part and parcel of the person. People in social interaction, thus, are living embodiments of social institutions.

Functionalist sociologists try to make it clear that the rules and the internalized roles comprising social institutions, and thus the institutions themselves, are *analytical,* not *concrete,* social realities. This means they are to be taken as realities that appear only upon analysis of social phenomena, and not as obvious facts of life that everybody confronts in their social lives. These patterns motivate, guide, and govern social interactions in the ways just discussed. The actions themselves, and the physical consequences of such actions, are the concrete manifestations of underlying institutional patterns.

In this light, the members of a congregation praying together in church, the service or mass conducted by the priest, and the church building itself, which they or former congregants have built, are all concrete manifestations of the institution of religion, with its relationship-guiding rules and identity-forming roles.

The social facts that Functionalists count and measure—rates of church attendance, marriage and divorce rates, employment, unemployment, and job-mobility rates, for instance,—are thus surface manifestations of the deeper, analytical social reality. They serve as evidence of the behind-the-scenes operations of the institutions of religion, the family, and the economy, respectively.

What are institutions made of? What are these patterns of action? Through the analytical lens of Functionalist sociology, we see them to be the underlying motivators, the guides and shapers of social interaction, institutional rules, and institutional roles.

SOCIOLOGY II
Myths, Powers, and Privileges

Activist sociologists don't like to talk seriously about social institutions in the abstract. What we have to deal with sociologically, they say, are the actual institutions as they are established in our society here and now, and the problems or the opportunities these particular institutions present to combatants in the struggle for social justice.

Functionalist talk about the inevitability or the logical necessity of such abstract institutions as religion, the family, the economy, and the polity (law and government) serves to persuade people in this society that class-conscious Christianity; consumerized, sexist suburban households; corporate capitalism; and corrupted democracy are inevitable and logically necessary parts of the way things are and must be. Functionalist abstractions, in other words, mask the reality of our contemporary social institutions. These institutions, Activists maintain, in fact camouflage the historically established structure of entrenched power and privilege.

Contemporary social institutions, from the Activist perspective, consist, upon first examination, of collections of carefully constructed myths asserting the rightness and inevitability of the alienating roles and relationships most of us are assigned in this society. They are firmly established myths, confirmed and propagated even by Functionalist sociology. For instance, the myth that big business, the military, and the government act as "countervailing forces" in the political system, when in fact they consistently collude with one another to make crucial decisions in their favor, is an important facet of the political institution in the United States (and many other nations) today (Mills, 1956). Similarly, the myth of "free enterprise" (which implies that businesses that make serious mistakes in the competitive market will fail) masks the fact that government, heavily lobbied and bribed by corporations, subsidizes and underwrites large corporations (like Lockheed) no matter what they do (see Zeitlin, 1970).

Behind the myths stand the establishments of power and privilege in this society. There is really only one set of genuine social relationships in contemporary society, the historically established relationship between the winners and the losers in the class struggle. Currently established social institutions are not alternative sets of relationships, they are justifications or smoke screens for winner-loser relationships. Such institutional false fronts are *mystifying* devices, cultural lies told by the winners to keep the losers naively in the game.

Activist sociology's first task is to help the losers see through the social institutional myths. The job of the Activist may be called *demystification*. Behind the myth of a free market economy is the reality of corporate monopolies and the alienated worker; behind the myth of government by and for the people stands the power broker with senators in each pocket, and the powerless voter with no meaningful choice to make at election time; behind the myth of equality before the law stands the rich man's lawyer bargaining him free while the poor man is sentenced for the same or a lesser crime. The list of myths to debunk goes on and on.

What are institutions made of? From the Activist perspective, the institutions in our unjust society are composed of social myths and the relations of power and privilege hiding behind them.

SOCIOLOGY III
Definitions, Accounts, Attributions

The first premise of Naturalist sociology is that only those things that can be directly observed will be admitted into the social scientist's gallery of exhibits. What then do we find in this gallery under the heading of "Observables—Social Institutions"?

Certainly invisible roles and rules will not be included. Nor will we find "myths," because one cannot observe a myth, one can only observe someone telling a story, and, perhaps, someone else calling that story a myth.

Naturalists claim we can directly observe only the words and symbolic actions by which social participants define their situations, account for their actions, or attribute motives to one another (see McHugh, 1968). Thus, institutions consist of institutional definitions, institutional accounts, and institutional attributions. They are seen by Naturalists to be, not rules and roles that somehow guide behavior, not myths and the privileges they protect, but commonly used sense-making devices. Institutional codes and conventions are social meanings that people use to make their actions meaningful.

We'd better pause here for an example of how a Naturalist observer might detect the existence and the operation of an institution as a sense-making device.

While participating in an occasion labelled in printed announcements "Cards Night" at a local church, I observed and noted down for future reference the following interchange:

A group of six men were playing poker at one of the tables, a few feet away from a table of five ladies playing bridge. The poker players joked, laughed aloud, and were generally rambunctious, whereas the bridge ladies remained quiet, restrained, and sedate. At one point in the evening, after a particularly raucous outburst from the poker table, one of the bridge ladies leaned across toward the men and admonished, "Shshsh! You're in church, you know!" A poker player waved her off with his cigar. "Naah! But this is cards!" he said, and the poker table roared with laughter once again.

This little anecdote is an illustration of social participants' use of "social institutions," or collections of institutional meanings with common-theme labels, to organize the sense and appropriateness of their interactive situation.

Note that the lady bridge player's admonition to the men, indicating that their behavior was inappropriate and deserved correction or scolding, invoked only the institutional label of the place in which they were situated. It is apparently enough to say, "You are in church," (because that is all she did say, apparently she assumed that that was all she *had* to say to do what she was trying to do), to indicate a set of boundaries differentiating appropriate from inappropriate behavior.

Similarly, the cigar-waving man economically answered the woman's challenge. (The economy of human actions in communicating so many complex meanings, and doing so much necessary interactive work with such minimal effort and time-use, is of constant wonderment to the Naturalist.) "Naah! But this is cards!" neatly counterasserts the priority of another social institution, namely, that form of recreational sport called "cards." The question, "whose behavior is appropriate in this situation?" is argued and apparently resolved (there was no further argument from the bridge table) by answering the question, "which institution shall be used to define the situation?"

The Naturalist's critique of other sociologists is also clarified in this example. We can see here that social institutions are not forces or constraints lurking in the background and "guiding" behavior or "mystifying" and "oppressing" social participants. They are, in this observed interaction, potential definitions of situation and the appropriateness of actions within it. These definitions are observably used by participants as instruments in their negotiations.

AN INNER VOICE

I can see the social system as being divided up into large institutional parts, like religion, economics, the family and so on. It seems to make good sense to say that these institu-

tions exist, and shape our everyday lives in different ways, according to the established pattern. But maybe they are just smoke- screens to hide the power games being *played behind the scenes. On the other hand, they could be devices that we all use to define our activities. It's just not clear yet which of these views is the most realistic.*

HOW ARE SOCIAL INSTITUTIONS RELATED TO ONE ANOTHER?

The relationships between social institutions may be seen as the functional or- ganization of the social system, as the distribution of power in the social arena, or as the interrelationships between social meanings. These three sociological views of institutional interrelationships find their respective bases in the understanding of *which* social institution is the basic institution, and which institutions are dependent upon it, peripheral to it, or derived from it. Functionalist sociology lo- cates the family as the foundational institution in the evolution of social institu- tions. Activist sociology avows that there is really only one institution that domi- nates social life, the economy. And Naturalist sociology maintains that language is the primary social institution, being the most commonly used and most fun- damental institution to the construction of all other institutions-in-use.

SOCIOLOGY I
Structures and Functions

The social system as a whole is composed of a number of institutional subsys- tems, each of which is responsible for carrying out a distinctive set of system- required functions. Social institutions are both the structural and the functional components of social systems; that is, the system's diverse roles are organized into structures such as the family, religion, the economy, etc., and these sub- structures fit together to form the overall social structure. Each of these institu- tional structures performs a distinct set of social functions, such as reproduction and nurturance, integration of values and beliefs, production and exchange, thus fulfilling the system's overall requirements for maintenance and continuity as a system.

The institution of the economy, for example, is mainly the structured or- ganization of occupational roles. These roles, hierarchically ordered in terms of power, prestige, and property rewards, make up an important part of the struc- ture of social stratification in modern societies, as explained in Chapter 5. The functions of the economic institution are basically to produce the goods and ser- vices necessary for the physical survival and the material enjoyment of societal members, and to distribute these goods and services among members in an or- derly manner for their consumption.

The fundamental functional requirements of any social system, its "functional pre-requisites" (Parsons, 1951) are carried out by a few core institutions that are central features of every social system. The family, or the institution of kinship, is acknowledged to be the *primary* core institution in every known or, according to many sociologists, any conceivable social system (Murdock, 1960). Almost equally universal are the core institutions of the economy, religion, and the polity.

These four core institutions together make up the basic structural backbone of any social system. Every member of a society plays the roles of child, parent, spouse, sibling, and the other roles in the kinship structure; every member does his or her part as employee, employer, buyer, seller, or consumer in the economic system; each has a role to play as priest or congregant, sinner or penitent, prophet or heretic in the religious organization of society; and every person in turn is citizen, taxpayer, voter, defendant, judge, or lawyer, prisoner or freeman in the polity.

In performing these roles, societal members simultaneously stabilize the internal structure of the social system and carry out the functions necessary for the system's growth and adaptation to external or internal stresses.

The family, in this regard, not only produces and nurtures new members so that the society can physically continue into the next generation, it also socializes future role incumbents, training them to be proper performers of their socially appropriate roles. The economy not only produces and distributes goods and services, it shapes the lives of its participants to fit more or less smoothly around their occupational roles, and integrates these roles in long-term relationships. Even conflict relationships, as between unions and management, between competing corporations, or between consumers and advertisers, may serve to bind the social system together in stable interactive relationships, rather than to tear it apart. Religion not only relates man to God in the proper manner, setting and reinforcing moral values for each societal member to follow in his own life, it also celebrates and teaches the unity and moral rightness of the social group, of the society itself as a holy entity. And the polity not only separates the rulers and ruled, the judges and the judged, into their appropriate role categories, it also binds them together in their common belief in the legitimacy of the society's political-legal procedures.

SOCIOLOGY II
Structure and Superstructures—The One Institutional
Reality and the Opiates of the People

Behind the institutional myths that, for instance, the family naturally requires male domination and female housewifery; religion requires tax-free real estate and male clergy; education requires degrees and the incarceration of whole youthful populations; politics requires fast executive decision making and governmental secrecy; and so on, there can be found one solid reality, and one genuine institution. The reality behind the myths is that people have to eat, goods must be produced and distributed, and large numbers of men and women performing many different activities must coordinate their activities and somehow cooperate in the vast human activity summed up under the heading of the economy.

Historically, whenever human beings have worked cooperatively to produce their daily bread and other necessities of life, they have generally produced a surplus. If this surplus were shared equitably among people, along with the work, society could be a humane paradise. Small groups, however, scheme and struggle to dominate the surplus, and when they have gained exclusive possession of it, they invent myths to justify their greed and perpetuate their elitehood.

Marx considered the economy the basic structure of society and the other, myth-encumbered institutions the *superstructure*. Activist sociologists make it their business to demystify the superstructure by unmasking the economic interests behind institutional false fronts. In its modern form, the truth of this Marxian insight is to be found in the dominance of conglomerate business corporations over every facet of life in the most modern of societies, what Activist Maurice Zeitlin calls "U.S.A. Inc."

Between the elite of the super-rich and the rest of us stands, as a major line of defense, the corporations. These legally established fictional persons have one simple purpose—to keep their blue-chip majority shareholders rich, and make them richer, by any means fair or foul. This may include bribing entire foreign governments, and bringing down elected presidents by hiring mercenaries, arming insurgents, and suborning the United States' intelligence agencies to plot and kill on behalf of a particular business corporation. It entails corrupting one's own government officials, falsifying the news, manipulating elections, controlling and directing what is studied and taught in universities, and propagating wars to sell more arms. The limited liability of the corporation, which protects the rich against the consequences of their greed, is firmly institutionalized in U.S. society. U.S. citizens only rarely discover for themselves the corporate power behind seemingly independent institutions.

★★

LEADING LIGHTS

Harvey Molotch on Oil in Santa Barbara

The case of the 1969 Santa Barbara, California, oil spill was a devastating blow to people's belief in the legitimacy of the institutional system. Sociologist Harvey Molotch claims that the accident itself, and its consequences for the local populace, was demystifying even without the aid of an Activist

sociologist to point out the moral of the story (Molotch, 1969).

People discovered through their own totally frustrated efforts to protect the California shoreline from further destruction by massive oil spills that: government regulatory agencies are owned and operated by the industries they are supposed to regulate; elected government officials at any level of government are powerless to confront large corporations on any issue; universities are owned, operated, and can be muzzled at will by large corporations; profit-making at any

cost to the environment or to other people's lives has been firmly institutionalized in this society, and there are no institutional means for countering this, or for pursuing any other goal.

★★★

In the Santa Barbara oil spill, the institutions of government and education were exposed, but only within a limited locality (the national institution of the "free press" did not point out the full implications of the story) and for a limited period of time (as with the war in Vietnam, people quickly seem to forget). Activist sociology is at work in a more continuous, and broader based frame of reference. They work to demystify all the false institutions. Religon diverts poeple from the struggle against social ills. The cults and dogmas that spring up and begin the dangerous process of institutionalization have to be demystified each time, starting with the question, Who really benefits? Government, no matter how often and how clearly its corruption is exposed, keeps rising Phoenix-like as the hope of idealistic people who see the need for social change but are conned into putting their efforts into the election of one more crook.

To further the process of revolution in modern Western societies, Activists must confront these and other false-front institutions. Significant change can only come when their legitimacy has been destroyed, one by one, in the minds and hearts of the people. That is why some have called the necessary path for a modern revolution "the long march through the institutions."

★★★

LEADING LIGHTS

Donald Hansen on Institutions as Ideologies

"Ideally, institutions are direct representations of the actions we have rationally and freely chosen, out of our clearly perceived needs. But, too easily, the link between human need and social prescription is lost. Out of hope, fear, and blindness, we simply follow the blueprints, uncritically and uncreatively. . . .

We are duped by elaborate sets of beliefs that make the conformity seem reasonable, that mask the reality of our situation and the reality of those who profit from our conformity.

These sets of beliefs, shared by men and women throughout society, are called 'ideologies.' They are, virtually, the 'masks' of institutions, leading us to identify incorrectly the sources of our troubles and to fail to see our possibilities. They even mask their own sources, leading us to think they are given by a god or that they have emerged through the working of human rationality over the centuries." (Hansen, 1976, p. 136)

★★★

SOCIOLOGY III
Language and Other Institutional Symbol Systems

Whereas the family is the core institution for Sociology I, and the economy is the core institution for Sociology II, Sociology III perceives language to be the social institution from which all others are derived, and upon which the others are modelled. It is also the institution whose uses in interaction can be most directly and commonly observed.

Language is a set of conventions that allow speakers and hearers, or writers and readers, to enter into and sustain meaningful relationships. All social relationships, all social interaction, must make sense to all participants. Language is therefore the crucial basis for the "social."

As an institution, language is surely the most conservative, most rigidly structured of institutions. Its words are written and defined in dictionaries, its grammars taught by rote for generations, its transmission from generation to generation precise even unto the minutest nuances so that one can distinguish a Brooklyn, or a Chelsea, or a Toronto accent. Therefore it is all the more remarkable that the most advanced linguists and sociolinguists should find that the outstanding feature of language-in-use is its creativity, its uniqueness from speaker to speaker and occasion to occasion. Speakers, even children, perpetually generate statements never before uttered or heard in the language, statements entirely correct and yet unpredictable from the rules of grammar or syntax. (See Chomsky, 1965.) What observers of language in social interaction see, in other words, is that speakers make language; language does not determine or program speech. After all, a language cannot be observed in the act of speaking a person, whereas our most commonplace observation is of people speaking languages.

The Naturalist's observation of all other social institutions in use in interaction reveals the same basic truth—interactants construct institutional forms or meanings in their interactions, using the institutions as instruments.

The way in which social institutions are observationally related to each other, then, depends on how participants in any particular occasion of interaction relate them. "Business before pleasure," "Blood is thicker than water," "Never borrow money from a friend," are cliches demonstrating the practice of relating social institutions with one another in social interaction. In such statements, we can observe participants making one institution prior to another, asserting the relative importance of different institutional relationships, separating institutional realms, and many other relationships.

Naturalists also consider the attempts of Functionalist and Activist sociologists to assert or prove the hierarchy of institutions functionally, historically, or scientifically to be prime exhibits in the gallery.

AN INNER VOICE

Which institution is most basic, the family, the economy, or language? We've been   *through the fact that my family is the basic institution for my introduction into society, my training or socialization as a social being, and family ties are still the ones that have the first and strongest claims on my loyalty and emotions. But it's also clear that the economy is where the power is in this society, and that you can find economic motives behind almost everything nowadays. "Follow the money," as they said in the film, All* the President's Men *and you find the basic truth about any social situation. Yet I can't deny that in order to talk about or act within any other social institution, I've got to use language, and follow all the conventions and rules of language as an institution to make myself understood. Not an easy question to resolve.*

HOW DO SOCIAL INSTITUTIONS CHANGE?

SOCIOLOGY I
Institutionalization, Differentiation, Bureaucratization

As we discussed in Chapter 7, the Functionalist theory of evolutionary social change holds that the process of *differentiation* is the central element in all societal change. Specifically, this means that as social systems evolve from simpler to more complex forms, more separate social institutions, more distinct sets of social roles and rules, emerge, or differentiate themselves, to perform distinct sets of social functions.

It is reasoned that whereas in extremely primitive societies the family may have performed all needed societal functions, more modern, complex societies have seen the differentiation of roles and rules around separate functions. The functions once performed by the family were then distributed over the core institutions of kinship, economy, the polity, and religion. These four basic institutions would represent the level of differentiation of, say, feudal social systems. We now experience the proliferation of institutions to cope with such functions of modern societies as: education, health care, mental health care, welfare, counselling, corporations, labor unions, advertising, entertainment, recreation, law, the police, the military, the civil service, professional politics, amateur and professional sport, and art, with new institutional roles and rules daily emerging to cope with newly recognized societal problems. In the past decades, we have witnessed the emergence of such institutions as environmentalism, poverty, nutrition, consumerism, meditation, abortion, women's rights, geriatrics, psychic phenomena, outer space, and communal living, to name just a few.

Functionalist sociology sees the process of differentiation as the general course of institutional change over the long run of social evolution. A few, all-embracing institutions combining the performance of many social-system functions in each institution differentiate into many more narrowly defined institutions, each performing perhaps a single social function, or at most a few functions.

This process has meant the progressive loss of social functions over time by the institution of the family, as each of the many functions it used to perform is taken over by a new, differentiated institution. (We shall deal with this proposition at length in the next chapter.) The addition of new institutions specialized to perform specific functions is an ongoing process that Functional sociologists call *institutionalization.*

Sociology I asks, how and why are new institutions formed? How do a set of differentiated social functions become a new collection of established patterns of action integrated around a central theme?

As an example, let us outline the rise of education as a distinct social institution. The teaching of the young in society was traditionally a family affair, according to the Functionalist reading of evolutionary social history. Progressively, from the apprenticeships offered by medieval craft guilds, through compulsory public education, to the vast bureaucratic machinery producing professionally taught courses all the way from prenursery to postdoctoral levels and even training for old age, education has been taken out of the realm of the family. During this process of differentiation, education has become more and more fully institutionalized.

Whereas the passing down of traditional folklore from the old to the young was an automatic feature of family interaction, we now have competing theories of education, professional educational theorists who argue and research the theories, and a large corps of professional educators who apply the latest educational theories in classroom practice.

Specialization is the first hallmark of institutionalization. When a form of social activity is being institutionalized, we find the generalists who had traditionally performed these and other functions displaced by specialists, who are chosen, trained, and dedicated to this single task as a profession. Every parent who has been convinced that the kindergarten or nursery school teacher knows best how and what to teach his or her child has experienced this facet of the institutionalization of education.

To speak in terms of social roles rather than of persons, as Functionalists prefer, it could be said that the function of education has been differentiated from other functions once performed by the family, and has become the nucleus for a new institution, education, through the formation and establishment of the role of educator. Educators are no longer simply the wisest elders in the family, they are professionally trained, career-oriented specialists in the function of education.

Within the institution of education, roles proliferate to perform ever more specialized subfunctions. Teachers at all grade levels and in all subject areas are trained more thoroughly in their specialities. Teaching the extra bright child or the slow or impaired is a career in itself. Curriculum development is recognized as a profession; school-government liaison positions become crucial jobs; and career professions for specialists, guidance counsellors, school psychologists, educational administrators, theorists, researchers, and teachers who teach teachers how to teach other teachers how to teach, all fill the ranks of the educational system.

Functionalist sociology warns that there is a danger point in this progressive development, a point of diminishing returns. In the development of every institution there comes a point in time when the performance of the social function for which that institution has been designed starts to take second place to the perpetuation, expansion, and aggrandizement of the institution itself. This is when institutionalization turns into bureaucratization, and an institutional "hardening of the arteries" begins.

Functionalist sociologists have made a study of bureaucracy and bureaucratization throughout the twentieth century (see Weber, 1905: Barnard, 1938; Blau, 1964; and Bendix, 1963, among others). These sociologists warn of the dangers our modern social systems face due to the ever increasing bureaucratization of social life.

Institutionalization is, among other things, the process of making the performance of a specific, differentiated social function into an ever more rational activity. Rational action in society, as Weber explained (Weber, 1905), is a kind of action in which the actor understands the technical relationship between means and ends, selects a goal or desired outcome that can be experienced and measured empirically, and consciously selects the means that will technically produce that desired outcome. The rational actor then is the one who manipulates things technically to achieve a goal, and who can see, touch, and measure the results of these manipulations to decide whether the goal has been reached or not, and if not, by how much it has been missed. We must realize, of course, that the vast majority of us act nonrationally most of the time.

Following Weber (especially Weber, 1905), Functionalists hold that tradition has been the major force governing social interaction, setting the rules and justifying reward and punishment throughout human social history. Even today, most of what we do in our everyday interactions we do because it has been done that way for years. We do not make calculated rational decisions about relationships between means and ends, in other words, we simply follow the patterns laid down for us by tradition and act in the appropriate manner for the situation we are in. Especially in family life, the most traditional of our institutional activities, we still behave in more or less traditional fashion, without much rational calculation as to outcomes.

But as modern social systems have become differentiated into specialized institutional subsystems performing specific social tasks, the pattern of organization and the mode of social interaction within the new institutions has become more fully rational. The major organizational instrument is bureaucracy, and the institutionalization of specialized social functions has meant the increasing bureaucratization of our social lives. What is bureacracy?

FOUNDING FATHERS

Max Weber on Principles of Bureaucracy

"I. There is the principle of fixed and official jurisdictional areas, which are generally or- *dered by rules, that is, by laws or administrative regulations. . . .*

"II. The principles of office hierarchy and of levels of graded authority mean a firmly ordered system of super- and subordination in which there is a supervision of the lower offices by the higher ones. . . . The principle of hierarchical office authority is found in all bureacratic structures: in state and ecclesiastical structures as well as in large party organizations and private enterprises. . . .

"III. The management of the modern office is based upon written documents ('the files'), which are preserved in their original or draught form. There is, therefore, a staff of subaltern officials and scribes of all sorts. The body of officials actively engaged in 'public' office, along with the respective apparatus of material implements and the files, make up a 'bureau'. . . .

"IV. Office management, at least all specialized office management—and such management is distinctly modern—usually presupposes thorough and expert training. This increasingly holds for the modern executive and employee of private enterprises, in the same manner as it holds for the state official.

"V. When the office is fully developed, official activity demands the full working capacity of the official, irrespective of the fact that his obligatory time in the bureau may be firmly delimited. . . .

"VI. The management of the office follows general rules, which are more or less stable, more or less exhaustive, and which can be learned. Knowledge of these rules represents a special technical learning which the officials possess. It involves jurisprudence, or administrative or business management. (Weber, 1905, p. 197—198)

◆◆◆

The modern bureaucratic organization of social institutions clearly is designed to make their performance of crucial social functions more efficient. Many Functionalists have gone on to show that even though such rule-bound, official, and abstract organization is the officially proclaimed policy in bureaucratic agencies, there is still a great deal of nonrational, personalized, informal social action that goes on in them. But Weber warned that bureaucratic organization can become too efficient. The rules, offices, professional training and hierarchy of control can come to be ends in themselves. Bureaucracy can then become, for all of us whose lives are organized by and through it, an "iron cage" that dehumanizes social life, and ultimately fails to perform the necessary social functions.

When is bureaucracy in social institutions too much? That is the question that Functionalist analysts of modern social systems still face.

SOCIOLOGY II
Debunking the Legitimation of Entrenched Power

Activist sociologists see modern social institutions, the components of our corporate capitalist systems or our socialist state systems, as barriers to the fulfillment of human potential in society. Activists therefore diagnose current institutional forms of organization as social ills. Helping others to see through the social lies is, as always, the first task for the Activist. Further, the "patient" must develop a willingness to get better. Sick institutions will crumble only when men and women jointly decide to tear them down, and erect humane, just institutions in their place.

But how did our current institutions get that way? How did they become sickening iron cages that alienate us from ourselves and from each other? How did we get an unjust legal system, a corrupt political system, a dehumanizing economic system, a meaningless, decaying religious system, a fragmented, frustrating family system, and an irrational educational system?

An Activist analysis of most modern social institutions in operation will show that their primary output in terms of social consequences is to keep the masses in their place. The goal of the elite is to perpetuate the institutions that keep them in power. The myths that make up modern institutions and which are their primary products serve this function.

Once a historically imposed form of social injustice has become institutionalized, it takes on the power and permanence of a natural law. It embodies its own social myth. It locks people into dehumanizing roles, making them the instruments of their own oppression and alienation. Institutions are the mental and physical cages in which we are all imprisoned. They are the instruments of repression, which, as we have discussed in Chapter 3, delude people into maintaining the system that oppresses them. The fight for freedom and justice must therefore always be a fight against the restrictions and delusions of sick social institutions.

Institutionalization, from this perspective, is not an inevitable, natural process as the Functionalists would make it out to be. It is the deliberate "carving into stone" of otherwise temporary victories in the class war, the entrenchment of power. It is a process that must be reversed, if we are ever to see movement toward a just social system.

The institutions must first be exposed, debunked, demystified, shown to be what they are—myths to make entrenched power seem legitimate. Let us return to the example of education and look at this institution through the Activist lens.

★★

LEADING LIGHTS

Ivan Illich on the Cultural Revolutionary

Ivan Illich doesn't call himself a sociologist, but he is a leader in the vanguard of social critics and analysts who fill our bill as Activists. He calls himself a "cultural revolutionary," and directs his attack on the ills of modern society, specifically at social institutions.

"We need an alternative program, an alternative both to development and to merely political revolution. Let me call this alternative program either institutional or cultural revolution, because its aim is the transformation of both public and personal reality. The political revolutionary wants to improve existing institutions—their productivity and the quality and distribution of their products. His vision of what is desirable and possible is based on consumption habits developed dur-

*ing the last hundred years. The cultural rev-
olutionary believes that these habits have
radically distorted our view of what human
beings can have and want. He questions the
reality that others take for granted, a reality
that, in his view, is the artificial by-product of
contemporary institutions, created and rein-* *forced by them in pursuit of their short-term
ends. The political revolutionary concen-
trates on schooling and tooling for the environment that the rich countries, socialist or
capitalist, have engineered. The cultural revolutionary risks the future on the educability
of man." (Illich, 1969, p. 181)*

★★

Illich's most frequent institutional target is education, that set of bureaucratically established myths that most of us in modernized societies take for granted.
Education performs such crucial social functions as, a) the secondary socialization of the young, giving them the skills and the motivations to perform their
complex adult roles; b) the pursuit and development of rational, technical solutions to the emerging problems a changing social system confronts; c) raising the
level of public literacy and knowledge required by participative political life; and
d) providing for individual self-discovery and personal advancement.

Supposedly in pursuit of these social goals, modern countries, both
capitalist and socialist, have poured billions of dollars into educational bureauc-
racies, allocating budgets second in size only to military budgets. Third world
countries spend even higher proportions of their gross national products on education (this is of course less money in absolute terms) trying to catch up to Western standards of education.

The results of this effort and expenditure, according to Illich's analysis and
documentation, are to make a "cult of the degree," to waste scarce societal resources (especially in the third world where such waste has tragic consequences), and most important, to perpetuate indivious class distinctions.

The cult of the degree, perpetuated by professional educators in their own
self-interest, is the myth that the number of years a person spends in school is an
indication of their general ability to cope with life. Degrees, diplomas, and certifi-
cates are granted primarily on the basis of years of schooling, so they become
the primary marks of competence. Persons compete with each other for jobs and
status on the basis of degrees, and countries distinguish themselves by having a
high number of average years of schooling per capita.

Paper qualifications issued by bureaucratically certified educational officials
become the sole means for measuring or guaranteeing the competency and
status of individuals and even of nations. Actual competency is not only ignored,
it can be seen to decline through neglect. So much money is spent on education
that the traditional means for instilling basic and even highly technical competency in a country's youth—apprenticeship, internship, on-the-job training, and
casual contact with adult role-models—all free exchanges between laymen—
become neglected, disused, and even shunned and despised.

Compulsory public education ensures that every person will come under
the tutelage of the professional educators. This means that not only is the only

legitimate pathway to success in life in the educators' hands, but also that at one level or another, that vast majority of the populace who do not earn an advanced degree have been measured and found wanting. To ask a person how many years of schooling he or she has had is to ask how far the individual got before he or she was rejected as no longer educable by the schools.

According to Illich, the schools fail an extraordinarily high proportion of the poor, and the ethnic or racial minorities, letting just a few of these slip by to the honored degree ranks to prove that the system is "fair." However this result may have been produced, Illich asks us to look at the effects. The losers in the class struggle are labelled as deserving losers. The rich and powerful have their degrees, or at least their children's degrees, to prove their superior social worth.

Compare the actual effects of schooling with the theoretical functions it is said to perform. The schools, right up to postgraduate study, serve as "holding tanks" to keep millions of young adults off the job market for many years. Unemployment would be unacceptably high if all these students were searching for work instead of in school. When they do leave school and hit the job market, more and more employers find them just as unprepared to do the job as unschooled youth, and have to train them on the job anyway. Many are overqualified for actually available jobs, which means their paper qualifications render them unsuitable for employment. The ranks of the unemployed are increasingly swelled with B.A., M.A., and even Ph.D. holders—again, even in the third world.

Ivan Illich argues that the true function of schooling is not to increase youths' abilities to produce or to create anything, but to train consumers:

> The more the citizen is trained in the consumption of packaged goods and services, the less effective he seems to become in shaping his environment. His energies and finances are consumed in procuring ever new models of his staples, and the environment becomes a byproduct of his own consumption habits. The design of the "package deals" of which I speak is the main cause of the high cost of satisfying basic needs. So long as every man "needs" his car, our cities must endure longer traffic jams and absurdly expensive remedies to relieve them. So long as health means maximum length of survival, our sick will get ever more extraordinary surgical interventions and the drugs required to deaden their consequent pain. So long as we want to use school to get children out of their parents' hair or to keep them off the street and out of the labor force, our young will be retained in endless schooling and will need ever increasing incentives to endure the ordeal. (P. 161–162)

Illich and his followers propose a truly drastic solution: the *deschooling* of society. Abolish compulsory education, they say, and pull all of that nonproductive money out of the educational bureaucracy. Let youths learn what they will through watching adults and asking questions, through apprenticeship, and through formal lessons in specific skills that they wish to acquire. But such lessons should be available to everyone and anyone, at any age, who wishes to acquire the skill taught. Reduce the system of education to anarchy, and let the people decide what they want to learn, how, and from whom, and, Illich predicts, genuine learning, of genuinely useful skills, will take place.

How to deschool society is a program still being worked out by the cultural revolutionaries.

The Illich attack on social institutions emphasizes the negative effects of the institutions on the society as a whole. Another mode of Activist attack focuses on the harmful effects of institutional involvement upon the individual, and advocates individual struggle against rigid social roles.

Institutionalized roles can be seen as distortions of the role player's true self. Institutions impose fundamentally negative conditions upon any human social relationship because they define, through social roles, what kind of people the partners in the relationship ought to be, and therefore prevent them from acting out and developing together who they really are. Men and women who begin to love one another for who they are, for instance, wind up judging, scolding, hating and even divorcing each other for the "housewife" or "breadwinner" the institution of marriage says they ought to be. Teacher and student, doctor and patient, policeman and civilian, executive and secretary—all of these relationship pairs interact with each other frequently, intensively, and intimately. Yet, because of the restraints of their respective institutional roles, they never get to know and respect each other as human beings, as full-fledged persons in their own right. I once knew a man who vowed he would never submit to surgery until he met a surgeon who really cared, personally, about *him,* and whether he lived or died. That man's prognosis is not good.

Institutional revolution will take place, according to this perspective, when large numbers of individuals independently assert their wholeness and humanity by breaking through the restraints of roles, by asserting their uniqueness and dignity regardless of the bureaucratic consequences. Those who summon up the "courage to be," to transcend roles and forge authentic interpersonal bonds across institutional boundary lines, are the true cultural revolutionaries. Those who liberate themselves from the bonds of role-playing, and thereby realize themselves, will shine as beacons of hope and courage for millions of others to follow.

In the dissolution of roles, the institutions themselves will dissolve in a bloodless, even soundless revolution. The dream is that there will come a day when so many have been liberated that "they" will declare a war, and nobody will show up to fight it for them!

SOCIOLOGY III
Useful Fictions

There is yet another, quite different, version of how institutions change. Sociology III agrees with Activists that social institutions are mythical entities that people could bring down just as they so assiduously build them up. But it also agrees with Functionalists that social institutions perform useful social tasks, even to the point of saying that people as social beings couldn't get along without them. The conventions that are thematically grouped into social institutions, Naturalists conclude, are immensely useful social fictions.

The usefulness of these fictions lies in the very fact that they can be set up and taken down again, like stage props in a play, for the interactive social occasion at hand. By definition, by mutual agreement, by command and compliance, or in many other ways, a scene can be established as an occasion of friendship, economics, politics, religion, kinship, or sport, and the attached sets of rules can be held to apply, giving our interactions their sense-making framework.

Institutionalization, then, for the Naturalist is the establishment of mutually agreeable sense in the course of any ongoing interaction. For the Naturalist, the institutions thus established are neither permanent structures nor mythical opiates. They are more like sand castles: tangible enough constructions of social participants, with definite, visible forms to them while they last, but subject to dissolution back into the malleable stuff out of which they were shaped, upon the next tide of social affairs.

Whether the bits out of which people form their meaningful social constructions are part of the human genetic heritage, or whether they are the primary elements of learned behavior picked up as children is not of major concern to the Naturalist. When one is admiring and learning to appreciate the design and usefulness of sandcastles, and the artfulness of their makers, one is not importantly concerned with where the sand came from.

Institution-building is the framing of interaction within a particular context of meanings so that it makes a particular kind of sense. Each institution labels a specific kind of sense, thus a specific kind of truth, a form of social reality. To observe institutionalization is to watch people making sense, to see them formulating and operating within the truth of religion, the sense of kinship, the reality of the economy, and the like. All of these institutional realms are commonsense worlds of reality, constructed within the more general framework of the primary institution, language.

One useful scheme for checking out the construction of a context of meanings is the basic story form used by journalists. Before you have fully described an event, the journalist's Rule goes, you must provide it with answers to the five "W" questions, What? Who? Where? When? and Why?

Assuming for the moment that the journalist's Rule is something like the general criteria everyday participants might have in mind when they make sense of their social situations, let us look at how the What? Who? Where? When? and Why? of social interaction becomes institutionalized.

What Is To Be Done?—The Institutional Motif

Social activities are often named by their participants with an explicit or implied institutional label attached. When asked, "What are you doing today?" if someone answers, "Going to church," or "Going to work," or "Going to school," or

"Going to the Game," the activities intended by these answers are clearly linked with the institutions of religion, the economy, education, and sport, respectively.

For Naturalists, it is in just such namings as they naturally occur, and in participants' references to the appropriate activities for the institutional situation, that the concrete existence of institutions is to be found.

The institutional heading provides the meaningful motif for the activities, and the activities, guided by participants' invocation of this motif, are the enactment of the social institution.

Institutional Identities

But institutions are more than "kinds of activities." They are also kinds of relationships between and among participants, and thereby provide a kit bag of masks of identity for the different players. The Who? involved in any particular situation might, in other words, be provided by the institutional identities taken on by participants. Reciprocally, by asserting a particular institutional identity, a participant is asserting the relevance of that institution for this situation.

The fact that language is the institution we are now constructing and being guided by in our ongoing interaction might be indicated by talk *about* our conversation (the institutional What?—that we are talking), and this could involve us in discussion of who is the speaker and who the hearer in a particular line of talk. What the speaker owes the hearer, or what the hearer has a right to expect from the speaker, could be the topic for talk about talk, specifically about identity rules and relationship rules in the institution of language.

Simultaneously, however, we might overlap another institution as relevant in the same situation. I might not only be the speaker and you the hearers, I might also be the professor and you the students. When I have asked my students to observe carefully the scenes of everyday activity in which they participate, they have most often perceived a great deal of complex institutional overlap of this kind. It is not only the overlap of language and some other institution, but also the overlap of kinship and religion, of friendship and education, of sport, economics, and politics, and so on.

This overlap situation implies that each of us may wear several different institutional masks of identity all at once. Somehow we all manage to negotiate this tricky and complex business with ease. Such is the artfulness of the Naturalist's favorite subject matter, the ordinary person.

The Appropriateness of Places—Institutional Space

Institutions are also kinds of places where kinds of participants perform kinds of activities. The church, the home, the office, the stadium, the courthouse, the school—these are just a few of the most obvious institutionally defined places.

But the definition works both ways. Once established as "the church," this space serves to guide our interaction inside it, to remind us of our appropriate religious roles and the appropriate religious behavior.

Spaces within which social interaction takes place derive their meaningfulness as places from their institutional identification. Naturalist research into institutional space seeks to discover how social interactants bestow meanings onto spatial environments, transforming them into social places. The other side of the coin is equally interesting. Once defined as a particular kind of place, how does a spatial setting exert control or influence over the activities taking place within it? Observations of this process make at least one finding repeatedly clear—both sides of the coin are perpetually being transformed and recreated. Even as the spatial setting is used to set boundaries on appropriate behavior for an occasion of interaction, it is being re-formed, is receiving new decorations of meaning from the participants. Every place has its history as well as its physical attributes, and that is why it is so difficult to speak about social space without also dealing with social time.

★★

LEADING LIGHTS

Laud Humphreys on Washrooms as Intimate Places

Naturalist Laud Humphreys (Humphreys, 1970), in observing the long-term patterns of interaction established among homosexual men in certain public washrooms (Humphreys took the participant role of "watch queen"), noted that the washrooms themselves were transformed by the participants into meaningfully private, special, erotically stimulating places. The history of past associations in and with the place would be discussed, interspersed with other conversation and activity, and participants came to feel that a particular washroom itself had inherently stimulating or erotic qualities. When *a "straight" outsider would venture into the socially decorated place for the purpose of using a public washroom, the contrast between the two institutionalized meanings of the place would become evident. The men would have to work to restore its wholeness. They did this mainly by jesting about the strangeness, the outsider quality, of the intruder into their private space. They even remarked how strange it was that the outsider should think this is just another public washroom, that he should be blind to the special qualities of this washroom.*

★★

Try the following experiment for yourself. Ask the new tenants or owners to show you around a house or an apartment that you and your family lived in for a number of years when you were younger. Say you're just taking a sentimental journey back to your youth, or doing a college assignment—they probably won't mind. But I predict that *you* will mind. You will be shocked and annoyed at how the new family is misusing the space in your old home. They don't know what is supposed to be family space, and what is clearly private space. Worst of all, look what they've done to *your* room!

The Institutional Clock

Institutional time is the kind of time (made up of sequences, durations, and frequencies) you experience when you are interacting under the official label of a particular institution. Prison time is "done" by inmates, work time is "sold" by workers, family time can be demanded by or freely shared with kin, religious time is "time out" from the work week, and so on. Institutions exist for the periods of time participants spend within their realms. They are particular forms of temporal order, just as they are particular forms of spatial order, and they can be seen to organize participants' experience of temporality (see Moore, 1963; Sorokin, 1964; DeGrazia, 1962).

Each social institution is a different kind of clock, with different intervals, and different meanings attached to the accumulation of temporal units. Kinship is measured from birth until death, and from generation to generation, celebrating birthdays, funerals, and daily meals in familial interaction. Religion also operates by the calendar, but this time is made up of Sundays, Saint's Days, and the progress of the soul from original sin to its eternal destination. The economy is made up of fiscal years, tax years, years to retirement, monthly salaries, weekly pay envelopes, daily piece work, and hourly wages. The polity careens from election to election. The new politics struggles against the old, the constitution has always been right all along, no matter how reinterpreted, and the life of the state is in its rise or in its decline, according to where one stands. Education clicks off standardized stages of mental development and ability, a sharp-edged temporal grid that also cuts off the slow, the backward, the retarded, and further separates the normal from the bright or gifted.

Everyone who participates in the multiplicity of institutional worlds making up modern social life not only wears a lot of masks, he or she wears as many watches, each ticking its own special time.

For Reasons of State—Institutional Framing of Motives

Finally, there is Why. Social institutions are themselves reasons, or motives, for our actions. They are available reasons we or others can attribute to our actions to make them sensible to others. It is only when people are called upon to account for themselves, or when others speculate upon "why he did it," that motives actually appear in observed social interaction. Talk about motives usually comes under the heading of gossip, but it can also be legal, medical, religious, familial, educational or economic talk as well.

Sociological Naturalism is perhaps the most different from other sociologies in this one regard: it does not inquire after the "truth" of motivation. It is not looking to establish scientifically *why* people behave the way they do. It is only interested in the motives people frame for themselves and others—the observable attribution of motives (Mills, 1940).

★★

LEADING LIGHTS

C. Wright Mills on the Attribution of Motives

Particularly in his contributions to the study of the "grammar of motives," C. Wright Mills demonstrated that he could take the role of Naturalist sociologist as well as being a leader among sociological Activists (Mills, 1940).

Mills proposed to "analyze the observable lingual mechanisms of motive imputation and avowal, as they function in conduct." He *defined motives as "imputed or avowed . . . answers to questions interrupting acts or programs," specifically, questions of the form "Why . . . ?" He called for the study of "the typical constellation of motives which are observed to be societally linked with classes of situated actions" (p. 908). Such observational studies are only now being seriously begun by sociologists.*

★★

One of the most useful features of social institutions is that in providing contexts of sense and meaning for our actions—identities, time, space, activities— they also provide typical sets of reasons for doing whatever we are doing, handily stereotyped motives that are acceptable to everyone.

I probably do not know, most of the time, the complex, detailed chains of motivation that may have produced my actions in a particular circumstance. I certainly do not know, ever, what particularly moved someone else to behave the way he did. But if either of us can say, with a vague degree of appropriateness, "It was a business matter," or "That's the way members of his family are," or, "It's the way friends behave with each other," that is enough for most intents and purposes.

Institutional labels announce standard motives. Just being in a bank is enough to assert some interest in money, just as being in a church indicates the probability of spiritual motives. Activities that announce their institutional meanings also announce the associated motivations. That is why motivation is such a rare and difficult activity to observe—most of it "goes without saying."

Thus, to answer our question directly from the perspective of Naturalist sociology, how do institutions change? First of all *they* don't do the changing. They *are* changed, by people, social participants who use them as instruments for their own purposes. And they are changed, if you will excuse the disrespect implied in the analogy, the way the bedsheets are changed, the way we change our clothing, the way we change our minds. Interactionally, participants can be observed to shift gears by changing into another institutional mode, either to meet and frame up a new situation, or even within the same situation, scene, or social occasion. The Naturalist perspective asks you to watch for institutional change in your own everyday life. At what moment, and through what interactional work, do we switch from acting just as friends to being buyer and seller? How does the meaning of space in my house become transformed when no relatives, but only a group of friends, are present? What happens to my interactional behavior when others signal to me that this is now religious time?

WHAT ARE SOCIAL INSTITUTIONS GOOD FOR?

It turns out that along the way to answering What are institutions made of? and How do institutions change?, we have been forced into answering our third question in advance of asking it. We have already said that institutions perform the required functions to keep the system operating, and form the system's major structural components, through the lens of Sociology I; that institutions serve to mask the true power structure and provide myths of legitimacy for the entrenched elites, and therefore more firmly establish the establishment, through the lens of Sociology II; and that institutions serve as definitional meaning-complexes, frames of reference, instruments for making sense out of immediate scenes of interaction for all social participants, through the lens of Sociology III. Let us then just recapitulate and elaborate this theme of institutional usefulness.

The basic theoretical argument of Functionalist sociology is that social institutions, and the particular formation of social institutions we happen to have, exist because they serve a necessary function for the social system. If the system is to survive and remain relatively cohesive and stable over successive generations, it must replenish itself with properly trained, properly motivated personnel. Hence, the family is necessary for reproduction and early socialization of the young recruits, and the institution of education is necessary for advanced, specialized socialization in a modernized society. If the system is to survive and remain relatively cohesive and stable, it must produce and distribute material necessities for the sheer survival of the population, and it must further produce and distribute whatever material luxuries are required to maintain at least the minimal level of satisfaction of the population's material demands; hence, the economic system. The system must maintain security of boundaries and advantageous relations with other social systems, and it must maintain law, order, and participative involvement, at least symbolically, within its own boundaries; hence, the polity. The theory runs right down the list of institutions, finding for each the contribution it makes to the functioning of the system, its reason for being.

Activist sociology insists on historical explanation for the existence of modern institutions in their peculiarly modern form. Corporate capitalism is the form of economic institution that has emerged in the West. This kind of an economy shapes and dominates the character, the structure, and the uses of all other contemporary institutions. The middle-class family, the facade of democratic politics, the charade of education of our youth, are the institutional myths that delude the masses. These myths serve to cloud the view of the people at large so that they cannot see clearly the activities of the elites, and their own chains of oppression. Functionalist sociology serves the purposes of the elites by making the institutional myths appear to be a part of the natural order of things. Until people begin to see through these myths, they will be unable to tear them down and cooperatively and freely build authentic institutions of their own.

From the Naturalist viewpoint, institutions are useful for, and everywhere used for, making common sense out of everyday social life. Language, first of all, is the most commonly used and useful institution. It is used to construct all of the other sense-making institutions. These institutional frameworks of sense, in turn, are used to construct a meaningful social environment surrounding any scene or occasion of social interaction in at least five dimensions. Social time, social space, social activity, social identity, and social motivation, are five dimensions in terms of which everyday scenes make sense to us, and we make sense of our lives as social beings. We build these meaningful frameworks out of kinship meanings, religious meanings, economic meanings, political meanings, art meanings, sport meanings, educational meanings, and the rest. In fact, it is only in use that social institutions are observable parts of social life.

What are social institutions good for? is the most important question one can ask about social institutions from any of the three perspectives. For Functionalists, institutions are defined and determined by the systemic functions they perform; for Activists, the institutions we experience in modern societies are exploitive devices; and for Naturalists, social participants can be observed to be participating "in" social institutions only insofar as they use them to make sense for and of one another.

❧❧

AN INNER VOICE

What would happen if we had a total social revolution and abolished all the oppressive institutions? No more family, no more economy, no more education, no more government or laws, no more religion. What then? What would we do in a state of complete social anarchy? Total freedom? Total chaos? Or total meaninglessness? Would we all then work together to establish new rules, new boundaries, new institutions to organize social life as we saw fit, according to our reasonable and cooperative human natures? Or would it be back to Hobbes' war of all against all? And how could we establish either total freedom or total war without the use of an established language? Suppose we could abolish only one institution. Which would cost us the least to lose, and gain us the most freedom by its abolition?

❧❧

---— DOING SOCIOLOGY ——

In the course of your regular clipping of the daily newspaper for your file, observe the layout of the newspaper as a whole, from page to page and from section to section. How have the editors of the newspaper divided the world into institutional realms? Have they covered all important institutions with one or more sections of the newspaper? Does this organization imply that the world of reportable events is "naturally" divided up into these institutional realms, or that the newspaper producers are helping to divide the world up that way in reader's minds? Develop Functional, Activist, and Naturalist analyses of the newspaper's "institutionalization" of the world, and present and debate your conclusions in a class discussion.

The Family

9

The family is a familiar institution in two distinct senses. It is the social institution with which each of us is most familiar. We probably first encounter the idea of social institutions through our experience of childhood's first and for some time only institution—the parents, children, and other relatives living together in our home. There is no other social institution that we take so fully for granted. Most of us have families, therefore we know implicitly what "the family" is, and we believe wholeheartedly in its existence as a fact of social life. In the second sense, the family is a familiar institution because it is one portion of our social lives in which we are interacting on familiar grounds. The family institution is where we are at home, in literal and figurative senses. It concerns our most intimate moments, our strongest emotions, our highest levels of trust and our deepest suspicions. Our kin are the social others we are closest to.

The consequence of this familiarity in both senses is that the family is the most difficult social institution to see, sociologically, and the easiest social institution to distort. It is difficult to be a sociologist of the family, because it is hard to step back from one's own personal involvement in family life, to take that sociologically necessary step into abstraction and statistical reasoning.

But the family can also be the most rewarding of social institutions to study for the same reasons. To add a sociological view, or even several sociological views, to the intimate knowledge one already has of this institution is to deepen and enrich one's total appreciation and enjoyment.

Studying the family sociologically has led some students into deep family problems; on the other hand, for some students it has provided solutions to family problems. No guarantee of safety or effectiveness is offered with this sociological introduction, however. It can only be said that the insatiable desire for the truth about all spheres of social life has led many sociologists into the sometimes sacred, sometimes profane, realm of family life.

Speaking sociologically, we may say that the institution of the family is that collection of established patterns of action that is integrated around the central theme of kinship. This is a particularly social definition. The family is a heavily studied institution, because it is totally concerned with relationships.

What are the differences between the ways that kin are expected to act and do act toward one another, and the ways in which they act and are expected to act toward nonkin? How are social participants identified, or socialized, or trapped in their kinship roles, by the patterns of action collected together under the heading, "Family"? And how does this social institution interact with the other major social institutions in society?

These are some of the general sociological questions framed by a sociological perspective on family life as a social institution. What does the family look like under the different perspectival lenses of Sociologies I, II, and III? What does your family look like if viewed from a Functionalist, an Activist, or a Naturalist point of view?

This chapter attempts to contrast as well as integrate the three sociologies' portrayals of the social reality of the family institution. To do this, we ask of each of our sociologies the following three questions: What, really, is "the family"? What is it good for? Will "the family" survive the twentieth century?

WHAT IS THE FAMILY?

SOCIOLOGY I
The Universal Institutional Structure of Kinship

From a Functionalist perspective social life is most significantly organized as a great system of mutually interdependent parts, components, or subsystems. The family is a major and crucial component of the social system. In fact, the functions it primarily performs—reproduction, nurturance, primary socialization, pair-bonding, control of sexuality, identification of offspring, intergenerational transfer of property and power, to name only some, make up the very life blood of the social system as a whole. The family can also be viewed as a subsystem in itself, with problems to solve, such as the balance between stability and change, or between cohesion and disintegration.

The family has been found to be a major institutional component in every known social system. In fact, recent compilations of reports by anthropologists, historians, archaeologists, and explorers show that the nuclear family unit, along with various forms of extensions, is a universal institution (Murdock, 1967). The nuclear family is composed of a conjugal pair and its recognized offspring. The problems involved in organizing, sustaining, and maintaining such units are equally universal. The variations in family structure from society to society, through history as well as in contemporary cultures, are also striking. The family unit may live in a home of its own, or the standard household may be composed of an *extended* family grouping (more than one conjugal pair plus their collective children). We shall examine such variations under the heading, "Will the Family Survive the Twentieth Century?" below.

Now let us look more closely, through the Functionalist lens, at the universal features of the nuclear family unit.

The nuclear family consists of the married couple and their legitimate (that is, recognized by society to be the rightful products of their marital union) offspring. Thus, this institution is the organization of the kinship roles of husband and wife, mother and father, parent and child, and brother and sister.

If it is true that the nuclear family unit is (with a few minor and explicable exceptions) the universal pattern of family life in all societies, then it must also be the case that monogamy is the most commonly recognized and approved form of marriage. Think about the necessary logical connections between these two, for a moment. Why would widespread polygamy (marriage between more than two partners), in the form of either polygyny (two or more women married to one man), or polyandry (two or more men married to one woman), or group marriage (two or more women married to two or more men) make the nuclear family structure extremely difficult to maintain? (A class discussion on this question will produce many more interesting answers than a text could, or should, provide. Therefore no answers are provided here.)

The same kind of empirical search across cultures and throughout history (also reported in Murdock, 1967) in fact shows that monogamy is the predominant marriage pattern. Although the polygamous variations are all to be found in one society or another, at some historical period or another, Functionalist sociologists conclude, after exhaustive comparative research, that within their own societies these deviations are exceptions to the rule, have exceptional causes, and require exceptional measures to handle their consequences.

In some societies where polygyny has been found, for instance, it is only the monarch who has many wives, whereas the rest of the population is traditionally monogamous. The multiwived ruler also has a staff of palace servants to keep his daily—and nightly—life organized and orderly, including state scribes or record-keepers to keep careful track of the order and standing of his many offspring. Cases of polyandry have been most often found among extremely poor groups of brothers who, between themselves, can only afford the purchase price and upkeep of one wife. Everyone suffers from the impoverishment of this relationship.

Monogamy is the preferred or normal pattern of marriage at the core of the nuclear family in all human societies, and in most of these societies extramarital sexual intercourse is officially forbidden even when it is tacitly acknowledged to be prevalent. This prohibition keeps sexuality within the bounds of marriage. Socially approved sex then is a nuclear-family affair, at least for adults, in most societies. This most explosive, most creative, as well as most potentially destructive of social interactions, is also carefully controlled within the monogamous nuclear family unit. The incest taboo is the third universal feature of the institution of the family (see Parsons, 1954). The incest taboo is "the prohibition of marriage and in general of sexual relationships between members of a nuclear family except of course the conjugal couple whose marriage establishes it." (Parsons, 1954.)

The nuclear family unit contains, then, both the only officially sanctioned and approved sexual relationship—the conjugal pair—and the most stringent prohibitions against sexual interaction to be found anywhere in society—the taboo against incest. Why should it amaze us that almost everywhere in human society, brothers must not fornicate with their sisters, nor fathers with their daughters, nor mothers with their sons?

For one thing, the taboo against incest seems to go against human nature, or at least against the animal nature of humans. We are naturally attracted, sexually, to those members of the opposite sex with whom we have much in common, with whom we have intimate day-to-day contact, to whom we have privacy of access, and toward whom we have developed intense emotional affection. What better natural candidates could there be for the object of our sex drives then, than our brothers or sisters, mothers or fathers, or pubescent sons or daughters?

It must take extremely powerful forces to curb our strongest natural desires. The universality of the incest taboo, and its apparent effectiveness, attests to the great power of social controls over individual actions.

The power of the opposed forces involved in this pattern of action also attests to great stresses and strains within nuclear families everywhere. Why do people put up with the incest taboo, and why does the family system expend so much of its power and energy to enforce it? We shall consider the Functionalist answer to this question under the heading, "What is the family good for?" Now we are only listing the basic universal features of family life.

The fourth and last family characteristic to be treated here is sexual division of labor, or role differentiation. The nuclear family as an institutional form universally comprises a structure of roles and role assignments that allocate different kinds of tasks to men and women.

Functionalists term the male role "instrumentalism" and the female role, "expressiveness." Functionalist sociologist Morris Zelditch (Zelditch, 1955) surveyed the anthropological accounts of nuclear family life in fifty-five societies and found that as a general rule, women assume an expressive followership role, while men take the instrumental leadership role. The man is the dominant member in the family, and the woman the submissive member, because of the different functions they perform in the family system and in the social system. As Parsons puts it (Parsons, 1954),

> An instrumental function is one primarily concerned with the relations of the group to the situation external to it, including adaptation to the conditions of that situation and establishment of satisfactory goal—relations for the system vis-a-vis the situation. Expressive function on the other hand is concerned primarily with the harmony or solidarity of the group, the relations internally of the members to each other and their "emotional" states of tension or lack-of it in their roles in the group. Zelditch makes it much clearer by applying this finding to "the American family" today (Zelditch, 1955).

★★

LEADING LIGHTS

Morris Zelditch on the American Male

"The American male, by definition, must   *"provide" for his family. He is responsible for*

the support of his wife and children. His primary area of performance is the occupational role, in which his status fundamentally inheres and his primary function in the family is to supply an 'income,' to be the 'breadwinner.' There is simply something wrong with an American adult male who doesn't have a 'job.' American women, on the other hand, tend to hold jobs before they are married and to quit when 'the day' comes; or to continue in jobs of a lower status than their husbands. And not only is the mother the focus of emotional support for the American middle-class child, but much more exclusively so than in most societies (as Margaret Mead has pointed out in her treatment of adolescent problems). The cult of the warm, giving 'Mom' stands in contrast to the 'capable,' 'competent,' 'gogetting' male. The more expressive type of male, as a matter of fact, is regarded as 'effeminate,' and has too much fat on the inner side of his thigh.''

★★

SOCIOLOGY II
The Exploitative Middle Class Myth

Activist sociology proposes that the most realistic way of looking at social life is as a large-scale arena within which the essential historical conflicts and struggles are fought. Within this arena, the myth of the family as a basic and necessary institution, and therefore the myth that our family roles are our most significant identities, serve primarily as a weapon wielded by the powerful to keep the masses powerless.

What is the family? The Activist does not ask this question in a world-historical context as the Functionalist does. The Activist asks what are the problems and troubles people experience with regard to family matters, and what are the emerging social issues concerning the late-twentieth-century family in industrialized corporate capitalist society, our own society.

The answer comes through loud and clear. The middle-class ideal of the nuclear family is a trap that destroys mature emotional relationships between men and women, humiliates, frustrates, and enfeebles women, and stunts or distorts the growth of children toward their human potential.

The family pattern imposed on everyone in this society is in fact a sickly distortion of the way we would organize our daily lives if we were free of economic pressures and conscious of our freedom to choose, that is, free of the mental control this society's propaganda exerts over us all.

People are desperately breaking out of this cage-like pattern every day, in increasing numbers, as the statistics on divorce show (United Nations, 1974). But they do not, by and large, have a sociological understanding of their troubles because, as the same public records show, most divorced people get married again soon after. They assume, apparently, that the stresses and strains of the first marriage were their own, or their spouses', personal problems and inadequacies, and failed to see the sickness of the pattern and the system itself. Thus, they walk right back into the trap.

The approach of Activist sociology to the family as a sociological problem is to listen first of all to those who combat its evils, who cry out against its inequities, who are beginning to mobilize themselves to fight for significant social change in this particular theatre of operations in the arena. The Activist concludes from these observations that the family is not a functioning subsystem of the social system, but a major battleground in the contemporary war of human liberation. The truth about the family as a social institution appears as follows:

The oppression, the alienation, the dehumanization of women in this society can be directly attributed to the imposition of the nuclear family pattern. This is not to say that all men, or men in general, are the perpetrators or the beneficiaries of this oppression. Men suffer from this cookie-cutter arrangement too. But women suffer most, and it is women who, in their burgeoning struggle for social justice, have begun to attack the nuclear family system as a major source of institutionalized injustice in this society.

★★

LEADING LIGHTS

Louise Mitchell on the American Female

To quote a self-identified "radical feminist" on the oppression of women by family rules and roles: "The situation of women is different from that of any other oppressed social group: they are half of the human species. In some ways they are exploited and oppressed like, and along with, other exploited classes or oppressed groups—the working-class, Blacks, etc. . . . Until there is a revolution in production, the labour situation will prescribe women's situation within the world of men. But women are offered a universe of their own: the family. Women are exploited at work, and relegated to the home: the two positions compound their oppression. Their subservience in production is obscured by their assumed dominance in their own world—the family. What is the family? And what are the actual functions that a woman fulfils within it? Like woman herself, the family appears as a natural object, but is actually a cultural creation. There is nothing inevitable about the form or role of the family, any more than there is about the character or role of women. It is the function of ideology to present these given social types as aspects of Nature itself. Both can be exalted, paradoxically, as ideals. The 'true' woman and the 'true' family are images of peace and plenty: in actuality they may both be sites of violence and despair. The apparently natural condition can be made to appear more attractive than the arduous advance of human beings towards culture. . . ." (Mitchell, 1971, pp. 99—100)

★★

Women are oppressed by being forced into the subservient, "expressive" role in the family, and in all areas of social life, regardless of their preferences or capabilities. The sexist ideology of the nuclear family allocates to women the unpaid, dishonored task of housework. For the more than 40 percent of women with jobs outside the home, housework—cooking, cleaning, and the rest—is an additional burden to their hours of commuting and wage labor.

The lower pay given to women for the less satisfying jobs they can get is justified or rationalized by various aspects of this imposed family role. Supposedly they are less effective at instrumental tasks, less aggressive, less practical, and less efficient than men. Supposedly child bearing and early child rearing prevent them from developing the professional skills and executive experience that carries successful men to the top managerial ranks. Supposedly they are "naturally" more capable of caring for houses and for children, and less capable of taking care of themselves, than are men. Therefore men must take care of their wives economically, while their wives take care of home and children.

The restriction of women to household tasks and insignificant jobs works in two directions to impoverish our society, according to this diagnosis. Women individually are denied the freedom to shape their own lives and to realize their human potentialities, and society at large is denied the creative energies and the socially constructive contribution of half of its adult population!

Dr. Benjamin Spock is recognized as the world's leading expert in early child care, and two of the world's toughest political-military leaders were Golda Meier of Israel and Indira Ghandi of India. Are we to assume that these people were all born into the wrong sex? The myth of sex-linked social capacities emerges directly from the myth of the necessity and inevitability of the nuclear family pattern.

The family is this society's bloodiest "Procrustean bed." Procrustes was a legendary Greek robber who insisted on the physical uniformity of his victims. Maniacally, he decreed that all must be of exactly the same height. Procrustes had a bed-shaped instrument built, which combined the features of the torture rack and the guillotine. Laid out on this couch, the victims who measured too short were stretched until they reached the required height, while those who were too tall were simply chopped off at the benchmark. The modern Procrustean bed of the nuclear family may stretch men all out of shape to make them fit the dominant, nonexpressive, competitive, and success-oriented ideal, while the women of our society are chopped short by it.

SOCIOLOGY III
The Chinatown Phenomenon

Naturalist sociologists combine an almost fanatical insistence on observation with the art critic's appreciation of what they observe. Within the Naturalist gallery are a number of careful descriptions of social activity labelled "Family Life." Except for this label, there are few similarities to be seen between any two of these descriptions. Observed with open eyes, the standard rituals of behavior that constitute family life appear to be exceedingly strange, even incomprehensible. Yet most family members consider their families normal and "just like everybody

||| else's family." This paradox is the double blind-alley down which an observational search for the truth about family life leads us.

★★

LEADING LIGHTS

Jules Henry on the Horrors of Family Life

Practicing as an Activist and as a Naturalist, Jules Henry observed the day-to-day interactions of the families of young people who had been committed to mental hospitals, most of them diagnosed as schizophrenics. Henry stayed as a house guest in their homes, participated in the meals and other routines of the household, and made careful, round-the-clock observational notes. He reports in a monograph titled Pathways To Madness *(Henry, 1971) how he was able to see family members driving one another mad and he presents enough of his raw descriptive data to enable his readers to see and understand this process as well.*

Through this work, Henry is trying to change our society on two fronts. He wants to dissuade mental health officials and professionals from viewing "insane" persons as emotionally impaired within themselves, and hence needing therapy to re-adapt them to their environments. In Henry's view mental patients are persons who appear to others to be "mad" because they are coping as best they can, as rationally as any one of us could, with continuously irrational, contradictory, maddening demands and cross-pressures from their families. Therapy, under this view, would be designed to cure the "mental illness" in the patient's family, not in the patient, who is merely the most vulnerable and symptom-displaying victim of the family's illness. On the second front, Henry wants his readers to begin to learn about their own family lives, to see in the madness he describes a reflection of such interpersonal destructiveness in our own homes.

Henry's Naturalist contribution is to lead us, by way of his careful descriptions and deep analysis of the meanings of the family interactions he observes, closer to a Naturalistic answer to the question, "What is the family?" Henry presents exhibit after exhibit of interactive exchanges over the course of the family's daily social life in which family members can be seen constructing, repairing, and maintaining what Harold Garfinkel (Garfinkel, 1967) and other Naturalists have called "the structure of normal appearances."

Henry observed parents starving a child by force-feeding it so brutally and angrily that the child could not eat. The parents have heard that it is quite common to have a child who refuses to eat, and that it is their duty as loving parents to feed the child, for the child's own good. They express their love for the child by forcing it not to eat, and they hate the child for not eating the food they lovingly supply. Their older child is an institutionalized mental patient, and they cannot understand what went wrong with this child because they had provided it with a "perfectly normal home life." The point of this story, together with the numerous other horror stories exhibited by Henry, is not that these families are doing abnormal and psychically destructive things to one another in the name of normality, but that whatever family members do to and with each other is considered, within that family, to be "perfectly normal" family interaction.

★★

Perhaps the point can be made more clearly if we turn to some observations of family life where mental illness or psychic destructiveness is not at issue.

In teaching a course on "The Sociology of the Family" to a class of seventy undergraduates at a suburban campus of a North American university, I assigned my students the task of "switching" families for one standard weekday evening at home, including the evening meal and subsequent interactive activities. Each student paired up with another of the same sex, approximate age, and where necessary and possible, the same race, nationality, religion or ethnicity, and general economic standing. The pair arranged in advance with their respective families to have the double stand in for the real family member at an evening meal at home, preferably scheduling both visits for the same night.

The stand-ins were instructed to attempt to participate smoothly and naturally in the preparation, serving, eating, and aftermath of the family meal, relying on their familiarity with normal mealtime routines in their own families. They were not to ask questions about "how it is done" or "what am I supposed to do" here. Then each student was scheduled to have a conference with the double to check out mutual misunderstandings and puzzlements after the fact, and to write up a descriptive report on what happened.

The reports universally emphasized and documented what we came to call "the Chinatown phenomenon." A then-current movie called "Chinatown" gave us our label for the recurrent pattern observed by the substitute family diners. In this movie, the private detective hero gets deeper and deeper into the labyrinthine mysteries of the economic-political system of Los Angeles and the even more mysterious relationships and personal histories of his client and her relatives. As the detective becomes progressively confused about what is going on in this case, he refers offhandedly to the good old days when he was a police detective assigned to the Chinatown beat. There, you never knew what the hell was going on either, but at least you knew you were an outsider in Chinatown and weren't *supposed* to know what the hell was going on! The point of the movie, and hence its otherwise irrelevant title, was that to probe deeply beneath the apparently normal surface of anybody else's life is to become as much a confused stranger as if you were a Caucasian cop in Chinatown.

That is how my student stand-ins came to feel after probing only enough to try to eat dinner "naturally" as a pseudo-member of somebody else's "typical" nuclear family. They found that they didn't know what to do next or how to do it appropriately, and they were so discomfitted by the fact that they couldn't understand what was going on or why that many of them could hardly eat, much less enjoy the food.

Keep in mind that virtually all of the social and economic variables that might be used to account for differences between family types or styles—economic class, regionalism, ethnicity, etc.—were controlled in this experiment by matching backgrounds. Further, despite the fact that each family had been asked not to treat the stand-in as a guest, but as the son or daughter of the house, in their ensuing conferences the student pairs discovered that in numerous ways, families had put on special manners and special modes of interaction for the guest. They had significantly altered their normal routines and did dinner so as to make the guest feel at home. It appeared that each family stereotyped or consciously normalized its family idiosyncrasies to present a more standard version of the "typical family dinner" for the guest. What then were the differences the student diners observed that made the encounter so strange and unpredictable for them?

How do you know when and if you have been called to the dinner table? Does the college-age son or daughter help with preparation or serving of dinner or simply go to the table like a guest? Do you go to a sink and wash up first, or go right to the table? Where do you sit? Do you wait for the mother to be seated, or let her stand and serve food while the rest eat? Is grace to be said, and if so, how and by whom? Do you place your napkin or serviette on your lap or under your chin, or leave it on the table? Do you drink wine before, during, or after eating, with or without toasting, or at all? Do you help yourself, wait to be served, or serve each other? Does one person speak at a time, does everyone speak at once, is there no talking at all during eating? Do you remain at the table until the meal is over or do you get up, walk around, and sit down again at will? Is there joking and laughing or must serious, quiet demeanor prevail? Are there subjects and topics about which one does not speak during the meal? Which topics? Are you expected to comment on the food as you first taste each dish, or will a general appreciation at the end of the meal do, or is no such comment called for or appropriate?

These are but a few of the behavioral puzzles the students reported they had to solve without adequate guidance from what was standard operating procedure in their own homes. This is to say nothing of the even deeper strangeness and incomprehensibility of the personal-history references and other pecularities of what was said in dinner-table conversation.

The students found themselves in "Chinatown" at each others' family dinner tables. Then they went back to home base and, at the next available opportunity, discussed the strangeness of the way the other students' family had dinner. In subsequent class discussions, they reported on the reactions of their own families, and these reports contained a remarkable similarity. All of the students' own families thought that the other family's practices were indeed strange, even abnormal, in some cases positively morally *wrong*. The right way, the normal way, the appropriate and typical way to have family dinner is the way *we* do it, the way *everybody* does it unless there is something wrong there, something strange about those people. *We* have dinner in *family* style, not like *that*.

What is the family? From the Naturalist's perspective, it is a convenient label used to normalize the unique, idiosyncratic patterns of action established within a particular household grouping, to generalize and typify the interactive behavior we experience among those we identify as kin. This normalization and generalization, this glossing over of the "Chinatown" strangeness and difference between one localized collectivity's standard practices and meanings and another's, is a cultural lie that allows us to live with peace of mind. The lie is that there exists something called the institution of the family, and we live in it and are organized in our behavior by it.

AN INNER VOICE

Now here's a social institution I can get my teeth into. It's there, no question about it, and the Functionalist research showing its universality certainly implies that it is created and sustained by forces above and beyond any of our single lifetimes. And after all, I've got one, of sorts. But perhaps it is oppressive, in many ways—how could this be fought? It would really take some doing, to my mind, to see something as solid and stable as the family as the creation of my own family member's definitions of things.

WHAT IS THE FAMILY GOOD FOR?

SOCIOLOGY I
Vital System Functions Performed by the Family

Functionalist sociology leads us to seek knowledge of the universal features of family life across cultures and throughout history. Then it asks, Why should these be the universal features? Why do all societies establish the nuclear family pattern? Why do most societies prefer monogamy? Why do all societies enforce the incest taboo? And why is there sexual role differentiation in most societies, with the men performing the "instrumental" functions, and women assigned to the "expressive" functions?

The general Functionalist answer to all such requests for explanation is to turn to the social system and assess its needs. The answer to all of the why's in the preceeding paragraph is that the system requires it so. There must be specific functions performed by these institutional arrangements that are so fundamental to the survival of any social system, that every society must have them or it wouldn't survive.

What are the societally necessary functions performed by the nuclear family subsystem, particularly by the elements of monogamy, the incest taboo, and sexual role differentiation?

LEADING LIGHTS
Talcott Parsons on the Main Function of the Family

We shall follow the theoretical reasoning of Functionalist Talcott Parsons (Parsons, 1955) in outlining the answer of Sociology I to this question.

For a social system to persist through time, it is necessary that its members not only reproduce biologically, but that they reproduce new recruits to the social system whose personalities are molded suitably for the needs of that social system. "It is be-cause the human personality is not 'born' but must be 'made' through the socialization process that in the first instance families are necessary. They are 'factories' which produce human personalities" (p. 124).

★★★

The first and foremost function of the nuclear family is reproduction of the species. But it is equally crucial for the social system that those who are reproduced be effectively socialized. For this a prolonged, intensive, and emotionally stable period of nurturance is required, long beyond the end of that natural period of time when biological nurturance is needed by the relatively helpless human infant. To become a minimally socialized human, an infant must receive the care and early supportive training that only a mother can be counted upon to provide for her own child. In addition, the child must "graduate" from the totally supportive, nurturing socialization of the mother to a second phase of socialization—the training in skills, discipline, and values that will prepare the child to learn and perform an adult role. Only the father (or, as in some societies, the mother's brother taking on the father role) can be relied upon to consistently and effectively perform this second crucial task of childhood socialization.

These two early phases are called *primary socialization.* Later, either the extended family or other specialized social institutions such as education may participate in the *secondary* socialization of the child. But the socialization process goes on throughout a person's life, and an even later crucial phase is also the unique responsibility of the nuclear family.

> The basic and irreducible functions of the family are two: first, the primary socialization of children so that they can truly become members of the society into which they have been born; second, the stabilization of the adult personalities of the population of the society. (Parsons, 1955, p. 128).

By being a mother and a father to their children, the conjugal pair of the nuclear family socialize themselves and each other, are even socialized *by* their infant children, into mature adulthood, the stage at which one has acquired a stable adult personality and can take on one's full share of social responsibility. Parenthood as well as childhood, then, are crucial periods in the molding of adequately socialized personalities.

Children become socialized by internalizing the models of the social system, its modes of acting and its values, that their parents provide for them. Parents become further socialized into mature adults by internalizing again, in a new context, the models their parents set for them as parents. They do this in order to properly perform their new roles as parents.

To focus on the socialization experience of one male-female pair,

Functionalist theory would say that this couple is first subjected to primary socialization within their respective "families of orientation" (the families into which they were born) and then subject themselves to further socialization within their "family of procreation" (the family in which they are the parents).

In order to have a stable social system in which most members are, most of the time, self-regulated, self-motivating, and self-disciplined functionaries of the system, this dual process of socialization must be relatively successful throughout the population. The combined structural characteristics of the monogamous, incest-taboo governed, sex-role differentiated nuclear family produce the long-term general conditions necessary for such success.

Monogamous parenthood provides for the necessary recognition, identification, and emotional bonding of father and mother with their child, as well as the loyalty and love that maintains long-term stability of the social bond.

The incest taboo regulates and stabilizes the relationships of authority, responsibility, and caring within the nuclear family structure. Lines of communication, of command, and of loyalty are stabilized by the taboo's control over the types of love that are allowed and encouraged between mother, father, sister, and brother. This internal organization of the nuclear family, sustained by these sexual limits, is the necessary social context for both types of socialization to flourish.

The differentiation of sex roles into "instrumental" functions for the father and "expressive" functions for the mother provides for the success of nuclear family socialization on both external and internal fronts. Externally, it is the father who must provide for the support and protection of the nuclear family group during those extensive periods of time when the mother's time and energies are completely taken up with child bearing, nurturance, and early child rearing. He must be socialized to take on instrumental functions in the outside economic and political world, therefore, as his specialty. Internally, the mother must be socialized as the expert in emotional and physical nurturance, the "expressive" functions. The adult male in his specialized capacity must also facilitate the child's transition into secondary socialization. Further, the continuity of the social system through the child's internalization of the adult models presented by parents depends on the presence of an adequate female model for daughters and an adequate male model for sons, to identify with and follow.

SOCIOLOGY II
The Substitute Arena

A militant feminist (Morton, 1970, cited in Mitchell, 1971) agrees with Talcott Parsons that the family serves the society in the capacity of "a factory." As an actual productive unit in society, as distinct from "the family" as an ideological myth, Morton argues, the family serves the changing needs of the capitalist industrial system. In earlier capitalist development, large numbers of workers were needed to man the assembly lines and the mines, and the family dutifully produced children by the dozen. More recently, advanced capitalism has required fewer laborers, but more highly trained and better disciplined workers in automated, capital-intensive plants and in the service sector of the economy. The family has adapted perfectly, producing fewer children per unit, but socializing each one more intensively and skillfully.

> The family is therefore important both to shoulder the burden of the cost of higher education, and to carry out the repressive socialization of children. The family must raise children who have internalized hierarchical social relations, who will discipline themselves and work efficiently without constant supervision. (Morton, 1970, p. 223)

The oppression of women in the Procrustean bed of the family is necessary to the capitalistic industrial state, say radical feminists. Sexism or male dominance based on the myth of "differentiation" operates to disqualify half of the potential aspirants to positions of authority and high reward before there can be any open competition on the basis of merit. The supposed openness of the society to upward mobility by achievement is thus closed by ascription for 50 percent of the population. This sexual caste system has obvious advantages to men in power.

Women in the work force are also socialized into selling their labor more cheaply, adding greatly to corporate profit margins. And the labor-value of women's housework is consumed entirely without cost to the corporate economy. Perhaps the major economic function of the nuclear family pattern, however, is to consume for an industrial economy that requires maximum waste, maximum turnover of new products, and maximum purchase of unneeded commodities for its continued expansion and profitability.

Compare the material requirements of a household set up among six college students for a few undergraduate years of off-campus living with those of the nuclear family household unit. (We shall consider various other long-term alternatives to the nuclear family under the next subheading, "Will the Family Survive the Twentieth Century?") The "roomies," even if they are well off, can get along quite well in one multibedroomed apartment, with one telephone, one stereo hi-fi set, one television set, one washer and dryer, one large set of dishes, silverware, pots and pans, one stove, one fridge, one dishwasher, one set of living room, dining room, and kitchen furniture, one collection of lamps and carpets, and perhaps even, in a pinch, the sharing of two or three automobiles among the six. To make the comparison fair, let us assume the six go on to marry six others of the opposite sex who have survived through the college years in similar style. The six couples then set up their typical nuclear family households, and lo and behold, the necessary commodities-per-capita triple in number even as their use is reduced to one-third. For twelve persons we now require the purchase of six telephones (plus extensions), six hi-fi's, six TV's, six washers and dryers, six stoves, six fridges, probably, in suburban America, *twelve* autos, and a partridge in a pear tree! Even with the inevitable arrival of two-point-six children per household, the economies-of-scale do not improve, for now we have nurseries full of cribs, garages full of strollers, and toy boxes full of roller skates to add to our collection, six at a time.

The advantages of the nuclear family pattern to the corporate capitalist economic system are not all directly and obviously economic, however. As the subtitle of this subsection indicates, the sociological function of the nuclear family system lies primarily in its use as a "substitute arena" for working out social frustrations through struggle and conflict.

German sociological "Founding Father" Georg Simmel has noted (Simmel, 1955) that it is in the most intimate love relationships that we, paradoxically and humanly, express our deepest and most destructive hostilities. That nuclear families are our society's bloodiest battlegrounds is a social fact reflected in our murder rates. The most frequent relationship between murderers and their victims is that of husband and wife, followed only by parent and child, other familial relations, and then unmarried lovers. Short of murder, we have enormous rates of physical violence between husband and wife, even if we only count the minority of occurrences that get reported as domestic disputes on police blotters, and even more horrendous rates of reported and unreported child abuse.

Activist C. Wright Mills calls for sociological imagination (Mills, 1961) to guide people in our society to see that their "personal troubles" are in fact largely treatable symptoms of "social issues." With revision, this can be applied to the Activist analysis of the modern family institution. The institutionalization of the nuclear family in our society convinces us that the circle of those others with whom we can legitimately share our triumphs and tragedies in life, with whom we can feel any deep group solidarity, is this pitifully small group of husband, wife, and children. The society is atomized, fragmented, not so much into isolated individuals, as into even more isolated because insulated nuclear family groups. We cannot develop solidarity with others who suffer the same economic and social injustices, our social class. We are injured by the society's injustices, but these remain the "hidden injuries of class" (Sennett, 1972). Instead, we are channeled into "taking it out" on our husbands, wives, and children, even as we take it out on ourselves (in suicide).

The millions of mini-wars raging within nuclear families thus prevent a full-scale, all-out class war in our society. In this way, the nuclear family functions to preserve the stability of the social system.

SOCIOLOGY III
Comforts of Familiarity

We observe ourselves and others in the act of glossing over the idiosyncratic rituals of daily household interaction and stereotyping our uniquenesses under the generalized heading of "normal family life." From the Naturalist perspective, this glossing, this stereotyping, constitutes the cultural lie called the institution of the family. The question, "what is the family good for?" can only be answered naturalistically by inquiring, observing, and analyzing what social participants use it for.

Why do people gloss over the idiosyncracies of their household rituals? Let us speculate a bit, and see if our proposed solution rings true.

The problem people face universally in their social lives is this: How do I construct for myself a space, a time, an identity, a recurring situation in which I can freely express the *private, personal* meanings of my everyday life? How can I do this in a wider social setting in which *universal* meanings, established ways of seeing and talking about things, seem to dominate?

Wouldn't a powerful solution to this problem be to define and characterize my private life as a publicly accepted stereotype, to give it a generalized label that makes it appear to be, in some sense, just like everyone else's private life?

Seen in this light, the paradox of the "Chinatown phenomenon" takes on a new meaning. The claim to a "normal family life" can then be seen as a very useful, even strategic, lie to cover and protect, with a veil of normalcy or legitimacy, the privacy and intimate idiosyncrasy of our actual home lives.

"The family" as a social institution in the Naturalist sense is therefore, among other things, an instrument or device that people use to effectively divide up their life-worlds between public and private realms. Behind this publicly acceptable label, people are free to construct their own worlds of private meanings. The nuclear family is the ultimate self-defined "we," protected and counterposed against all others "out there" in society.

WILL "THE FAMILY" SURVIVE THE TWENTIETH CENTURY?

SOCIOLOGY I
Lost Functions, New Functions, the Specialized Family

Functionalist sociology views change in the structure of the social system and its parts as a long-term evolutionary process. In this view the family has an evolutionary history as a subsystem in its own right, as well as an evolving relationship with other institutional subsystems and with the social system as a whole. The overall course of societal evolution has been the transition from traditional to modern structures and values. The family also has traditional as well as modern forms, with several varieties in between.

The traditional family pattern, to be found in ancient societies as well as in contemporary social systems that have not yet been modernized, is the *extended* family. The traditional family household includes not only the married couple and their children, but also the grandparents. It also may typically include the brothers and sisters of one or both parents and their spouses and children.

Cousins, uncles, nephews, and nieces may therefore all be included in the traditional family household group. Add to this the fact that each couple would be traditionally expected to produce large number of children, and we have a much larger group, numerically, and much more complicated internal organizational patterns in the traditional household than anything we might experience today.

Beyond the household grouping, kinship relations with members of the extended family, grandparents, uncles, aunts, cousins, great-uncles and great-aunts, great-grandparents living or deceased, and second cousins, are important and obligatory features of everyone's interactive social life in the traditional family pattern. The traditional family thus organizes the major portion of roles and relationships in the traditional social system. For most members of this system, the family is the all but comprehensive institutional structure.

The functions performed by the traditional family are also comprehensive. The production, distribution, and consumption of material goods may all be carried on within the family. The family may embrace the exercise of political authority, the establishment and application of legal rules, and the relative distribution of rights and power. All the socialization of the young, from primary nurturance to technical training for adult roles, are handled by kin. Worship is conducted in family ritual, and the health, recreation, and welfare of each member is a family affair, from the cradle to the family cemetery.

The transition from traditional to modern family patterns can be measured, in the Functionalist view, by the progressive loss of members of the household, of serious relationships with nonhousehold kin, and of traditional family functions.

Through the process of modernization, the traditional family household has been whittled down in size to the isolated nuclear family today. The grandparents, now colonized in retirement homes, were the last to go. Relations with outside kin have been progressively reduced to the greeting cards and pro-forma holiday gatherings we still feel obliged to maintain. And the functions performed by the traditional family have been successively taken over by the specialized institutions of the state, law, corporations, the educational system, church, communications industries, health care, welfare, and the like. (We don't have space or time here to go into the Functionalist explanations for why modernization of the social system has entailed all of these losses by the traditional family pattern. Let us merely consider the fact of this loss, and its consequences for the future of the family.)

We are left with the modern nuclear family and its attenuated functional responsibilities. But even this truncated structure is in the process of further breakdown under the relentless assault of social change. Divorce rates continue to rise in all sectors of modern society, until amost one out of every two marriages contracted today can be expected to terminate long before "till death do we part" (Reiss, 1976, p. 308). Larger and larger numbers of married women, even with young children, are taking up full-time jobs outside the home. Children are nurtured and trained in nurseries and day care centers by professional child-care personnel at younger and younger ages. Projecting these continued losses to the not-so-distant future, we confront the possibility of the functionless nuclear family. Will the family then become extinct as a general social institution?

Functionalist Talcott Parsons argues that despite all of these indications, predictions of the death of the nuclear family pattern are, at the least, premature (Parsons, 1955). Divorces are concentrated among those most recently married, couples without children, and there is a high rate of remarriage among divorced individuals. "Even though married before and divorced," Parsons says,

> once people settle down to having children there is a relatively high probability that they will stay together . . . . In spite of a situation where it has become economically easier than ever before for single women to support themselves independently, the proportion of the population married and living with their spouses is the highest that it has ever been. . . .(p. 128)

Parsons claims that the loss of functions previously performed by the traditional family does not imply that the modern nuclear family is a weaker, less important, institution, but that the modern family has emerged as a more specialized institution, depended upon even more exclusively than before by the rest of the social system to perform its specialized, differentiated "root functions." In addition, Functionalists argue that the modern, specialized nuclear family has developed new functions to fulfill the new requirements of the modern social system.

The "root functions" of the nuclear family, the socialization and stabilization of the personalities of children and parents, as we discussed before, must still be performed, and there is no other social institution or agency, emerging or foreseeable, that could adequately substitute for nuclear family organization in performing them. Parsons predicts that the nuclear family will continue to be minimally necessary through and beyond the twentieth century, even in the most modern of societies.

Further, beyond these root functions, there is reason to believe that the nuclear family pattern will continue to grow into an even more important functional subsystem in modern social systems. As social life under modern conditions grows ever more demanding in terms of occupational skills, more and more bureaucratic, and more and more complex, there is less and less room in the public world for the "other side" of the human personality to express and satisfy itself. The bonds and satisfactions involved in interaction between husband and wife and parents and children will be called upon more and more exclusively to provide the sole "life support system" for our emotional needs, for our nonrational expressiveness, for trust, warmth, laughter, and, yes, most of all for love.

SOCIOLOGY II
Human Alternatives to the Family

Will the family survive the twentieth century? From an Activist Sociological viewpoint, a better formulation of this question would be, "Should the family survive . . . ?" And the obvious answer is, "not in its present dehumanizing and oppressive form, not if we can help it." The nuclear family as universal cookie cutter, as an imposed standard that cuts and stretches like a Procrustean bed, is nothing but an impediment to the realization of social justice, human freedom, and a healthy society. It is useful only to the economically and politically powerful. If the rest of us are to overcome our powerlessness, the family institution as it is generally established today must be overthrown. Individuals must struggle to realize the uniqueness and strength of their true selves, breaking out of the mold of standardized roles and routinized relationships. And the society at large, we the people as a group, must break through the family myth to see clearly and realistically whom we should trust, and whom we must fight, who are the true friends and enemies of our vital interests as a class.

This does not necessarily mean the elimination of the family altogether, but the elimination of its present oppressiveness. From the feminist perspective, for instance, women seek liberation from the confines of this single family mold. Not the complete abolition of the family,

> but the diversification of the socially acknowledged relationships which are today forcibly and rigidly compressed into it. This would mean a plural range of institutions where the family is only one such institution, and its abolition implies none. Couples of the same or of different sexes—living together or not living together, long-term unions with or without children, single parents—male or female—bringing up children, children socialized by conventional rather than biological parents, extended kin groups, etc.—all these could be encompassed in a range of institutions which match the free invention and variety of men and women. (Mitchell, 1971, p. 151)

The family in a healthier future, then, would have a diversity of structural arrangements, chosen to suit individual needs and imposed on no one. Just as in a "deschooled" society (see Chapter 8) education would still go on, but in a wide variety of freely established ways, so in a future "defamilized" society the intimacy between couples, the socialization of children, and the organization of private households would still go on, but in new patterns. "Freedom from the family" would mean the freedom of every individual and group to establish or alter their familiar relationships as they saw fit. This freedom of choice would reverberate throughout economic and political sectors of the society as well. Free women, free men, and free children living in freely organized familial groupings—communes, cooperatives, extended families, or nuclear families—would be much less vulnerable to mass propaganda and manipulation from the top. A revolution in family life would be a major step toward total social revolution, and the establishment of a free, just, humanly healthy society.

SOCIOLOGY III
Continuity of the Paradox

Naturalists observe the institution of family as the use by family members of the concept and terminology of the family as protective coloration, as publicly acceptable camouflage to preserve the privacy of family life. Interestingly, the diversity of actual household practices, activities, and relationships that we could observe if we were allowed to see behind all of these family veils of normalcy would probably approximate, if not exceed, the diversity and variation desired and proposed by Activist "family revolutionaries." In other words, both the standardization measured and explained by Functionalists, and the diversity and free choice envisioned as a utopia by the Activists, are probably coexistent facts of family social life in our society today, and for all we know or could know, they were facts of life in past societies and are for contemporary "traditional" societies as well.

One of the most striking features of "traditional" family life as I have observed it in various regions, among different classes and ethnicities, and in rural and urban areas in India, for instance, is the incredible diversity from family to family. Somehow the surface uniformity of traditional family customs can be preserved even where the household unit may vary in size from two to forty, where its composition might be the nuclear family with two children, or five unmarried sisters over sixty and their over-ninety mother, or six single brothers and sisters in their twenties, or two unrelated couples and their children—or anything else you could imagine. In addition, in a society in which the traditional, standardized family pattern is said to be even further organized and routinized by religion, one finds that each and every family has its own unique combination of rituals, spiritual beliefs, hierarchy of gods, and prayers—its own religion!

The future in this modernized society in which we live might well hold, then, the even greater richness, freedom, and diversification of patterns of family life in actual private practice that is sought and struggled for by Activists. But from a Naturalist perspective we would also expect that the standardization of the fronts we put on our private family lives will continue to be sustained and developed as well. Both of these are the products of human social creativity.

AN INNER VOICE

The question still remains, should the family survive? As the training ground for conforming system members, as the oppressive rules and roles that keep women as well as men locked in stereotyped identities, as the *"chamber of horrors" described by Henry? Do we need it? And what would we invent to replace it? I wonder what the rest of the class—and the rest of my generation— thinks?*

DOING SOCIOLOGY

Pair up with a member of your class whose background is most similar to yours, and switch places for a family dinner. Do your experiences bear out the "Chinatown phenomenon" described above?

10

Magic, Science
and Religion

How are the institutions of magic, science, and religion related to each other in society, and how are they distinct from one another? What different facets of these relationships and distinctions can be seen through Functionalist, Activist, and Naturalist sociological lenses?

First we will look into the general problem of how social institutions overlap and become entangled, no matter which lens we look through. Then let us see how magic, science, and religion overlap, and how they might be disentangled for a clearer view of what these three institutions do for us, what they do to us, and what we do with them.

Magic, science, and religion are three social institutions found in every society. All three are involved in social participants' eternal quest for the truth about life, for certainty about the world, and for surefire cures for the crises of life. They are social instruments designed to capture three distinct types of truth for their users.

THE PROBLEM OF INSTITUTIONAL OVERLAP

The most bedevilling logical, strategic, and observational problem for the sociologist interested in studying social institutions is the overlap and intermingling of one institution with another, often several others.

The Functionalist sociologist finds that the logical conceptualization of any single institution and its specialized social functions is made difficult by functional overlap. The polity is functionally responsible, for instance, primarily for the maintenance of law and order, the protection of the social system against outside threats, and the legitimation of the demands the society makes upon the individual. But the political system in modern societies also manages much of the economy; nationalism can come to serve as a substitute religion; and through its public school system, the state takes over more and more of the family's function of socializing the young. At the same time, politics and legislatures are influenced (an Activist would say manipulated) by economic forces; religious allegiances and conflicts can determine electoral outcomes (was Al Smith unelectable because he was Catholic?); and family ties can be stronger than political rules, with important consequences for government (the "Kennedy dynasty," for instance). Where then, functionally speaking, do economy, religion, and kinship end and the polity begin? To handle this problem, Functionalist sociology makes logical definitions of the boundaries between institutions, by constructing a model or an "ideal type" (Weber, 1905) of a social institution in "pure" form. Then the realities of overlap can be seen as overlap, while the logical distinctions between overlapping institutions are maintained.

For the Activist, the social arena is clouded over, the struggles going on within it intentionally made obscure, by the overlapping of institutional myths and realities. The powerful elite try to keep our collective attention rooted to "political" struggles between parties, candidates, and levels of government in order to mask the economic realities of corporate moves to control national and world political events. The family, as we saw in the previous chapter, serves as a convenient arena within which we can vent our frustrations, diverting our attention from the real struggle going on outside. The Activist's task is to sort out these engineered institutional overlaps, to distinguish between the institutional myth up front and the concrete reality of institutional control behind.

The Naturalist who tries to observe social interaction defined or acknowledged by participants to be "political" or "familial" or "economic" is confronted directly with the puzzle of overlap, but it is a problem the sociologist cannot solve from this perspective. Participants in interactive occasions appear to be donning two or more institutional masks of identity at once, more often than not. The activity of shopping for the household groceries in the company of a friend, for instance, involves us as participants in the institutions of the economy, friendship, and the family in a very complicated mix. When the friend asks us who we intend to vote for in the coming election, given the outrageous price of instant coffee, who is to say which institution is going on here? All we can say in general, at the outset, is that institutional overlap appears to be a complex fact of everyday social life, but participants seem to be able to negotiate the complexity quite handily, and sort it all out as a matter of course in their fateful progress toward the checkout counter. Once again, it appears that we are more skilled at figuring out society as participants than as sociologists.

Now let us look at the overlap problem in the case of magic, science, and religion.

Malinowski's Functionalist and Naturalist Distinction Between Magic, Science, and Religion and Its Activist Implications

Anthropologist Bronislaw Malinowski's classic essay, *Magic, Science and Religion* (Malinowski, 1948) will serve as our primary text in this discussion. Malinowski argues that there are universal principles of human social interaction

and social structure to be found in the daily lives of the tribal peoples of the Trobriand Islands in New Guinea. He describes the actions he observed in careful
detail, and taking up the theories advanced by the world's great thinkers on
magic, science, and religion, holds each of them up to the light of his observational experience for criticism and appreciation. In this he is practicing in the
modes of both Functionalist and Naturalist sociologies. As Robert Redfield puts it
in the book's introduction,

> Malinowski's gift was double: it consisted both in the genius given usually to artists
> and in the scientist's power to see and to declare the universal in the particular.
> Malinowski's reader is provided with a set of concepts as to religion, magic, science,
> rite and myth in the course of forming vivid impressions and understandings of the
> Trobrianders into whose life he is so charmingly drawn.

Through Malinowski's observant eyes, we watch the islanders go about the
complicated business of their daily lives. We see how they manage, through the
use of scientific, magical, and religious technique, to keep their bodies and souls,
and their social system, together.

Malinowski observes that when the islanders poison the lagoon to harvest
fish, when they plant, tend, and harvest vegetables by the cycle of the seasons,
when they build oceangoing canoes that will not tip or drag unnecessarily in the
water and wind, and when they navigate hundreds of miles of open ocean by
the stars, they use sets of calculated, rational, generationally developed under-
standings of nature that correspond to most Western notions of natural science.
The ends are practical, the means are purely technical, and the islanders' understanding of the relations between means and ends is theoretically logical. This
knowledge, this accumulated truth about nature and our predictable relations
with it, and the calculated application of this knowledge to practical goals, is the
institution of science.

When crises erupt in the lives of particular members of the society, or when
the tribe as a whole confronts tragedy or triumph in events beyond anyone's
control, we then see the practice of religious rites. Marriage; birth; initiation to
manhood; death, dying, burial, and mourning; sea-storms; drought; victory or
loss in war; exceptional harvest or island-wide blight are all occasions for ritual
directed toward the gods, in thanks or in supplication. The celebrations of religious beliefs are also seen as actions, ritualized into traditional religious
techniques, taken toward specific goals. But the kinds of goals or end results
sought, as well as the types of actions seen as means toward those ends, are
quite different in the case of religious activity than in scientific social action. In the
scientific realm, the ends sought are rationally calculable, measurable, observable consequences of the means used—the *empirical* ends of fish in the nets,
yams in the larder, return to the desired harbor, or the speed of the canoe. Religious rituals are directed toward ends that cannot be seen or measured, that are
difficult to separate out from the means themselves—placating angry gods, satis-

fying the demands of long-dead ancestors, the emotional reintegration of the family and tribal group after the loss of a member through death, the future success of a marriage or a career. All of these things are believed to be insured by the proper performance of the religious rite, but they are goals that cannot be calculated or observed directly—*nonempirical* ends. Often, the ritual celebration is seen as an "end in itself"—its mere performance satisfies the deeply felt need that motivated it.

Religious ritual as a *means* to these nonempirical ends is also a different kind of activity than the application of scientific technique, in Malinowski's view. No one knows, or even dares to ask, how or why the performance of the ritual ceremony satisfies the gods, or guarantees marital happiness, or speeds the progress of the dead one's soul to a peaceful resting place. Scientific means toward ends are rational because the practitioner knows theoretically, logically, how and why the technique produces its practical results. Religious means, by contrast, are nonrational because the person who prays or dances or chants religiously simply believes the action has the desired or required effect. This belief or faith in the efficacy of prayer and ritual is a major component of the desired effect itself. The rational understanding of the relations between means and ends that characterizes scientific action, therefore, can have no place in religious action.

Magic is practiced when individuals are faced with uncertainty, risk, and circumstances beyond the control of practical technique. When a tribesman wants a certain woman to fall in love with him, when, out of revenge, he wants his neighbor's crop to whither and die on the vine, or his teeth to fall out or his sexual organs to shrivel and fall off, when he wants to be cured of an illness for which no scientific medicine or treatment is known or effective, when he wants to end the drought or stop the excessive rains, he calls in the magician. The magician is a technician who is believed to have the power to manipulate supernatural forces. Magical technique is called upon to produce end results that are just as observable, measurable, practical—*empirical*—as those produced by scientific action. The magician bases his claim to fame and his professional fees on the practical, observable success of his spells and incantations, and is usually seen to be successful on the basis of the human propensity to forget many failures or negative outcomes as long as there are a few spectacularly positive results to remember, and build a reputation upon. But the positive results of the magician's activities are always seen as specifically miraculous events. Magically produced events are miracles because it is not known, and in principle cannot be rationally known, how and why the magical technique or means has produced the desired ends. The power and mystery of the magician lies in his or her ability to produce empirical ends through the use of nonrational means.

The different relationships between means and ends described here forms the essence of Malinowski's distinction between the institutions of. magic, science, and religion in Trobriand society, and by extrapolation, any society.

In diagramatic form, here is a distillation of Malinowski's distinction:

| | Ends | |
Means	Empirical	Nonempirical
Rational	I. SCIENCE	II. (impossible)
Nonrational	III. MAGIC	IV. RELIGION

(I am indebted for this schematization to the late Rex Hopper, in classroom teaching at Brooklyn College.)

In Cell I we have the institution of science, defined now as a form of social activity: the application of rational means (understood in rational, theoretical terms to be logically related to outcomes) to the production of desired empirical ends (observable, measurable, practical outcomes).

Cell II is a logically impossible alternative, because rational means cannot be applied to nonempirical ends. If the ends or outcomes cannot be observed, calculated, and logically understood, then the means cannot have been rational, which by this definition requires logical understanding of the relations between means and ends. Rational means can only be logically applied to empirical ends.

In Cell III of the table we have the essence of the social institution of magic, now defined as a form of social activity: the application of nonrational means (no one understands why and how the magician's powers work, only that he exclusively possesses them) to the production of desired empirical ends (like the scientist's ends, but beyond the knowledge and certainty of science).

Cell IV is the realm of religion, now defined as a form of social activity: the application of nonrational means (as in magic, no one knows why or how prayer and ritual work) to the production of desirable nonempirical ends (the results of prayer and ritual occur in the supernatural realm of the gods, outside of mortal observation or calculation).

To shorten this definition, we could say that science is the use of rational technique to produce practical results; magic is the use of mystery to produce practical results; and religion is the use of mystery to produce mysterious results.

Malinowski made these distinctions on the basis of his observations of the social life of a small "primitive" tribe of Trobriand Islanders. But he claimed he was observing the universal principles of human social life as they are expressed or exhibited in a particular case. Let us follow up this generalization by applying these definitions of magic, science, and religion to our contemporary social system. Looking through our three sociological lenses, what is the social reality of magic, science, and religion as social institutions today?

SOCIOLOGY I
The Advance of Science

Taking magic, science, and religion as patterns of social action, as institutionalized ways of dealing with the problems of social life, Functionalist sociology views magic and religion in much the same way as it views the family as a social institution. These two institutions have progressively lost functions and adherents over the course of social evolution into modernity, though they survive even in modern society as narrowly specialized institutions. The institution that has taken over the traditional functions of magic and religion, and that now stands as the dominant truth-seeking and problem-solving institution, is science. The rise and advancement of scientific method, and technique, and increased popular accep-tance of this institution, coincided with the loss of faith in and reliance upon religion and magic. The development of science into the dominant mode of truth-seeking has meant, in Max Weber's perceptive phrase, "the disenchantment of the world" (Weber, 1946).

The modern social world is a world no longer filled with religious meanings and magical mysteries. We have come to demand and expect the certainties of science in answer to all of our important questions about how to cope with the problems of our lives. Scientific technology over the past two centuries has given us mastery over nature to replace our former religious acceptance, passive and fatalistic, of God's inscrutable plan. In place of magical attempts to manipulate our social and personal fates, we now have political science, the science of economics, psychology and psychiatry, and even the science of society, sociol-ogy. We demand empirical proof for all of these scientific claims to truth, and we receive practical benefits in the form of material well-being beyond the wildest dreams of primitive or traditional men and women.

◆◆

FOUNDING FATHERS

Max Weber on the Limitations of Science

There is a price to pay for all of our scientific gains, in the Functionalist view. The disen-chantment of the world has left us bereft of a sense of ultimate meaning, and of any sense of our place in a coldly material, mechani-cally functioning physical universe. Our al-most total reliance on scientific truth may turn out to be an overreliance.

As Weber put it, "Who . . . still believes that the findings of astronomy, biology, physics, or chemistry could teach us any-thing about the meaning of the world?" He quotes Tolstoy as saying, "Science is mean-ingless because it gives no answer to our question, the only question important for us:

'what shall we do and how shall we live?' "
Weber goes on, "and still less can it be proved that the existence of the world which these sciences describe is worth while, that it has any "meaning," or that it makes sense to live in such a world. Science does not ask for the answers to such questions. . . . Natural science gives us an answer to the question of what we must do if we wish to master life technically. It leaves quite aside, or assumes for its purposes, whether we should and do wish to master life technically and whether it ultimately makes sense to do so." (Weber, 1946, p. 146)

◆◆

This limitation of science convinces Functionalists that though science dominates and will even further dominate the modern social world, though science may disprove and displace every religious claim to physical and even social truth about the world, religion, at least, among our three contending institutions, will continue to perform vital functions for the social system, for our lives in societal interdependence.

The "root functions" of religion, to reuse Parson's phrase about the family (Chapter 9) are, in Functionalist terms, to orient societal members at large toward the ultimate meanings, the core values of their actions and their lives, and to integrate and sustain the integration of individual members and disparate groups within their social system as a whole. These have always been the major functions of religious activity and will continue to be the functions needing to be performed by the specialized but still vibrant modern institution of religion.

FOUNDING FATHERS

Emile Durkheim on the Functions of Religion

Founding Father Emile Durkheim analyzed anthropological field reports about religious practices among tribes of Australian aborigines (Durkheim, 1912) for an answer to this dilemma. He concluded that the dual needs of human beings for a sense of the ultimate purpose of their lives, on the one hand, for an obligatory sense of belonging to a social group, on the other hand, can only be fulfilled by religious belief and ritual practice, whether in primitive tribes or in modern social systems. Religion, thus, is a functional necessity in any society.

If the family is crucial to the social system in socializing individuals to become loyal, functioning societal members "from the bottom up," so to speak, religion is a crucial functional institution in orienting and integrating system members "from the top down." The social system's functional requirement for this integration of members in an essentially nonrational manner leads the Functionalist to expect and predict a continual resurgence of religious belief and practice at the society-wide level, despite the domination of the modern worldview by science. The recent election of a "twice-born" president of the United States, among other indications of renewed religious activity, would tend to confirm this expectation. If it was ever true that "God is dead" among a certain segment of the population in the 1960s, we can be confident that He will continue to be reborn in slightly different, perhaps more contemporarily relevant, forms.

As to magic, there have always been, and there always will be, areas of social life that are characterized by uncertainty, risk, and chance. Meteorologists will never be able to predict with absolute certainty that next Saturday's picnic will not be rained out; mathematicians still do no better at the roulette wheel than the average sucker with a hunch; "lucky in love" is still the only true hope of the computer-dating service customer; you'd just as well consult your astrologer as your psychiatrist if you want to know if you'll recover the things you've lost; and if you want your rival's sexual organs to shrivel up and fall off, don't call the American Medical Association, find your neighborhood witch. The institution of magic, the application of mysterious techniques, superstition, luck charms, and incantations to the intractible problems of an always risky social life, will also continue to thrive in society no matter how modern and scientific it becomes.

The general Functionalist point is, if there are social functions that need to be performed, there will be social institutions developed, revived, and sustained to perform those functions. As long as there are practical needs that cannot be fulfilled in rational, technical ways, as long as there is uncertainty and risk in our social lives, we will have magic.

SOCIOLOGY II
Instruments of Oppression

Activist sociology also views the historical relationship of magic, science, and religion as a series of victories of the scientific attitude over the superstitions of magic and the mass illusions of religion. The rise of the bourgeoisie against the feudal aristocracy has coincided, as an intellectual struggle, with the replacement of magical and religious belief with scientific rationality. The technological power over nature placed in our hands by modern science gives us material resources and a degree of freedom from backbreaking toil beyond the dreams of earlier societies. But the the revolution of science and the promise of freedom and dignity of technology has not gone far enough. They have been appropriated as instruments of oppression by contemporary bourgeois and corporate elites.

The Functionalist myth that each of these institutions has its specialized and continuing functions masks the reality of power and oppression in our corporate capitalist society (no less than in socialist totalitarian states). The reality is that science is used to function in the interests of the elite, while religion keeps the masses in thrall, and magic doles out "consolation prizes" for society's losers.

FOUNDING FATHERS
Karl Marx on the Humanistic Potential of Science

As a Founding Father of Activist sociology, Karl Marx would have approved of Malinowski's definition of science as the application of rational means to empirical ends, because it is based on, and retains ultimate respect for, the actual activities of men and women coping with the contingencies of life. Malinowski's depiction of science, in fact, closely corresponds to Marx's ideal of nonalienated productive labor, or as Fromm restates it, "The concept of the active, productive man who grasps and embraces the

objective world with his own powers . . ."
(Fromm, 1961, p. 43).

The ideal of nonalienated human labor expressed by Marx requires a knowledge of the relationship between means and ends, just as Malinowski defines scientific activity:

"A spider conducts operations that resemble those of a weaver, and a bee puts the shame to many an architect in the construction of her cells. But what distinguishes the worst architect from the best of bees is this, that the architect raises his structure in imagination before he erects it in reality. At the end of every labor process, we get a result that already existed in the imagination of the

laborer at its commencement. He not only effects a change of form in the material on which he works, but he also realizes a purpose of his own that gives the law to his modus operandi, and to which he must subordinate his will." (Marx, Capital, *I, cited in Fromm, 1961, p. 41.)*

The promise of true science is to enhance the capability of every person to cope rationally with material and social realities in the world, to work his or her creative will upon the objective materials of existence, to realize the complete and authentically human self in scientific, that is, fully conscious and productive activity.

◆◆◆

What the Activist sees in the contemporary social arena under the label of institutionalized science, however, is quite contrary to this humanistic ideal. The products of scientific research translated into technology consist, in terrifying measure, in the instruments of advanced scientific warfare. Peacetime technology is focused on the invention and variation of marketable commodities, whose uselessness or harmfulness has to be covered up and sold through mass propaganda campaigns called advertising. Scientific research as a creative end in itself has no place in the competition for research funding.

Professional scientists have become a minor elite unto themselves. Hiding behind the Weberian claim that scientific analysis cannot lead to moral judgments, they refuse to accept responsibility for the moral and social consequences of their research activities. Their scientific activities are not only thus separated from their moral, political, and social roles, science is separated from the layman as well by smoke screens of jargon, by levels of professional training and rank, and by the failure to make a true scientific education available to all. This is the twofold alienation of the institution of science as seen through an Activist sociological lens. As a result of this alienation, much of the "science" that filters down to the nonexpert is presented in the form of technological miracles performed by practitioners imbued with mysterious powers—the perfect replication of Malinowski's definition of primitive magic.

An Activist critique of our society's domination by and through professional experts of all kinds, scientific as well as quasiscientific, shows that the practice and the power of magic is all-pervasive in modern society, not the residual and insignificant remnant of a specialized institution as depicted by Functionalists.

The elite experts dominate and delude laymen and clients in every institutional sphere of the contemporary arena through mystification. The power of scientific knowledge to transform the relations between human beings and nature for everyone's benefit is misused to produce benefits for individual or corporate clients who can afford to pay them. Knowledge of the functioning and health of the human body is mystified by the medical profession and held as the Private possession of doctors, instead of extending medical education to make each person his or her own best physician. Knowledge of the law is mystified by lawyers, instead of being translated into public education about how to protect and defend one's own legal interests. Knowledge of technological devices — automobile, washing machine, radio, clock—is mystified by mechanical engineers and repairmen so that one dare not tinker for fear of the consequences.

Science as an institution may indeed dominate our modern society, but as the application of rational means toward empirical ends, it hardly pervades it. We live in a world of mysterious gadgets and mysterious relationships between things, presided over by expert practitioners who have the exclusive power to make things work. Surely, this is the age of magic, not science, for most of us.

As for religion, the application of nonrational means to nonempirical ends is merely an irrelevant hangover from a dim, deluded age gone by, from this standpoint. Institutionalized religion from this perspective, is and always has been a counterrevolutionary force in human society. The demands and the struggles of the masses for concrete benefits, such as economic and social justice and freedom from domination by others, have traditionally been met with offers of "spiritual" rewards instead. You save your soul, and I'll invest my profits, say the elites through their religious spokesmen. Be patient, slave, you'll get justice in heaven. Blessed are the poor. Your sufferings under my heel are the expression of God's will, so take your complaints to the head office. You'll never get justice, so try bliss instead, you'll feel better.

By keeping religion alive, through manipulated revival upon revival, the elite strives to sustain and deepen the mystification and alienation of the people. But science, with the aid of the Activist, is progressively eroding religious delusions. As a social institution, religion is on its way out, despite occasional indications of resurgence.

What science could be, as a liberating force for human potential and self-realization, and as a generator of a technology to meet every person's material needs, is a crucial feature of the just and free social future Activists are fighting for. To take science and technology out of the exclusive possession of the experts and put them in the hands of people at large would also mean the end of magic as an instrument of oppression. These are the actual and potential relationships between the institutions of magic, science, and religion as seen through an Activist sociological lens.

SOCIOLOGY III
Overlapping Observations: Scientific Religion, Magical Science, Religious Magic

What the Naturalist observes when the inquiring lens is turned upon these three realms is a dense and confused overlap of the three modes of action distinguished conceptually in Malinowski's theoretical scheme.

There are strong elements of religion to be found in modern science. The public faith in science to provide the ultimate answers to all of life's questions and problems raises science to the level of a folk religion. Scientists with well-deserved reputations for making profound discoveries in their technically specialized fields are called upon by the mass media to pontificate on the great political and moral issues of the day, elevating them to the status of high priests or gurus. Perhaps their ability to grapple with fundamental natural forces and principles is generalized in the public mind into a special sort of communication with the gods. Science itself, as it has been institutionalized in modern society, no longer appears as a mere instrument of human inquiry, invented and constructed by men and women for their own practical ends, but as a mysterious power over and above human will and purpose, with a destiny of its own. Such is the grip of science as a self-generating, sacred entity upon our consciousness that "scientism," the emulation and imitation of scientific ritual even where no scientific or practical end is sought, has become a widespread practice.

The corollary to this is the scientization of modern religion. "The family that prays together, stays together," is a popularized, vulgar example of the increasing use of religious practice as rational means to empirical ends. Religion as a consciously chosen means to mental health, crime prevention, weight loss, cure for drug addiction, or business success (because a card-carrying Baptist can be trusted with your money, for example) clearly begins to approach Malinowski's definition of scientific activity.

The overlaps between magic and science in our contemporary social lives are perhaps even more dense. The practice of astrology is becoming daily more accessible to every intelligent person through books, the press, and even educational programs, as an instrument for making practical predictions and decisions on the basis of mathematical calculations of probabilities, themselves based on accumulated statistics about past relationships between dates, seasons, and types of social events. At the same time, the science of astronomy becomes ever more distant and incomprehensible to the layman, requiring sophisticated and arcane knowledge of electronics, optics, topographical reading of radiographic scans, and advanced mathematical calculations. Both are nominally dealing with "the stars." Both are technically based on mathematical probabilities and correlations between observed events. But can either be clearly distinguished, according to Malinowski's definitions, as purely magic or purely science? And is it conceivable that astrology is becoming more scientific, while astronomy is becoming more magical, each as a social institution?

The Activist viewpoint, that technological miracles appear to consumers and users as magic in our society, is of course also observably true. Our everyday relations with the products of science are often decidedly magical in nature. We still ritualistically kick the tires of new automobiles to "test" their soundness, and the incantations to be heard over a balky carburetor on an icy morning would put many a primitive witch doctor to shame.

When the application of science and technology to supposedly technical problems fails on a grand scale, as it did in the case of the scientific warfare carried out by the United States against the relatively primitive people of Vietnam, the confusion of magic with science *and* with religion deepens. We blame the magicians for failing to use their powers correctly (Halberstam, 1972), we question our faith in science itself as the ultimate answer-giver, and we begin to doubt the sacred purpose and moral rightness of the national god, the social-system religion.

Perhaps there are elements of Malinowski's magical scientific, and religious definitions necessarily involved in all of our human social activities. The wish to manipulate and foresee all the contingencies in a risky venture, supposedly characteristic only of magic; the need to know that we know what we know, supposedly reserved for science; and the pure leap of faith into belief in the rightness and inevitability of what we must do, supposedly the preserve of religion—are these not the intermingled constituents of all social action? If so, we should be able to observe the activity patterns of magic, science, and religion in every exhibit of social interaction, interwoven in the fabric of our everyday social lives.

*   *   *

We should not end this discussion without a Naturalist sociologist's note on Malinowski as a sociological Naturalist.

In 1966, Malinowski's widow Valetta Malinowski (he died in 1942) had his early diaries translated from the handwritten Polish and published under the title *A Diary in the Strict Sense of the Term*. The diaries cover the periods from September 1914 to August 1915, and October 1917 to July 1918. The second period was when Malinowski did his field research in the Trobriand Islands.

The diary is a remarkable document because it fully and honestly expresses the complex, emotional, irrational mixture of experiences of a social naturalist in the field before everything has been boiled down to neat ethnographic description and logical analysis in the research report. The clear distinctions Malinowski made in his written work between magic, science, and religion as elements in the social actions and lives of his native subjects blur and fade in his private accounts of his own actions and experiences while he was studying them. Consider the overlap and the meaning of magical, scientific, and perhaps even religious elements to be seen in *Malinowski* as a social being, in the following diary entry:

1.17.18 Woke up at 7:30: After writing diary went to <u>sopi</u> for gymnastics, under the palms, near the mangroves. Running, then very intensive exercises. Also, planned the day and *steel my thoughts*. Gymnastics removed slackness but introduced a certain nervous tension, *nervous irritability* insomnia, which I have not had for a long time. Worked 2 hours in the morning; Campbell arrived; this irritated and depressed me—like a customs search on the border—a little afraid he might cause me some unpleasantness; then again *bother*, waste of time, and I don't like him personally. Talk during which I was expansive. Then a short letter to E.R.M. Gymnastics; I tried to concentrate, to take the proper attitude. . . . Gymnastics calmed my nerves, restored my balance and put me in an excellent mood. With gymnastics and a regular mode of life I should keep healthy and carry out my scientific plans. The only danger is overstraining my heart. Ergo: take intellectual work, everyday difficulties, efforts lightly, "not take them to heart." Absolutely eliminate personal rancor, excitement, etc. Cultivate *sense of humor* (not the English one, but my own) . . .

Then lunch with a fellow and talk—about what?—In the afternoon: I lay down for a quarter hour, and started work—bwaga'u business. At about 5 stopped, was fed up. Excited, impossible to concentrate. Ate pineapple, drank tea, wrote E.R.M., took a walk: intensive gymnastics. Gymnastics should be a time of concentration and solitude; something that gives me an opportunity to escape from the *niggers* and my own agitation. Supper with a fellow who told me stupid anecdotes, not interesting at all, about Kiriwinian ethnology. I listened and dozed and nodded: what a brute. Short letter to E.R.M. I thought about her intensely again: the only woman for me, the incarnation of everything a woman can give me. Some fellow sang during the night, this annoyed me, I couldn't fall asleep. Slept badly. (Pp. 187—188)

What kind of sense do you suppose a Trobriand native anthropologist, watching, questioning, and recording this day in the life of Malinowski, would make of the cultural pattern of the West as represented by him?

─────────── DOING SOCIOLOGY ───────────

Carefully review your own personal journals, and bring to a class presentation and discussion at least one clear example of each of the activity patterns described by Malinowski as magic, science, and religion.

Epilogue: Invitation to Sociology as an Amateur Sport

11

In this brief concluding chapter, I wish to make three basic points:

a) Sociology, in all its many versions, has become too highly professionalized.
b) Sociology can best be advanced, practiced, and enjoyed by amateur sociologists.
c) You are cordially invited to consider yourself an amateur sociologist, and to begin enjoying your lifetime practice.

Professionalization is one major feature of the more general process of bureaucratization that characterizes modern society. From the Functionalist sociological viewpoint, it makes for the most efficient organization of a set of functionally important occupational roles. From the Activist standpoint, the only function served by professional standards, associations, and mystiques is to enhance the power and privilege of the self-serving professional elite. From a Naturalist perspective, professionalization is a device for stabilizing, concretizing, and making secure and permanent a field of knowledge or skill, against the uncertainties that might otherwise paralyze social action.

Functionalist sociologist William Goode has noted that "an industrializing society is a professionalizing society" (Goode, 1961, p. 902). He lists ten characteristics of the professionalized occupation, but claims that these derive from only two "core characteristics" of professions: "A prolonged specialized training in a body of abstract knowledge, and a collectivity or service orientation."

Further, Goode says that these characteristics imply

> *social* relationships; they assert obligations and rights between client and professional, professional and colleague, or professional and some formal agency. Consequently, an important part of the process by which an occupation becomes a profession is the gradual institutionalization of various role relationships between itself and other parts of the society. (P.903)

Professionals, in other words, as compared to the amateur practitioner of any art, science, or sport, are institutionalized, in all three sociological versions of this term: they are more highly organized in their practice, which is probably a paid career occupation rather than a casual avocation. Professionals possess and wield important powers vis-a-vis clients, who need the services and lack the knowledge and skills because they are, after all, only laymen. Finally, professionals transform the uncertainties of common sense into the certainties of professional judgment in order to facilitate remedial action.

It is my contention that sociology as a field of inquiry has become overly professionalized in recent years, and that such professionalization is anathema to the growth of any kind of sociological knowledge. The professional organization of sociologists, the professional powers of sociologists and sociological findings, and the professional drive toward useful certainties all get in the way of *doing sociology*—that is, of applying scientific methods of inquiry to the puzzles of social life.

Sociology's ultimate subject matter, from any sociological perspective, is paradox. The individual is society's product, yet society is the product of individuals. The victims of class exploitation are willing partners in the creation of the illusions that give power and legitimacy to their exploiters. Naturalistic description of social interaction requires the use of language plus the assumption that there is something outside language to be described, yet it is always language-in-use that makes up the social interaction we can observe and describe. The sociologist is always an intimate part of the phenomena he or she must get outside of for objective, scientific study.

Professionals in any field cannot afford to acknowledge or deal with paradox. They must deny paradox, apparently resolve discrepancies, and transform uncertainty and contradiction into certainty and order. That is what their clients hire them to do. That is what their specialized training is supposed to equip them to do.

Therefore, a professional sociologist is a contradiction in terms. Much of sociological theory and practice today is based on the premise introduced early on into the field by Emile Durkheim, that only the professionally screened and trained applicant can be trusted to do sociology (Durkheim, 1895).

There was a time not long ago when most universities did not recognize sociology as a legitimate academic discipline. Full-fledged professionalism was not an easy achievement for sociologists. There were social theorists, social critics, and social observers aplenty, in and out of universities, but not many departments of sociology, journals of sociology, classes in sociology, or sociology textbooks. Far back in the history of the discipline we find Auguste Comte, unemployed during most of his sociological career, holding unofficial seminars among his cronies and those rare students who would come just to hear what a thinking man had to say. Comte developed the foundation for modern sociological theory in this disestablished manner. Herbert Spencer, a little later in the chain, wrote his major treatises on sociological topics as a private scholar, unaffiliated with any university department or professional association. And Karl

Marx of course had no academic tenure, no graduate students, and no professional colleagues to chat with over lunch at the faculty club.

In the early years of this century in the United States, sociologists tended to be primarily moralistic social reformers—either Christian, Marxist, or anarchistic in orientation—and therefore were despised by established academics in the fields of economics, psychology, and philosophy (Page, 1964; Becker, 1963). At the same time, many sociologists condemned the academy for remaining irrelevant to social issues and social needs.

The mutual contempt between sociologists and established academicians can perhaps best be exemplified by reference to the career and writings of Thorstein Veblen, who did manage to acquire a number of academic jobs by posing as an economist (Veblen, 1917). At each of several universities, however, he quickly revealed himself to be really a sociologist, and an Activist as well. This, combined with his disrespectful, amorous, and irregular personal style, got him fired, again and again, despite the public success of his written works. Veblen's conduct in the university setting was always seen as "unprofessional."

Sociology had to fight its way into university curricula and budgets by proving that it wasn't really just a branch of economics, or a part of psychology, or a new version of history. It also had to overcome the suspicion that its practitioners were disreputable scoundrels, wild-eyed utopian dreamers, rabble rousers, or dilettantes. Professional standing was finally achieved in the last forty years.

Sociologists are now, by and large, as professional as dentists or accountants, though not as highly paid or as socially valued. They belong to international, national, regional, and local professional associations, and are flown to the annual meetings at university expense to present research findings to their peers. This research is heavily funded by governments, foundations, institutes, and private corporations. As respectable academics, sociologists now handle their share of the student load, and their departments are generally expanding in size, even in times of general university retrenchment and budget cutting.

The profession now possesses a mysterious language, or jargon, and a set of computer-oriented mathematical techniques that appear sufficiently arcane and exotic to the layman. Thus armed with the elements of the "professional mystique," sociology screens out the merely curious and produces professionally polished, dedicated, career-line sociologists.

It has taken a great deal of trouble, effort, and time for several generations of sociologists to reach this plateau of a thriving profession. What could be wrong with this? How could the characteristic features of professionalism get in the way of doing sociology? Yet, I would argue, some of the necessary elements for doing a social science are weakened or even eliminated by professionalization.

I think that the creativity at the heart, and at the developing edge, of any science, is bound up with an attitude and a practice of playfulness on the part of creative scientists. Scientific creativity is of course the only source of new and fruitful ideas in any field, its very life blood as an ongoing intellectual enterprise. Without new ideas, a discipline dries up and becomes a meaningless ritual, a going-through-the-motions parody of a true science. If I am correct in believing that such new idea production is necessarily a playful sort of activity, done for the fun of it, then professionalism is clearly antagonistic to a creative, developing sociology.

Consider first the choice of a topic or problem to study. Should it be a playful choice, or a professional choice? If it is a playful choice, the topic will be something that intrigues me as a researcher, that tickles my fancy, that pricks my imagination, that fascinates me and perhaps even obsesses me emotionally. I pursue the answers to my questions because I am pursued by them, not for any practical, logical, relevant, or even academic or scholarly reason. I am possessed, as Max Weber phrased it, by a demon—by a passionate, personal need to know, which is a perfectly subjective, irrational motivation. A professional choice of topic, on the other hand, is based on a number of much more rational, and even bureaucratic, considerations. Will my colleagues be interested in it, will they consider it a valid and rewarding contribution to the discipline, can I get funding for the research, is it the kind of question I am technically trained and qualified to answer, is the topic relevant to the concerns of other sociologists, to the interests of funding agencies, to public issues and concerns of the day?

Which would you expect to produce a more creative sociology?

Professionalization involves the formal codification of rules of procedure for the professional in his practice. Applied to sociological research practice, this means increasing emphasis on following methodological *rules for discovery* of new facts about social life. But sociology's special subject matter concerns it centrally with the *discovery of rules* in social life. It is only by somehow getting outside the rules in various creative ways that sociologists can see them and present them for public viewing. To the degree that the sociologists are professionally bound up with a set of prescribed rules for research, they are necessarily blind to their subject matter!

In the same way it is more difficult to "see" institutions the more fully one is a committed member of an institution, such as a profession. It is more difficult to take a skeptical, outsider's view of the concreteness and inevitability of any societal arrangement, the more fully one is oneself an insider in, say, the profession of sociology or the role of the academic.

In general, the relationship between the sociologist and the subject matter necessary for the production of sociological insights is totally contradicted by the requirements of the relationship between the professional and the clients.

Clients demand services for fees. As Ronald Reagan said, in his California gubernatorial campaign of 1964 (and here he was talking about all university academics as hired professionals), "The taxpayers of this state are not about to subsidize idle intellectual curiosity." Results are what professionals in any field must publicly, observably produce for their clients. The work of the professional is done for a fee, not as an end in itself. And sociology just isn't the same when it is done for a fee. The difference between doing it for fun and doing it professionally seems to me to be even greater in social science than in sex. But more importantly, clients come to rely on the productions of professionals to fill their own very real needs. This quite naturally leads them to demand the professional's services, and to demand that the results be useful and helpful. It is obvious that the freedom of sociological inquiry, to choose its own puzzles and to range over social life at will for interesting problems to solve, will be narrowed, channeled, and curtailed by the demands of clients, at the very least.

The Activist would carry this point even further. A sociologist who works as a professional for a clientele can be nothing more than a paid propagandist for the social elite, a part of the power structure. How can a hireling of the power elite critically study, expose, and combat this elite? Professional sociology is a self-contradiction, from this perspective, which Activist sociologists have experienced often in their conflict-laden careers. The more openly and competently they do Activist sociology, the worse their "clients," be they universities, granting agencies, or research institutes, treat them. Activist sociologists really ought to do something else for a living, if they wish to continue their critical, curative practice as sociologists. The kind of medicine they practice is definitely not consciously desired by the sickest "patients," and they must operate, not like professional M.D.'s, but like prophets crying out in the wilderness.

The major consequence of professionalization for Functionalist sociology is that as the field becomes more respectable, the research tends to become more and more ritualized, more highly codified and less creative or flexible. The major consequence for Activist sociologists is that they become even more the odd-person-out as their professionalized colleagues reject their critical work, and the power elite ranged against them comes to include more and more of their own colleagues. The major consequence for Naturalists is that the client's demands for relevance, for results, for news from their researches tends to distract them from the free pursuit of irrelevant, inconsequential questions like "How is the everyday world made to appear as commonplace as it is?"

If sociology is to continue as the free "application of scientific methods of inquiry to the puzzles of social life"—that is, if individual sociologists are to define the mode of application, to choose the applicable scientific methods, to select the interesting puzzles, to develop their own images of the nature of the subject matter, and to do all of this for their own reasons—then the consequences of professionalization must somehow be avoided. How can this be done?

My solution is a radical one, akin to Illich's deschooling of education. I propose that we de-professionalize sociology by transforming it into a primarily *amateur* pursuit. The transformation will be nonviolent and noncoercive. All it takes is an ever-increasing number of sociologists practicing as amateurs to bring the *institution* of sociology down. As in the case of prostitution, when there are enough people around who are doing it for free, the profession becomes superfluous.

WHAT WOULD AN AMATEUR SOCIOLOGY BE LIKE?

Sociology as an amateur pursuit would most likely develop even more diversity, more incompatible images and versions of social reality, than the profession has within it today. The general tendency, however, I think would be in the direction of greater development of what are called in this text Naturalist and Activist sociologies. The image of people as active change agents in society, or as creative formulators of social reality, underlies both of these kinds of sociology. By contrast, Functionalist sociology views human beings as the products, the victims, or the puppets of the social system. Sociology I therefore is more compatible with a fully professionalized sociology, a sociology of system-integrated experts, whereas a sociology of amateurs would be made up of everyday people, self-consciously creating and re-creating their own social worlds. Doing sociology would therefore be not a job or a profession, but a form of recreation.

Deprofessionalizing sociology would in itself be an acceptance or a recognition of the validity of the basic tenet of Sociology III, or Naturalist sociology: There can be no greater expert about anyone's social life than the person living that life. Amateur sociology would then be like one group of experts telling another group of experts how "we" create and experience "our" social reality, and asking for an answering description and display in return. The "we" and the "our" in each instance of this kind of show-and-tell would have to be made up as a situationally satisfactory group identity for the purposes at hand, and recognizably so.

For instance, who could know better how bureaucracy works than career bureaucrats? As amateur sociologists, they would be encouraged to display their self-knowledge and their skilled artistry in making bureaucracy work to other amateurs.

The sport of sociology would be in becoming increasingly adept at seeing "how it is done by members like us," and reporting this to others who are interested.

Sociological education would also have to undergo serious transformation. Sociology courses, instead of being dedicated to the recruitment and training of professional sociologists, would have to take seriously the task of challenging and equipping amateurs to take on sociology as a lifetime sport, hobby, or recreational activity. Amateur sociology in the classroom would rely heavily on what the students can teach their professors. In actual practice, most introductory undergraduate courses are now split between these two tasks. The rise of amateur sociology would resolve the professor's dilemma in favor of amateur coaching rather than professional training.

It may have crossed the reader's mind that this introductory text favors the amateur sociology approach over the professional screening and training methods. Certainly it does. The introductory student is encouraged, urged, invited, to begin now to do sociology, and to do it as an end in itself, for what it is worth as a recreational activity.

This openness does not mean, however, that the amateur sociologist can't get better at the sport with further effort and coaching. The levels of skill and artistry that can be achieved by dedicated amateurs are probably infinitely high, and certainly not even dimly perceived at present.

The sociology of the past hundred years has produced a tremendous variety of instruments for viewing and analyzing different forms of social life, but it has also resulted in the establishment of a professional sociological bureaucracy, with all the strains toward orthodoxy that this entails. The sociology of the next hundred years will advance furthest and fastest in the direction of many different heterodoxies, each displaying different facets of social life anew. This development requires the phasing out of professionalism, and the burgeoning of amateur sociologies.

Amateur sociologists would probably form groups, loose associations to assemble and present and argue their observations, findings, and theories with one another. They might communicate through newsletters and they might even establish journals to publish their works in addition to writing in the popular press and magazines. But they would not adopt the two professional "core characteristics" defined at the beginning of this chapter by Goode, and their social implications. That is, the body of knowledge of amateur sociology would be the always accumulating and always radically revisable knowledge of social reality, including the sociologist's involvement in it, that sociological activity continues to produce. This body of knowledge would be viewed as the barest, most superficial gleaning of what can be known, sociologically, so that its possession would only define the enormity of one's sociological ignorance. And the "prolonged specialized training" of the amateur sociologist would consist of a lifetime of amateur inquiry into the puzzles of social life.

Secondly, the "service orientation" of the professional would be completely eschewed by the amateur sociologist. There would be no clients, no services, no fees. Doing sociology in this new context is firmly and exclusively an end in itself, the pursuit of social knowledge in perfect personal freedom.

Amateurism implies more than just the lack of professionalism. The word itself means "lover," and in the case of amateur sociology, it means a deep, respectful, and abiding love for one's subject matter, the puzzles of social life. This also means that, as in other forms of love, the satisfaction is in the doing, as an end in itself, not as a means to some other end.

This introductory text is an invitation to you to pick up and try on a variety of sociological lenses, and to begin a study of your own social life and its interconnections with everyone else's social life. Choose the puzzles that fascinate and worry you; take up the viewing lens that helps most to clarify those puzzles, or that leads you into deeper and even more fascinating puzzles. If you are fortunate, from my point of view, you will be caught and held in thrall by the social realities and the social mysteries that you begin to see. You will find these lenses difficult to put down. You will want to make "amateur sociologist" one of the significant labels or masks of identity in the kit-bag of your multiple social self. And you will join the great sport, the great art, the great human science, of amateur sociology. Welcome, lover.

Bibliography

Agee, James. *Let Us Now Praise Famous Men.* Boston: Houghton Mifflin, 1960.

Arendt, Hannah. *On Revolution.* New York: Viking Pr., 1965.

Barnard, Chester I. *The Functions of the Executive.* 1938. Reprint. Cambridge, Mass.: Harvard U. Pr., 1968.

Becker, Howard S. *Outsiders: Studies in the Sociology of Deviance.* London, Free Press of Glencoe, 1963.

_____. "Whose Side Are We On?" *Social Problems*, Winter 1967, pp. 239–247.

Bell, Daniel, ed. *Toward the Year 2000: Work in Progress.* Boston: Beacon, 1968.

Bendix, Reinhard. *Work and Authority in Industry.* New York: Harper & Row, 1963.

Berger, Peter. *Invitation to Sociology: A Humanistic Perspective.* New York: Anchor, 1963.

_____. *Pyramids of Sacrifice.* New York: Basic Books, 1974.

Bittner, Egon. "The Police on Skid-row: a Study of Peace-keeping." *American Sociological Review* 32(5) (1967): 699–715.

Blau, Peter M. *Bureaucracy in Modern Society.* New York: Random House, 1964.

Brinton, Crane. *The Anatomy of Revolution.* New York: Prentice-Hall, 1938.

Cannon, W. B. *The Wisdom of the Body.* New York: Norton, 1932.

Casanova, Pablo Gonzalez. "C. Wright Mills: An American Conscience." In *The New Sociology,* edited by Irving Louis Horowitz. New York: Oxford U. Pr., 1965.

Castaneda, Carlos. *The Teachings of Don Juan.* Berkeley: U. of Cal. Pr., 1968.

_____. *A Separate Reality.* New York: Simon and Schuster, 1971.

_____. *Journey to Ixtlan.* New York: Simon and Schuster, 1972.

_____. *Tales of Power.* New York: Simon and Schuster, 1974.

Catton, William R. *From Animistic to Naturalistic Sociology.* New York: McGraw, 1966.

Chomsky, Noam. *Syntactic Structures.* The Hague: Mouton, 1965.

_____. *At War with Asia.* New York: Vintage, 1970.

Clarke, Robin, and Hindley, Geoffrey. *The Challenge of the Primitives.* London: Jonathan Cape, 1975.

Cleaver, Eldridge. *Post-Prison Writings and Speeches.* New York: Random House, 1969.

Cloward, Richard A., and Elman, Richard M. "Advocacy in the Ghetto." *Trans-Action* 4 (1966): 27—35.

Coles, Robert. *Children of Crisis: A Study of Courage and Fear.* Boston: Little, 1967.

Comte, Auguste. *The Positive Philosophy of Auguste Comte.* 3 Volumes. 1855. Translated by Harriet Martinson. Reprint. London: Bell, 1896.

Davis, Kingsley. "The Myth of Functional Analysis as a Special Method in Sociology and Anthropology." *American Sociological Review,* December 1959, pp. 757—772.

Dawe, Alan. "Two Sociologies." *British Journal of Sociology* 21 (1970):207—218.

DeGrazia, Sebastian. *Of Time, Work, and Leisure.* New York: Twentieth Century Fund, 1962.

Demerath, N.J. and Peterson, Richard A., eds. *System Change and Conflict: A Reader on Contemporary Sociological Theory and the Debate over Functionalism.* New York: Free Press, 1967.

Domhoff, G. William. *Who Rules America?* Englewood Cliffs, N.J.: Prentice-Hall, 1967.

Douglas, Jack. *The Social Meanings of Suicide.* Princeton, N.J.: Princeton U. Pr., 1967.

Douglas, Jack, ed. *Understanding Everyday Life.* New York: Free Press, 1969.

Durkheim, Emile. *Suicide: A Study in Sociology.* 1897. Translated by J.A. Spaulding and G. Simpson. Reprint. New York: Free Press, 1952.

———.*The Rules of Sociological Method.* 1895. Translated by Sarah A. Solovay and John J. Mueller. Edited by George E. G. Catlin. Reprint. Glencoe, Ill.: Free Press, 1962.

———. *The Elementary Forms of the Religious Life.* 1912. Translated by Joseph Ward Swain. Reprint. New York: Collier, 1954.

———. *The Division of Labor in Society.* 1893. Translated by George Simpson. Reprint. Glencoe, Ill: Free Press, 1964.

Eisenstadt, S.N. "Social Change, Differentiation, and Evolution." In *System Change and Conflict,* edited by N.J. Demerath III and Richard A. Peterson. New York: Free Press, 1967.

Frank, Lawrence K. *Society as the Patient.* New Brunswick, N.J.: Rutgers U. Pr., 1948.

Fromm, Erich. *Marx's Concept of Man.* New York: Ungar, 1961.

Garfinkel, Harold. *Studies in Ethnomethodology.* Englewood Cliffs, N.J.: Prentice-Hall, 1967.

Glazer, Myron. *The Research Adventure.* New York: Random House, 1974.

Goffman, Erving. *The Presentation of Self in Everyday Life.* Garden City, N.Y.: Doubleday, 1959.

———. *Asylums.* Garden City, N.Y.: Doubleday, 1961.

Goode, William J. "Encroachment, Charlatanism and the Emerging Profession:

Psychology, Sociology, and Medicine." *American Sociological Review,* December 1960, pp. 902—914.

————. *The Family.* Englewood Cliffs, N.J.: Prentice-Hall, 1964.

Gouldner, Alvin W. "Anti-Minotaur: The Myth of a Value-Free Sociology." *Social Problems,* Winter 1962, pp. 199—213.

————. *The Coming Crisis of Western Sociology.* New York: Basic Books, 1970.

————. *For Sociology: Renewal and Critique in Sociology Today.* New York: Basic Books, 1973.

Gracey, Harry L. "Learning the Student Role: Kindergarten as Academic Boot Camp." In *Readings in Introductory Sociology,* edited by Dennis Wrong and Harry L. Gracey, New York: Macmillan, 1972.

Habermas, Jurgen. *Knowledge and Human Interests.* London: Heinemann, 1972.

Halberstam, David. *The Best and the Brightest.* New York: Random House, 1972.

Hansen, Donald A. *An Invitation to Critical Sociology.* New York: Free Press, 1976.

Hayden, Tom. *The Love of Possession Is a Disease with Them.* Chicago: Holt, 1972.

Henry, Jules. *Pathways to Madness.* New York: Random House, 1971.

Hobbes, Thomas. *Leviathan.* Oxford: James Thornton, 1881.

Hollander, Xaviera (with Robin Moore and Yvonne Dunleavy). *The Happy Hooker.* New York: Dell, 1972.

Hopper, Rex. "The Revolutionary Process." *Social Forces* 21(1950): 270—279.

Horowitz, David, ed. *Radical Sociology: An Introduction.* San Francisco: Canfield, 1971.

Horowitz, Irving Louis. "The Life and Death of Project Camelot." In Horowitz, *Professing Sociology: Studies in the Life Cycle of Social Science.* Chicago: Aldine, 1968.

————. and Liebowitz, Martin. "Social Deviance and Political Marginality: Toward a Redefinition of the Relation Between Sociology and Politics." In *The Sociology of Dissent,* edited by R. Serge Denisoff. New York: Harcourt Brace Jovanovich, 1974.

Humphreys, Laud. *Tearoom Trade: Impersonal Sex in Public Places.* Chicago: Aldine, 1970.

Illich, Ivan. *Celebration of Awareness, A Call for Institutional Revolution.* New York: Doubleday, 1969.

Johnson, Chalmers. *Revolution and Social System.* Stanford: Hoover Institute Studies, III, 1964.

Kozol, Jonathan. *Death At An Early Age.* New York: Bantam, 1970.

Laing, Ronald David. *The Politics of The Family.* Toronto: Canadian Broadcasting Corporation, 1969.

Liebow, Elliot. *Tally's Corner: A Study of Negro Streetcorner Men.* Boston, Little, 1967.

MacIver, Robert M. *Society*. New York: Holt, Rinehart, 1937.

MacKay, Robert W. "Conceptions of Children and Models of Socialization." In *Ethnomethodology*, edited by Ray Turner. Baltimore: Penguin, 1974.

Malinowski, Bronislaw. *Magic, Science, and Religion*. 1925. Reprint. Garden City, N.Y.: Doubleday, 1954.

————. *A Diary in the Strict Sense of the Term*. Translated by Norbert Guterman. London: Routledge, 1967.

Marcuse, Herbert. *Eros and Civilization*. Boston: Beacon, 1955.

Marx, Karl, and Engels, Frederick. *Manifesto of the Communist Party*. 1848. Reprint. New York: International, 1948.

————. "Theses on Feuerbach," 1888. Excerpted in Marx and Engels, Basic Writings, edited by Lewis S. Feuer. New York: Doubleday, 1959.

————. *Economic and Political Manuscripts of 1844*. New York: International, 1964.

————. *Selected Writings in Sociology and Social Philosophy*. Edited by T.B. Bottomore and Maximillian Rubel. Baltimore: Penguin, 1964. (Written 1843—1871).

————. *Writings of the Young Marx on Philosophy and Society*. New York: Doubleday, 1967. (Written 1843—1845).

McHugh, Peter. *Defining the Situation: The Organization of Meaning in Social Interaction*. Indianapolis: Bobbs-Merrill, 1968.

Mead, George Herbert. *Mind, Self, and Society*. Chicago: U. of Chicago Pr., 1934.

Merton, Robert K., and Nisbet, Robert. *Contemporary Social Problems*. New York: Harcourt Brace, 1961.

————. *Social Theory and Social Structure*. New York: Free Press, 1949.

Mills, C. Wright. "Situated Actions and Vocabularies of Motive." *American Sociological Review* 5 (1940): 904—913.

————. *White Collar*. New York: Oxford U. Pr., 1951.

————. *The Power Elite*. New York: Oxford U. Pr., 1956.

————. *The Causes of World War III*. New York: Simon and Schuster, 1958.

————. *The Sociological Imagination*. New York: Oxford U. Pr. 1959.

————. *Listen Yankee: The Revolution in Cuba*. New York: McGraw, 1960.

————. *Power Politics and People: The Collected Essays of C. Wright Mills*. Edited by Irving Louis Horowitz. New York: Oxford U. Pr., 1963.

Mitchell, Juliet. *Woman's Estate*. New York: Random House, 1971.

Molotch, Harvey. "Oil in Santa Barbara and Power in America." *Sociological Inquiry* 40 (1969): 98—115.

Moore, Wilbert E. *The Conduct of the Corporation*. New York: Random House, 1962.

————. *Man, Time and Society*. New York: Wiley, 1963.

Morton, Peggy. "A Woman's Work Is Never Done." Leviathan 2(1): 27—45.

Mullins, Nicholas C. *Theories and Theory Groups in Contemporary American Sociology*. New York: Harper and Row, 1973.

Murdock, George P. *Social Structure*. New York: Macmillan, 1960. (1959): 203—212.

Nettler, Gwynn. "Ideology and Welfare Policy." *Social Problems* 6 (1958—1959): 203—212.

Nicolaus, Martin. The Professional Organization of Sociology: A View From Below." In *Radical Sociology,* edited by J. David Colfax and Jack L. Roach. New York: Basic Books, 1971.

Ogburn, William F. *Technology and the Changing Family.* Boston: Houghton Mifflin, 1955.

_____. *Social Change.* New York: Viking, 1932.

Page, Charles Hunt. *Class and American Society: From Ward to Ross.* New York: Octagon, 1964.

_____. and Talamini, John T., eds. *Sport and Society.* Boston: Little, 1973.

Parsons, Talcott. *The Social System.* Glencoe, Ill.: Free Press, 1951.

_____; Bales, Robert F.; and Shils, Edward A. *Working Papers in the Theory of Action.* Glencoe, Ill.: Free Press, 1953.

_____. "The Incest Taboo in Relation to Social Structure." *The British Journal of Sociology* 5 (1954): 101—117. Reprinted in *The Family, Its Structures and Functions*, edited by Rose Lamb Coser, New York: St. Martin, 1954.

_____, and Bales, Robert F. *Family Socialization and Interaction Process.* New York: Free Press, 1955.

Pettee, George S. *The Process of Revolution.* New York: Viking, 1938.

Quinney, Richard. *The Social Reality of Crime.* New York: Dodd, Mead, 1970.

Rainwater, Lee. "The Sociologist as Naturalist." In *Sociological Self-Images: A Collective Portrait,* edited by Irving Louis Horowitz. Beverly Hills, Calif: Sage, 1969.

Reiss, Ira L. *Family System in America.* New York: Holt, 1976.

Riesman, Paul. "Review of the First Three Don Juan Books." In *Seeing Castaneda,* edited by Daniel Noel. New York: Capricorn, 1974.

Ritzer, George. *Sociology: A Multiple Paradigm Science.* Boston: Allyn and Bacon, 1975.

Sacks, Harvey. "On the Analyzability of Stories by Children." In *Ethnomethodology, Selected Readings,* edited by Roy Turner. Baltimore: Penguin, 1974.

_____. "Notes on Police Assessment of Moral Character." In *Studies In Interaction*, edited by David Sudnow, New York: Free Press, 1972.

Sahlins, Marshal D. and Service, E. R., eds. *Evolution and Culture.* Ann Arbor, Mich.: U. of Michigan Pr., 1961.

Scheff, Thomas. *Being Mentally Ill: A Sociological Theory.* Chicago: Aldine, 1966.

Schutz, Alfred. *Collected Papers I: The Problem of Social Reality.* The Hague: Martimus Nijhoff, 1962.

Sennett, Richard, and Colb, Jonathan. *The Hidden Injuries of Class.* New York: Knopf, 1972.

Simmel, Georg. "The Sociology of Sociability." 1892. Translated by Everett C. Hughes. Reprint. *American Journal of Sociology,* November 1949, pp. 254—261.

————. *The Sociology of Georg Simmel*. 1908. Edited and translated by Kurt H. Wolff. Reprint. Glencoe, Ill.: Free Press, 1950.

————. Conflict and the Web of Group Affiliations. 1893. Translated by Kurt H. Wolff and Reinhard Bendix. Reprint. New York: Free Press, 1955.

Skinner, Burrhus Frederic. *Beyond Freedom and Dignity*. New York: Knopf, 1971.

Smith, Dorothy. "Woman, The Family, and Corporate Capitalism." In *Women in Canada*, edited by Marylee Stephenson. Toronto: New Press, 1973.

Sorokin, Pitirim A. *Sociocultural Causality, Space, Time*, New York: Russell & Russell, 1964.

Speier, Matthew. *How to Observe Face To Face Communication: A Sociological Introduction*. Pacific Palisades, Calif.: Goodyear, 1973.

Spencer, Herbert. *The Principles of Sociology*. New York: Appleton, 1898.

Stark, Werner. "Herbert Spencer's Three Sociologies." *American Sociological Review*, August 1961, pp. 515—521.

Stein, Maurice R., and Vidich, Arthur J., eds. *Identity and Anxiety, Survival of the Person in Mass Society*. New York: Free Press, 1960.

Stoddart, Ken. " 'Pinched'; Notes on the Ethnography of an Argot." In *Ethnomethodology*, edited by Roy Turner. Baltimore: Penguin, 1970.

Stone, I.F. *In a Time of Torment*. New York: Random House, 1967.

Sudnow, David, ed. *Studies in Interaction*. New York: Free Press, 1972.

Thomas, W. I. *The Unadjusted Girl in Social Behavior and Personality*. Chicago: Social Science Research Council, 1951.

Toch, Hans; Grant, J. Douglas; and Galvin, Raymond T. *Agents of Change; a Study In Police Reform*. New York: Wiley, 1975.

Toffler, Alvin. *Future Shock*. New York: Random House, 1970.

Turner, Roy, ed. *Ethnomethodology*. Baltimore: Penguin, 1970.

United Nations. *Demographic Yearbook, 1973*. New York: United Nations, 1974.

Veblen, Thorstein. *The Higher Learning in America*. 1917. Reprint. New York: Hill and Wang, 1968.

Ward, Lester F. *Applied Sociology*. Boston: Ginn, 1906.

Weber, Max. *From Max Weber: Essays in Sociology*. 1905. Edited and translated by Harris H. Gerth and C. Wright Mills. Reprint. New York: Oxford U. Pr., 1946.

————. *The Theory of Social and Economic Organization*. 1905. Translated by A. M. Henderson and Talcott Parsons. Reprint. New York: Oxford U. Pr., 1947.

————. *Methodology of the Social Sciences*. 1904. 1905. 1917. Reprint. Glencoe, Ill.: Free Press, 1949.

————. *The Protestant Ethic and the Spirit of Capitalism*. 1930. Reprint. New York: Scribners, 1958.

————. *Economy and Society*. Translated by Ephraim Fischoff. New York: Badminster, 1968. (From various writings of Weber, 1900—1919.)

Wrong, Dennis. "The Oversocialized Conception of Man in Modern Society."
    American Sociological Review, April 1961, pp. 183—193.
Weinstein, Deena, and Weinstein, Michael A. *Living Sociology: A Critical Intro-
    duction.* New York: McKay, 1974.
Zeitlin, Maurice. *American Society, Inc.* Chicago: Markham, 1970.
Zelditch, Morris. "Role Differentiation in the Nuclear Family." In *Family, Sociali-
    zation and Interaction Process.* New York: Free Press, 1955.

Index of Terms

Achievement versus Ascription,   Sociology I; when a person is awarded a social position with its attendant honor and rewards, on the basis of inherited characteristics or family name, that is called status allocation by **ascription**; when the same type of position is awarded on the basis of proven competitive merit, on the other hand, that is called status allocation by **achievement**; see p. 129.

Alienation,   Sociology II; literally, the separation into alien parts of anything that is by nature an organic whole; applied to social life, it refers to the fragmentation of the social self, the tearing away of the natural bonds between people and their work, and the splitting up of natural human communities, all of which occur in sickly societies, and represent the major symptom of social illness in modern times; see pp. 5, 24, 113—115, 117—118, 157, 169, 181, 198—199, 221—222.

Amateur Sociology,   Sociology III; see pp. 227, 231—233.

Analysis,   Sociologies I, II, and II. In Sociology I, analysis is the splitting of the whole social system into its constituent parts in order to explain how they fit and function together. In Sociology II, analysis is, as in psychoanalysis, the diagnosis, therapeutic involvement, and prescriptions for cure of the societally ill "patient." In Sociology III, analysis is the interpretation of meanings to be found intricately woven into the fabric of every social puzzle; see pp. 102, 169, 192.

Anomie,   Sociology I; a French word meaning the complete lack of standards or rules for social conduct, a form of social breakdown that occurs during times of rapid or sudden social change, and causes great personal distress among members of the society; see pp. 109—113, 116—117, .146, 152.

Attributions,   Sociology III; the only observable aspect of many imputed social facts. Attributions are what people say their own or other people's motives are. The rightness or wrongness of actions or persons is attributed, and therefore consists, observably, only in attributions; see pp. 189, 191.

Futurism, Futurists,   Sociologies I, II, and III; see p. 153—154, 162.

Hierarchy,   Sociologies I, II, III; in general, an arrangement of things one above or below the other. One can see such an arrangement as an inevitable and necessary feature of the social system (Sociology I), as the basic injustice of social inequality (Sociology II), or as something people do in interacting with one another (Sociology III); see pp. 102, 122—143, 172, 176, 180, 212.

Identity,   Sociologies I, II, III; Is personal identity something that is implanted in the individual by society, is it something a person naturally has, but that may be taken away or distorted by an oppressive society, or is it something that is created in social interaction, something different for each situation that arises? See pp. 63—78, 119, 186, 191.

Ideology,   Sociologies I, II; a set of self-serving beliefs, usually with the standing of natural laws or scientific facts fraudulently claimed; see p. 175.

Incest Taboo,   Sociology I; a basic rule for preserving social order; see pp. 195—196, 203, 205.

Inequality,   Sociology II's morally tinged word for social hierarchy or stratification; see pp. 122—142.

Institution, Institutionalization,   Sociologies I, II, and III; in general, a collection of established patterns of action integrated around a central theme; see pp. 10, 165—192, 192—213, 214—226, 228, 230—231.

Interaction,   Sociology III; what there is of social life to be observed; see pp. 7, 25, 58—59, 70—72, 90, 92, 98—99, 138, 167, 171, 176, 179, 195, 210, 215—216, 225, 228.

Interpretive, Interpretation,   Sociology III; see p. 25.

Intersubjectivity,   Sociology III; the socially necessary belief that if I were in your place, I would see things the same way you do. On the basis of this belief, we construct the fiction of an objective reality; see pp. 26, 31—32.

Involvement,   Sociologies I, II, and III; see all of Chapter 2 and pp. 63, 79—99, 193.

Labels, Labelling,   Sociologies II and III; attributions of identity often mistaken for inherent characteristics of those labelled; see pp. 25, 63, 71—73, 107—109, 119, 171, 185, 189, 208.

Legitimation,   Sociologies I, II; see p. 134.

Meaningful Social Action,   Sociologies I, III; "Human behavior when and insofar as the acting individual attaches a subjective meaning to it," by German sociologist Max Weber's definition.

Typification,   Sociology III; the kind of social definition we all commonly do in order to identify one another as belonging to particular classifications or categories of persons.

Value Judgments,   Sociologies I, II, and III; what one must avoid making in order to remain objective and scientific, according to Sociology I; what one must make consciously and openly in order to see social reality honestly, according to Sociology II; what *all* statements of fact about social life really come to, according to Sociology III; see pp. 20, 44, 59, 76.

Variable,   Sociology I; a quantity that may be seen to increase or decrease in relation to some other quantity; see p. 17.

Verstehen,   Sociology III; a German word used by Max Weber to identify the form of understanding necessary for the comprehension of social interaction, that is, the sympathetic identification of the viewer of an action with the intentions and meanings implied by the observed actor in his act; see pp. 22—31, 34.

Index